The Catholic Demonologist Handbook
A Comprehensive guidebook to understanding, diagnosing and solving Ghost and Demonic Hauntings.

```
[Underground Edition] v1.0
© 2008-2010 Kenneth Deel / Swords Of Saint
                 Michael
```

CONTENTS: TOPIC INDEX TABLE

DEDICATION 8
INTRODUCTION 8
ABOUT THE AUTHOR 10
A WORD ON MY PRACTICED METHODOLOGY 14
FOR THE NON-BELIEVERS 18
TO THE WOULD BE DEMONOLOGIST 23
WARNING YOUR BELIEF IS ABOUT TO CHANGE 26
A SPIRIT CAN NOT ENTER 30
EXORICSTS AND EXORCISMS 31
WHAT IS DELIVERANCE? 34
TRAINED EXORCIST IN A FEW WEEKS 35
GHOST HUNTERS 36
WHAT IS SPIRITUAL WARFARE? 36
PRAYER SAID BEFORE YOU BEGIN STUDIES 38
IDENTIFYING THE BASIC TYPES OF SPIRITS 41
NOTES ON 'DIAGNOSING' A HAUNTING 42
INDICATIONS OF A TRUE HAUNTING 44
HAUNTED 'HOT SPOTS' VERSUS 'RESIDENTIAL' 45
THE OWNERS CAN HELP THEMSELVES. 47
'BACK DOOR' METHODS 48
BOUND BY RULES: THE LAW OF INVITATION 49
HOW OUR WORDS ARE BINDING 50
WHY ARE YOU HAUNTED? 51
GHOST HUNTERS BEWARE! 54
AN UNHEALTHY INTEREST 56
THE NAMES OF DEMONS 57
THE MASQUE OF 'ANGELOLOGY' 59

READING BOOKS ON SATANISM, BLACK ARTS   63
WHAT IS A "CURSE"?   64
REINCARNATION   67
ABOUT WITCHCRAFT & OCCULT PRACTICES   69
TESTING FOR "CAUSE AND EFFECT"   72
OUIJA BOARDS   73
DEMONS CAN'T SPELL?   75
ORACLES OF COMMUNICATION   77
THE GHOST BOX (A.K.A. FRANKS BOX)   79
EVP (ELECTRONIC VOICE PHENOMENON)   82
SINFUL SEXUALITY   84
ALTERED STATES OF CONSCIOUSNESS   84
"PSYCHIC-MEDIUMS" / "SENSITIVES"   85
REBORN AFTER NEAR DEATH   88
ASTRAL PROJECTION   89
BABY BIRTH AND BABY BLUES   90
A RECENT DEATH OF A PERSON   91
SPECIFIC TO HOUSE HISTORY: 93
SUICIDE AND MURDER   93
GRAVE SITES KNOWN AND UNKNOWN   93
CHANGING PROPERTY LANDSCAPE   94
"PORTALS"   95
HOME/BUILDING RENOVATIONS?   97
WHY ARE SOME "HAUNTED" AND OTHERS NOT   100
SCIENCE – NATURAL: 102
PARAPSYCHOLOGY: THE PSEUDO SCIENCE   102
HISTORY - WHEN IT WAS ALWAYS 'DEMONS'   103
SCIENCE DEBUNKING PARANORMAL   104
A BALANCE OF 'SCIENCE AND FAITH'   107
PARAPSYCHOLOGY: THOUGHTS CONTRARY TO.   109
COLD SPOTS   109
RESIDUAL HAUNTS AND APPARITIONS   110
'BLACK SHADOWY BEINGS'   112
PURGATORY PART 1   113
EMF EFFECTS AND METERS   113
POLTERGEIST   114
REAL OR IMAGINATION?   118
HOW DO WE DISCERN?   119

WHAT ARE ORBS? 122
BI-LOCATION CAN APPEAR AS A "GHOST" 124
DREAMS INDICATE A 'PRESENCE' IN ROOM 125
FIELD INVESTIGATION NOTES 127
MORE THAN ONE WITNESS 127
TO 'PROFILE' THE CLEINT(S) / WITNESS 128
LEARNING FROM CATHOLIC PROTOCOLS 129
TYPE: DEMONIC-NON-HUMAN 130
THE NATURE OF DEMONS. 130
DEFINITIONS & THE ORIGINAL MEANING 131
"EXORCISM" AND "POSSESSION" 133
WHEN 'THEY' CAN BE SEEN 135
TYPES OF DEMONS – PT 1: REVEALING TRAITS 137
THE 'SIX' STAGES OF THE DEMONIC 138
POSSESSION IN FAQ 141
'TEST' TO SEE IF SOMEONE MAYBE POSSESSED? 145
SOME COMMON SIGNS OF POSSESSION? 150
WHY… GOOD PEOPLE BECOME POSSESSED? 151
"BAD SEED" CHILDREN INHERENTLY EVIL? 153
INDENTIFYING 'DEMONIC' 157
RELIGIOUS PROVOCATION INVESTIGATIONS 157
HISTORICAL DESCRIPTIONS OF DEMONS 160
THE 'GREY VEIL' 160
RECOGNIZING BY ACTIONS 163
INDICATIONS - OTHER SENSES 165
RECOGNIZING BY APPEARANCE 167
SHADOW PEOPLE, BLACK FORMS 171
TYPES OF SHADOWS 177
MY EXPERIENCE WITH 'SHADOWY BEINGS' 179
WHEN TO CALL A HAUNTING "DEMONIC" 184
"MASQUARADE" / A CASE STUDY: A UFO ALIEN 187
GHOST OF CHILDREN 191
ANIMAL GHOSTS & SPIRITS 193
THE DEMONIC REALM 196
THE MIRRORED WORLD BEYOND 196
A SIGNATURE COUNT OF "THREE" 198
THE NUMBER "6" AND "666" 199
THE SIGNIFICANCE OF 3AM 201

THE 3 AM APOCALYPSE THEORY   203
MORE SYMPTOMS OF THE DEMONIC HAUNT   203
"THE BORROWERS"   203
YOUR ABILITY TO 'THINK' AND DREAMS   205
EFFECTS ON RELATIONSHIPS, MARRIAGE   207
LISTEN TO THE CHILDREN   209
PRAYER FOR OUR CHILDREN   212
DEMONIC ENCOUNTERS: SPIRITUAL ATTACKS   214
"TEMPTATION" – 214
CAN DEMONS READ YOUR "AURA"?   216
YOUR 'PERSONAL DEMON(S)'   218
CAN DEMONS READ MINDS?   219
CAN A DEMON HEAR PRAYERS? 220
TYPES OF PHYSICAL ATTACKS   222
SPECROPHELIA 223
PROGRESSIVE STAGES 'SEXUAL ENCOUNTERS' 225
INCUBUS-SUCCUBUS   226
'DEMONIC INDUCED DEATH'   230
OLD HAG / SLEEP PARALYSIS   231
DIFFERENCE BETWEEN SP AND AN ATTACK: 240
A DEFENSE, WHEN YOU CAN'T MOVE OR SPEAK   247
MYTHS & MISCONCEPTIONS 'DEMONIC SPIRITS   248
WHAT ARE THE NEPHILIM?   254
TYPE: GOOD-HUMAN SPIRITS   255
CASE EXAMPLE OF A GOOD SPIRIT   257
PURGATORY - "ALL GHOSTS 'NOT' DEMONS"   259
TYPES OF 'PURGATORY GHOSTS   259
GHOSTLY APPARITION: PROM TEENAGER   272
THE BATTLE BEGINS - WARFARE SOLUTIONS   270
THE SPIRITUAL ARMOR OF GOD   273
I - PREPARATIONS   275
'SAFE' ADVICE TO "FIELD INVESTIGATORS"   275
DON'T GO IN WITH 'ALL GUNS BLAZING'   279
THE POWER OF 'FAITH AND GRACE'   283
CATHOLICISM FOR DUMMIES   285
THE "ROMAN RITUAL" VS. 'DELIVERANCE'   290
YOUR DELIVERANCE TOOLKIT   292
PRECAUTION: AVOID DEMONIC "RETALIATION" 293

BLESSING OF OBJECTS   293
BLESSED SEA SALT AND CANDLES   294,295
SAINT BENEDICT MEDAL   296
CRUCIFIXES (NOT PLAIN CROSSES)   303
AURA OF BLESSED WATER: A SCIENTIFIC STUDY   306
WHY 'JESUS' NAME CAN AFFECT EVIL SPIRITS   308
MIRACULOUS MEDAL (OF BLESSED VIRGIN MARY)   309
FRANKINCENSE AND MYRRH NOT SAGE   312
DISPOSING OF 'UNHOLY' ITEMS   313
BUILD YOUR SPIRITUAL ARMOR   315
PRAYER: "ACT OF CONTRITION"   315
UNIVERSAL SOLUTIONS AND UNDERSTANDING   316
CHANGES TO MAKE PSYCHOLOGICALLY   319
CHANGES TO MAKE TO YOUR ENVIRONMENT   325
BREAKING CURSES   327
BREAKING CURSES PRAYERS   328
VII - THE DELIVERANCE   334
DELIVERANCE PRAYERS   334
NOTES ON FURTHER TAKING ACTION   336
MORE ON "CATHOLIC EXORCISMS"   337
POST – PREVENTION MEASURES   340
THE 3 KINGS BLESSING   341
BOUNDARIES OR YOUR PROPERTY OR HOME   343
PROTECTION PRAYERS   346
A WORD ABOUT "MIXED FAITH" SOLUTIONS   348
HOW LONG WILL A "SUCCESSFUL" EXORCISM LAST?   349
THEY RETURN SOON AFTER A CLEANSING?   350
THE LORD HELPS THOSE WHOM HELP THEMSELVES   353
DEALING WITH CHILDREN WHO "SEE GHOSTS"   356
PRAYER: GOOD-HUMAN SPIRIT HAUNTINGS   365
INVESTIGATORS DEMONIC HAUNT "CHECK LIST"   373
FIELD INVESTIGATORS CLIENT QUESTIONNAIRE   378
ACKNOWLEDGMENTS & RECOMMENDED READING   392

DEDICATION

For my parents and my friends who encouraged me to complete this book. And a special thanks to my other "mentors" such as Lorraine Warren, and various clergy who were often my inspiration.

INTRODUCTION

In a way this book can be considered a "Self Help Guide" for what some refer to as a "problem haunting". It is also a definitive guide to "Demons and Ghosts" in their behaviors, origins, and their very existence, more so in how they might affect us. A "Demonologist" handbook as I am mainly adding info that applies to the work I do. However please note reading this book cover to cover will not by default qualify you as a "Demonologist", just that you will have much information all combined into one resource, that otherwise might take as much as 25 or more years to accumulate. I expect it will expedite training for anyone who seeks a better understanding and knowledge of these topics, where they can indeed help themselves as well as to help others who might be living through a "problem haunting". I decided that I'm not going to waste valued print trying to sway skeptics away from their closed minded viewpoints. As I find from personal experiences, it is a waste of my time and theirs, and there is not enough pages or books in the world to convince a skeptic in such belief systems.

As it is also not my intention to try to convince you that *ghosts* exist, or even to change your denomination of Christian faith to '*Catholic*'. You will find, however, that I will make a case that may provide 'food for thought' that may lead to such changes. However, I do not intend to be "politically correct" either, at the expense of the truth. In this work, to do so is misleading, and can be dangerous. We should never try to avoid hurting someone's 'feelings' at the expense of the hard facts.

I don't expect to be Popular in what I say in this book, it isn't about being "P.C.", or sparing the feelings of others who might not be "Christian". I go for the facts and that beyond a mere Christian perspective, as the truth can be told from other points of view as well just as clear. So in this book, I may 'ruffle some feathers'- but my approach in doing so is in a more logical manner, and not merely using "holy scripture" to make my point. Or forcing a belief system upon someone that I don't feel has it's ground in truth based on my experiences and case studies. I will also try to explain 'universally' as well, so that any person of faith can better understand. Let us pray that I succeed.

There is a fine line between an interest in just merely wanting to learn about demons and ghosts for a personal knowledge, and to satisfy a certain curiosity on these topics. And those who have an unhealthy interest and fascination in this. I sincerely hope this information somehow comes to use in helping oneself or others who are afflicted by these spirits, as that is the true intention of this book.

LAYMEN TERMS

This can be a sort of "handbook" for those who do indeed seek answers to an age old phenomenon in haunting and paranormal experiences. The goal is to provide this information in more of a laymen's approach. Skipping the *'Latin', church lingo*, as I will keep it plain and simple. Simple words and analogies to better educate and pass on what I know to the reader in an easy to understand fashion. (As *with those "For Dummies" or "In a nutshell" series of books*) You will find I don't spend much time quoting 'scripture' either. I don't feel a need to add more pages proving biblical support to what I know is fact. What I tell in this book does not go against Catholic or true Christian teachings. Even as though some of this in this book, you might hear for the first time.

This isn't to say some will try to argue that, however please note, some of the information here is quite the 'uncommon knowledge' to those even with the proper education and experience in this line of work. So, the goal is to help you understand the phenomenon better, and to use this knowledge to help others and to help yourself as needed.

ABOUT THE "UNDERGROUND EDITION"

As you might have an early copy of this book. You'll see that it looks to be more of an *Underground publication*, rather than a mass marketed paper back or hardcover book you'll see on the New York Times best seller list, or found in the inventory at your local Barnes and Noble. This is a special early release edition, likely personally signed, and although it is a 'full copy', I expect at some point, at a later date to have the book released through a major publisher (TBA). In short, please excuse any spelling, 'typos' and grammar errors you might find in this text book.
-Thank you!

ABOUT THE AUTHOR

I am now a <u>retired</u> "Catholic Demonologist", these two words describe, my personal faith, and how I work and my area of interest and "expertise", if you will. My study, research and experience over the last 32 years was toward 'Demonology" and "Ghosts", with church doctrine (The Catechism), and theology being obviously a part of it. And have been involved with "Deliverance", (i.e. ghost busting), for the past 29 years as of the first printing of this book. If I go yet further back into my life, it entails having paranormal experiences since I was about seven years old.

So as my approach is more of that from a 'Christian-Judeo' perspective and as a "Catholic" I lean to "Catholic" solutions, and when they have a real problem haunting they are open to that. The track record for Catholic methods, as revealed in public media, can almost speak for itself, as it already has a sort of common 'built in' for
acceptance for most people.

Please note that I am not an official church appointed "Catholic Demonologist"; only a bishop appointed clergy is fully recognized by the Roman Catholic Church itself, as an 'official' church Demonologist. *(Beware of Catholic 'laity' who claim to be otherwise!)* I have attained the respect from my peers, and work with Catholic clergy, as well as with 'other Christian denominations' on occasion, however I am not a 'Catholic insider'.

I have to go about the same "red tape" as many others do, unless I somehow know clergy local to your area. As I build a personal network of such clergy, we hope this will better expedite help through the church where exorcisms are warranted. *(This is being done through the **www.SwordsOfSaintMichael.org** as I write this)*

As I have had my own personal 'paranormal experiences' I have had since I was very young. Back then, my parents would tell me that I am simply 'dreaming', or experiencing 'twilight dreaming', 'night terrors' (*psychological*), or sleep paralysis (*medical*). But I suspected even at this early age, that what I was experiencing was none-of-the-above, and it was indeed "*supernatural*". (Looking back I realize I had a Saint Benedict medal around my neck since I was very young. So I imagine things could have been far worse to not have extra protection and prayers provided by my parents. Without telling me these things were real and feeding these 'beings' more with a child's fear that would escalate much higher, if they were told they were in fact real encounters. And not "just a bad dream."

As a teen, a more serious study began on noted subjects after one night a friend had witnessed "A dark figure hunched over my bed" which is one of the 'shadowy being(s)' I have been seeing for years. This was when I was only seventeen. Let me just say that having another person validate you are not 'imagining it' was a huge turning point, and most certainly it had more so prompted a serious research and study of the paranormal. Most certainly a self study alone of my personal 'experiences' made it easier to discover some of the truths about the paranormal. As being able to "test" would be spirits, what DOES affect them, and what does not.
 However, back when I began studies in the late 1970's, there was little to no mention of black shadowy figures, creeping black forms, or fiery disembodied faces. Just stories in which describe the old gray and blue classic traditional ghost. This was all of course before the retail print of classic cases told such as with '**The Amityville Horror**', and the book "**The Demonologist**, which introduced some elements as these 'black figures' into the mainstream. However, some uncommon books from our personal library, such as on the life of (Saint) Padre Pio and Cure D'Ars, made mention of such phenomenon long before.

Since I was a child, my family had attained many books that grew into a large library that came to serve on the subjects of Theology, and topics of 'Spiritual Warfare', and so forth. This included Biographies of Saints, as well as other text material that did relate to the study and knowledge of 'demonology'.

All of these sources provided answers over the years, and to our benefit, many of these books were discarded after the closing of Saint Louis area convents & seminaries. Including books from the library of Saint Louis University, which also ended up in my family's possession all starting back in the early 70's. So I essentially acquired my knowledge from church documents, clergy, literature, publications & books not sold in retail stores. Basically attaining an uncommon knowledge, that is for "Catholic laymen".

In addition to reading many books such as those, and from these studies of ghosts, demons, and the supernatural in general. I also gained from talking with "mentors", which were many. Spiritual advisors in priests, some were in my family as we have many Catholic clergymen in my family, although now that I am older sadly, most are now either retired or have passed away. My mother and father were married by mom's cousin in Saint Louis; a Catholic "bishop", my son was baptized by cousin "Father Bill". My parents themselves are also considered my mentors; my father is quite the theologian of the Catholic faith and it's history. And both are very devout "traditional" Catholic. "Deliverance" and "demonology" is nothing new to my family. I have also been involved with several "prayer groups" and 'deliverance" teams since the early 80's. Personally involved in help through the years, including providing advice on the *World Wide Web* since 1996.

The paranormal is often related to 'spiritual warfare', and I consider it to be more so a spiritual matter of religion, this is my view first and foremost. However, we seek through a team effort to get the whole picture investigating with a parapsychology approach (first), and the analysis of the physical and mental health of the 'witnesses' in order to 'cover all bases' before concluding there is an actual haunting involved. Beyond simply a Demonologist by study, I also have many of my own paranormal experiences that begin at my childhood. I lean towards a more traditional and reverent Catholic church, a pre-Vatican II era, which is the mindset I grew up with in my family who are very devout in their faith. I do not work under 'official' church authority, for I am not clergy. But I will go to the church when the need is justified. I am also not an 'Exorcist', nor would I perform the Roman Ritual, that is for an ordained Catholic priest to do, this is another area where church assistance is required, as I follow the guidelines laid out by the church.

My goal is always to CLOSE the case, not simply investigate, gather evidence, wave some 'sage', and leave...

There **ARE NO GUARANTEES** in this. It more relies on the people themselves. More often God truly can better help those who help themselves.

Those who will read this book will find that I do not stray from what is considered traditional Catholic church doctrine. Where many others may. Mixed faiths in haunting help is a dangerous game, I don't recommend it for anyone who endeavors in "deliverance". However I do know when to think outside the box, as no one person has all of the answers. And research is an ongoing task, as is the nature of '**spiritual warfare**'.

A WORD ON MY METHODOLOGY

I am not an "Exorcist", that is not what I do. In an analogy of a car repair guy, the difference between a "Demonologist" and an "Exorcist" can vary as between the guy who diagnoses the problem and recommends a solution (Demonologist), versus the guy who then removes the defective part and replaces it with a new one (Exorcist). Being armed with the knowledge and understanding of an Exorcist is part of the required skill to investigate claims of the paranormal and discern the type of spirit, diagnose, recommend a solution as to help in the 'healing'.

Which might entail contacting a qualified "Exorcist".

I investigate the claims by various means when it is warranted, starting with thorough personal interviews, truly "listening to the client". A scientific team might be called in to gather evidence 'if needed', *(but mainly to try to gather physical evidence on tape/film for example)*. But I approach these as more of a 'spiritual' than a 'scientific' methodology, of course, never setting aside a notion it can indeed be merely a "medical" or have 'natural' explanations. But, part of my investigative work involves clearly defining 'natural' from 'supernatural' or paranormal. 'Good' or 'Evil', 'Human' or

'Demonic'. True demonic cases leave clear footprints enough for those who know what to look or listen for, some of us in the field can identify the dark spirit is present without dragging in a full team with equipment. And as we know the demon to be elusive, purposely avoiding a capture, such an investigation will too often turn up nothing. Thus, it is not alone reliable means to effectively diagnose a haunting. As I suspect a true haunting, I arrange for "prayer teams", as I also submit 'prayer requests' to specific communities and organizations, even through my own parents, who themselves are very devout Catholic/Christians and more knowledgeable on these topics than most "Demonologist" out there, as some few know. So we offer these prayers for those tormented by the evil ones, and through these 'positive' intercessions from Heaven, it is more to help these people to 'help themselves'. A good precaution even if you are still unsure about the haunting's origins, as our prayers are never wasted.

Let me stress again, I am not an *'Exorcist'*, as I never claimed to be, and I don't generally *'bless'* homes, or do what people refer to as a '*cleansing*', I am not a Catholic priest . Although I will '*cleanse*' my own house from time to time, as I do recommend that everyone should do this by default in their own home.   As we own our homes, as I detail later in this book, we have certain authority over our property.   So as we would '*invite*' or *command* some spirits to leave, these actions have more of an effect when it is done by the owner, than it would to have just any Joe Schmoe do the same. So in this I will at times, instruct a person or family on how to do an effective 'cleansing' themselves. Again to better "*help them to help themselves*". A doctor can at some point advise a diabetic to "*lay off the sug*ar", and follow a special diet, but he can only do so much.   As it is up to the individuals themselves at some point to follow the advice to "*help themselves*".   And we certainly hope they don't let things go to where some more drastic measures are needed. In case, a full blown exorcism would be considered as they let things go so far, such 'extremes' are the only solution to help them.

As a "*Demonologist*" I do all of the initial "leg-work" prior to these final "*deliverance*" phases. This is where these third party deliverance team(s)/ exorcists enter the case, and this includes Protestant ministers, not just Catholics, who are more accessible yet effective enough in many cases. So after my diagnosis and recommendation it is more so up to the people who are having the problems and it is the job of the deliverance team/exorcist to work with the person to rebuke the offending spirits. Although I actually find that many haunting cases in general can be solved without anyone but the "Priest" or an "Exorcist" physically stepping foot inside the home.

As in my approach is more so from a *Christian-Judeo perspective*, this is understood by clients as I try to make it clear, when I am contacted. As some lower level solutions I can provide can be stated with a more "*universal*" understanding, if the client requests a faith practitioner outside of my 'belief system', sometimes the best I can offer is a referral to someone who might be able to help them. However, most often when the haunting is extreme enough, they will "try anything" for a solution, even if they are NOT Catholic, or Christian, or even Jewish themselves.

I myself am independent of what are called *'deliverance teams'*, however, the client is a *'client for life'*, during the entire process I might talk with the client for a great number of hours, to help keep their 'spirits high' in the least, to help them understand what they are going through. (*Note I cite "Spiritual Warfare Advisor", "Catholic Faith Advisor" as another part of the job description.*) I often find that I actually spend more time talking with these victims than anyone during the process of the 'healing' and after.

THE COUNSELOR

This role goes beyond giving advice, as often times people need to hear words of encouragement, coaching on 'positive' thinking, and so forth, as demonic infestations can be very taxing on one psychologically, (*as that is a part of it*), so I try to do what I can to keep their spirits higher.

At some point I might recommend a 'Psychologist/Psychiatrist, (medical doctor), or as is more often the case, a 'spiritual advisor' (only true ordained clergy), based on the client/family denomination or faith, this is more so common to 'possession' cases. This may involve an entire family, which may require a form of therapy to get through those darker times. I can also serve to advise clients of the Catechism of the Roman Catholic church as well as other Christian faiths in general, that is again, a part of "helping them help themselves" steering them into the right direction, as spiritual problems more often entail spiritual solutions. I might have to "dig deeper" just to get a better understanding of "why" the haunting might be there to begin with, and to better recommend an effective solution. But this goes a long way, often I find I can help people through intercessory prayers without even stepping foot into one's home. Really all that is needed is a clear diagnostic of the haunting. Then I go to recommend, and help apply the appropriate 'solutions'.

A "Spiritual Advisor" will help them be more active in 'their' church (for example), in ways that will better help with the 'healing' process. A Catholic priest for example, can help them to make a 'better confession', where this for myself can otherwise be, to say the least, a bit 'awkward', (*probing deeper into one's more personal life, as when helping them examine their spiritual life for 'sin'*). So I prefer leaving it up to their church priest / minister, although that isn't always how it follows that route...

FOR THE 'NON-BELIEVERS'

To the typical 'demon skeptic', we are placed all together into one box, and labeled as just another superstitious, faith based 'bible pounding' Christian type. I might add unfairly placed in a category with groups that say that **"Paisley prints are of the Devil"**, **"all hauntings are demonic"**, in saying we essentially blame demons for everything... Personally I find it disrespectful and annoying, but I am not really offended by this, although it can be a bit 'insulting' to me. When some act as I am blindly following some 'bogus religious' doctrine or a "bible only" philosophy in my beliefs, with absolutely no 'scientific backing' whatsoever. Perhaps the denial is part of being 'afraid' of accepting the reality that not only are we not alone in the universe, but we share the same multi-dimensional space as Evil Demonic beings and God's Angelic army who are at war with one another, trying to work to sway us to their sides.

Now if you believe in ghosts, think back. Remember how when you told (some) others of your encounter with a ghost, how they made you feel? They might have tried to say you were 'crazy', 'doing drugs' or even 'dabbling in witchcraft', for you to have experienced such things. Yes, it is quite offensive to have someone draw such conclusions. One can feel alone, confused, wondering themselves if it was indeed merely an 'over active imagination'. But I guess we were to believe our imagination only conjures up 'nightmarish' encounters. (*Nothing that a teenage boy would purposely imagine.*) When you approach a skeptic you will find they seem to never have an open mind to believe, unless they experience it first hand and had seen it themselves. Why we expect anything different is beyond me, perhaps we are looking for validation such as I got when I was eighteen and my friend also witnessed what I saw one night in a shadowy visitor. I was both relieved and frightened a bit after this.

It meant all of those years it wasn't my imagination as I thought. Suddenly my world was much different. And suddenly skeptics have two people telling the same story, two witnessing the same thing from different visual perspectives in the same room. Describing the same exact thing. Imagine that! But the skeptic will still ignore and turn away from truth.

We realize that *"demon"* is a label some people advert from because of its ties with 'organized religion'. The problem is some of these abusive relatives, preachers, and others who turned you away from the faith by subjecting you to extreme fundamental ideas as in how '*you will go to hell*' if you do this -or- that, is doing more the 'work of the devil' themselves, just look at the result after all. As I have children now, I rediscover some lessons in physiology. How we all don't respond to one type of 'motivation'. It is McGregor's "theory x" that is more the negative reinforcement, that would be trying to frighten someone to go to church. McGregor's "theory Y", would be in motivation about the 'positives'. I say this because if they drive away people, and not bring them closer to God, they are ineffective and counterproductive as a '*Minister*' or a "*Demonologist*". And like it or not you will be giving out your share of 'spiritual' advice and this is a note to use your empathy in determining what type of motivation they may need. While perhaps some may believe the 'fallen angels' label of these creatures might be debatable. I still feel that their existence, habits, and their very nature, is not, to me this has proven itself overtime beyond a mere "theology". Of course to not believe nor understand their origins and history is to lack an understanding in part, of what motivates them. Quite frankly, we should not let childhood experiences of a 'forced' attendance of 'Sunday services' with grandma, be a reason to ignore truth. Sure church can be 'boring' to some, but we are not at 'mass' to be 'entertained'. The problem here is people turn their back on all of the doctrine because of a disagreement with a few points. I have to say again regardless of your past experience, truth is truth, and ask that you don't turn completely away. For the sake of you and your family.

The fact is that these negative spirits were never human, and have existed for ages, and they are our enemies by their actions. They 'do' recoil to holy symbols, and certain words mentioned that we call 'prayers'. The name of 'Jesus' spoken does often send them fleeting, even if the words are said by those who don't believe in him as anything more than a prophet. They are 'provoked', as lighting a fire under their feet, and they can't ignore the proximity effect or the utterance of certain words and names that relate to 'religion'. And regardless if it turns some people off, because it is 'religious', the facts still remain. These things occur so much; one has to ask why these spirits continue to validate the age old faith based religions such as the Catholic-orthodox teachings have provided for the past two-thousand years. So even they alone can validate the faith for us. And this is one reason why God might allow these infestations to occur, as to help send some, who have fallen away, back to him. And solidify their faith when they see how his 'positive' grace can affect the 'negative' evil of the demonic. Again, why do they continue to display the very nature the church has outlined over and over again for the past two-thousand years? We continued to learn through the experience and writings of 'deliverance & spiritual warfare' counselors, exorcists, and of course those true demonologists, who existed throughout history.

In short, this is a witness to the "cause and effect" of things considered 'religious', it's what indeed brought me back to the Catholic faith and solidified it. Plus through this age old Christian faith, they had the answers like none other could compare. Now I don't go around bible quoting really when I try to educate those of the reality of these menacing spirits. Part of this is simply a preference, second "I don't need to", as 'bible only' denominations may be as hard to convince all ghosts aren't demons as much as an atheist is to convince of the reality of 'demons'. Plus, there is no need for me to become a 'preacher' and quote bible passages, which for many is a complete turn off, and as I mention can be 'counter productive' to the work. We can educate by other sources, experienced sources other than the good book alone as I trust many of you will also, as this book and others serve to further your studies and understandings of this work. I find with that 'bible only' mindset, these are the same ones who speak of *Heaven and Hell* only, so therefore, in their view, there are no 'other' planes of existence. Here again, I know better. Now as for myself, I didn't build a belief nor a knowledge of 'demonology' on the 'bible alone', it is an acquired knowledge passed on by church scholars, clergy and other theologians over the past two equates to one thousand plus years of Christian history through the ages.

My point is, if I relied on the bible alone as many other Christian denominations, I would be missing too much information that is needed to educate one of 'demonology'. I can't say "That is not in the bible" and ignore what I have come to experience and learn firsthand. When I realize the bible is in fact 'incomplete' as history dictates.

In short, through my own paranormal experiences I have found what I have learned from them parallel what I again was taught, basically learning of it again through my demonology studies. The study only validated what I found out for myself previously with firsthand experience. A very uncommon occurrence no doubt, but I feel everything happens for a reason. Now just because you don't care for the governing body of the church, and the bad public relations from the media such as with that more recent point in history where there was the over publicized 'pedophile priest', that the media ran with for a while, this should be a reason to ignore sound church doctrine. If one really has a problem with the Ten

Commandments in general, one should really think about re-examining one's lifestyle if you disagree with this. After all aren't we told of *"charity, compassion, hope, to "love your neighbor as yourself"*.
So why are people turned off by Christian doctrine? Why blame God for bad people of the cloth and in the ministry? And the world problems, that are the result of turning your back on God?

As for myself, I look past the bad clergy, and don't label the whole church because of a few bad apples. I also ask to not be labeled as some blind faith driven fool, and I ask to consider me more as a 'Teacher', not a 'Preacher', however a 'Professor of the subject Demonology studies', may better apply as I have spent over 30 years of my life on this. I call myself a Demonologist because it IS the area of expertise, in it I am a specialist. The title makes it easier to be recognized for what I specialize in, so that those who seek my advice and help can more easily find me.

But let me close with this metaphor:

Consider the '**non-believers**' as those who think the world is 'flat'.
'**The believers**' of course as being the ones who have written it is round as we know today. I am the explorer in heart, say a merchant, who comes upon something unexpected. As I was on a trade route, I discovered an alternate path that essentially proved the world was indeed not flat by sailing around the world. Now I would still get opposition from the 'skeptics' or 'non-believers' Unless maybe I took them on a voyage on this same route, of course in knowing skeptics, this is certainly no guarantee they would have the intelligence and wisdom (which is key) to understanding what has just occurred, even with their first hand witness experience. They may flat out remain close-minded and biased toward such a belief regardless. Likely I

would not have wasted my time as an explorer trying to convince the 'others', it is more so a waste of valued time. Instead I would seek to counsel others who believe in the plot course they could take to get to these destinations along this new route. So naturally after discovering this for myself, I find myself gravitating to those who have already written and spoken of the truth I have just discovered for myself. But I realize I may never get non-believers, who don't understand or believe what I experienced.

AN EXORCIST, DEMONOLOGIST, AND A 'GHOST HUNTER'

I want to describe in detail the difference between true 'Exorcist' and those who can be called 'Demonologist".

TO THE WOULD BE DEMONOLOGIST

First, I want to say although this can be a handbook for those seeking the studies of demonology, it is not going to certify you as a *"Demonologist"* simply because you read and memorized it cover to cover. I will say however, I believe that many who might even already call themselves *'Demonologists'* currently will find a great deal of things in this book they did not know previously. It just goes to show after even 10-20 years in studies and experience in the field you can still know so little. I hear of one young gentleman who is very confident in their knowledge and in reading one article on their website they make an absurd statement that **"Demons can't spell"** on an OUIJA board. It bothers me these misinformed people are taking on *"demonic cases"*, and saying more or less **"If you insist on using the Ouija board..."**, to warn them to stop using if the spirits can't spell because it is then a "demon". Well we argue most often it is a demon, and always a negative spirit. So there is no SAFE usage of this board. The supposed "*Religious Demonologist*" is ill advising on this one thing, how many other things is he spreading about the web and by other means that is totally false?

As he cites "*seventeen years*" in this field, I have to say to you the reader, to never think you have reached the point where you know everything. There are many points to consider in ongoing research that I continue to study, even after over 32 years. So never reach a point where you think you have all of the answers, and you ignore someone who has many years and experience over you on these topics, to where you are too grounded in a 'belief', (*which may be completely wrong, as this "Demons can't spell" notion).* The scope of this book is to simplify the diagnosis and solution to all 'hauntings'. And because of the many variables as to the spiritual, medical and psychological makeup of the people themselves. We can find the location and even what they might have in their possession, can play a part. And therefore each case is a unique study in itself as many variables play an important part as to why they are *haunted* and how to solve it. We are often working with people directly, and we have to be "empathetic" to a point of dealing with people as a Psychologist would. Bad 'people skills' should indicate that you should avoid certain aspects of this work when you deal directly with people on any level as with this. No matter what knowledge you have acquired in dealing with people, this can be where you 'drop the ball' and fail to help them. In saying this, it goes well beyond mere knowledge to be a supposed "*Religious Demonologist*". So no matter how vast this book is, it cannot change the way one may not be naturally "geared" for this type of work. There are many Priests who are not. So pray for your 'calling', rather than to take this on as a sort of "Career choice". In this you either have a calling from God, and should pursue the studies and work, or you don't.

In which case you should seriously consider staying away from it. Note however, as I have indicated, if you don't pray enough it will affect your life, even if you DO have a calling. Their reason is to intimidate you away from this work, so there is one less person out there armed with the proper knowledge who can "fight the good fight" against this evil. Some people might feel this work "rubs them the wrong way", but the simple truth is that some will have a true 'calling', and then back away because it starts to affect their lives too profoundly, as well as their family. When it may just be a matter in which they have NOT stepped up their spiritual life to a level where they can be more so protected from the effects of these spirits. Never take it for granted and wait to get hit with say 'financial hardships' and your baby is waking up screaming at night, your son speaking of his fear of night time "shadowy visitors". Even as you take on these studies, before entering into the actual field work, you will have to change your whole life around this. And use these extra measures of protection for your family as well as yourself, so that they are not affected. This might be one reason why people who do such work should be at least in their mid 30's. The wisdom of age will help us with these cases, and we are not so 'reckless' and become more settled as we grow older. Thus it is easier to not be swayed into social peer pressures in parties, and even teenage crushes that are going to affect our relationship with God, as these things can be occasions of sin.

Not to sound preachy, but we have to realize how these "free will choices", in our thoughts, words and actions might be offensive to others and to God. And at the same, these things empower evil spirits, as we appease them by turning our backs on God. As I say:

"you cannot expect to rebuke one demonic spirit while appeasing another."

So, in this, I recommend that you do yourself and those you care about a favor and stay out of this work if you are not ready to set aside your younger years of a "singles" life, trust me on this! You are not going to be an adventurer like Indiana Jones, but more like a "Priest" or an "Exorcist". Be prepared to start praying and going to church more often like one, if you want to survive. I have to say to be leery of those calling themselves a *"Demonologist"*. People should realize that simply making a choice to specialize in demonic haunts doesn't make one by default worthy of a title such as with a 'Demonologist.' As with reading this book will not make you one, anymore than visiting a Zoo makes you a 'Zoologist'. There is so much more to it than a few years of study, and it must be from the right sources. As my own 32 years of serious studies are ongoing, I never want to assume I have all of the answers. Only God does have all of the answers after all. Today, even my father will still always have a new book he's reading about 'spiritual warfare', and other related topics. I have bought him books for his birthday and Christmas all throughout the years. So, some say for me, it is more so a 'generational' practice to study and apply this knowledge. This beyond the many clergy in my family. So in a way, one could say, that 'Demonology' is sort of a 'family business', my legacy, as far as a knowledge and understanding. I now more realize even with that, it chose me, I didn't so much choose it, as I have had paranormal experiences since I was at least 7 years old. As that did kindle a search for answers, but in my case there was a wealth of knowledge almost at my finger tips throughout the years, so I wasn't limited to book stores and libraries alone.

There were many mentors of Catholic clergy and faith within my own clan. Books within my own house, my parents were already quite diverse on these topics before I was old enough to understand them.

WARNING! YOUR LIFE IS ABOUT TO CHANGE!

For some whom aren't familiar with these topics, it can be quite a shocking dose of a lesser known reality. At some point you might want to back away from the studies so that you don't become too engulfed in them.

It can effect you psychologically, make you bitter, cynical, hard to live with. Don't expect others to share your interest in these topics and it will be hard to contain your studies to yourself. Although we are seasoned adults now, it can still hit you like your first experience in watching a Horror movie as a child, which yes, can include frightening nightmares . Imagine having to tell your child monsters are real? But more so many years later after they reached adulthood, they will read on and learn what they experienced as a child. And it was actually not their imagination as their mom and dad had them believe.

Now before you give a phone call to mother and ask her '*why?*' I have to say, in thinking back, that this was the 'best decision'. In my Case I wore a Saint Benedict medal around my neck since I was at least nine years old, they could have been quietly praying behind the scenes for me, and my protection, while telling me it was my '*imagination*' as to not feed these hidden beasts with more of a child's fear. Which also is giving them 'recognition' rather than by simply ignoring them. And this in some phases is the best solution as it was in my case, as with many cases of children seeing 'monsters' in the closet or under their bed. (*When they are at school or at grandma's, have your home and their room and closet blessed.*)

So now that you are an adult, and more or less we can say it could have all been real, it will forever change your life and how you view the world. As it did with me. You might see things more as they really are, even as a basic understanding of 'positives' and 'negatives'. The (positive) purity of honey, love and light, the negative foul stenches of spoiled milk, cold, hate and darkness. And you will see how these absolutes affect one another. How these 'negative' entities for example advert from these 'positives', and cling to those 'negative' things. It is these traits that help us to better understand their very nature as well as how to combat them in "*spiritual warfare*" and "*deliverance*". And the very nature of these entities we call **'demons'**.

As you read on, you will become more aware of their habits, how they work, and their very nature. And as they know this, that is a 'dangerous knowledge' acquired, and they might try to directly show their disapproval or try to, (in the least), intimidate you from learning more and continuing your studies and work. After all *"knowledge is power"* in this war for yourself and as you might
affect others.

At the corner of your eye you might see them, visitations at night, suddenly waking at 3 AM. Doesn't mean in this case you are suddenly with a Demonic "infestation". It is just that you are being "visited", this differs from a true haunting that 'lingers'. However, we still need to take action daily to keep them from gaining any foothold in our homes and our lives. I know of some who are hit hard with financial bad luck, and have no idea that can be caused by demonic spirits. I can attest that this is a common way we can be affected, and another reason alone to pray so that these hardships will not take hold.

In 2002 I started to write the book again, I was a few years into my marriage and my first child was born. Some effects started quick after I began writing, experiences at night, in shadowy beings crawling up the wall, my son became affected as well. So I decided to back away and had lost the notebook I was writing
much of this in.

A few years after, I started to write it again, my son was almost five, and by then he was profoundly afraid of the dark. One night a transformer blew around 10PM, he screamed, and I ran to be with him. I stayed with him for 2 1/2 hours as we awaited them to replace the transformer. During that time he told me of things he experienced. "Pixies" as some might call them; he described them in too much detail. Yes I have heard of these before and it often didn't entail something necessarily 'good'. Around that time, it was the habit of my son to be placing toys in the hallway before bed that were colored 'black'. A toy vacuum cleaner, a pinball machine, all things a boy shouldn't be afraid of in the least.

I understand the reason for this, as I prepare my room differently than most adults. I close closet doors to cover the deeper dark inners of the inside; I move or hang up black clothes draped over the back of a chair, etc. I understand how, dark spirits like to hover close to dark objects and shadows when they lurk. We can see the darkness move, as he did. So, I didn't find it odd he was doing the same thing, when I never mentioned to anyone, not even my wife, I would do those last minute tasks just before bed without
mention of reason.

One night, he had awoken calling for me, I awoke and witnessed a smaller size cat shadow running up my shelf vertically, as I entered his room, he said: **"Delilah was in his room"** (*A black cat we had then*), this when his door was closed, and that cat was sleeping on the couch in the living room as she normally did that time of the night. But how about these two black cats, or a witness of several in his room that <u>do not</u> live in our house?

I stepped up prayer life with a daily rosary and these things backed off. So without further details, a step up in my spiritual life was necessary, even in writing just this book, without dealing with client cases of hauntings. These things can stir them up. Just be aware of that! As anytime you are seen as a threat they will try to punish you or intimidate you from proceeding. And this is often at the expense of your family. So take measures to protect them all. No need to detail why you give your son a "*Saint Benedict*" medal to wear exactly, just do as my parents did with me, and I had also done for my son. In saying it is for "protection".

Much of what you can do, can be done without the family being affected at all…

…if you pray to keep it at bay.

A SPIRIT CAN NOT ENTER

One morning I got up to start breakfast on the usual Monday morning. My son was already up, and told me a *"kid was outside his window"* and he was pacing back and forth outside of it. It was 20 degrees in the fall, with still morning darkness at 5:30 AM. And this boy as he described him wasn't wearing a jacket, just a blue T-Shirt, which was odd in itself. This didn't make sense, there was no access to cut through our yard on that side of the fence, as he thought maybe the kid was doing that. Our fence is blocked by shrubs; it would be easier to go through the gate on the other side, which was 'open'. We find that spirits will linger at a point of entry, when they can't get in, a manic pacing back and forth. This from study and experience I can say was likely 'not' a friendly spirit. The night before, I was tired and ready for bed, and I did the last things. I remembered I did 'not' yet say my daily prayers for protection and 'cleansing'. These can take 15 minutes to say and let me tell you sometimes it is too easy to let a drowsy body over come us, and just say `"I'll skip it tonight"`.

I went ahead and did them, and it might have been more needed than I would have thought. When we do these prayers a barrier is created that will lock out these infesting spirits. And in my line of work they will always try to get at me or family members, to affect us, and our lives. As sort of an act of revenge. This is true for anyone who does this work, not specific to me. We were just able to validate again here how these prayers are needed, and how you must push yourself to do them. Because we often can see what the results are and what is really lurking on the door step wanting in.

The reason 'salt' is said to be poured across door thresholds, the "Three Kings Epiphany" or blessed oil is placed over doorways, is because these spirits 'do' seem to have a limit. They perhaps symbolically use a door or window to enter your home. People ask now why don't they just go through the wall, for whatever reason they often can't enter by this way. And we will find it might even be a good practice to have a window open when doing prayers of deliverance. I am not sure about this as far a spirit 'leaving' but there seems to be indications that also might be true.

AN 'EXORCIST'

To clear up any misconceptions, it is indeed true that the Catholic 'Roman Ritual' does require prior consent for the local Archdiocese (*Bishop*). And it must be performed by an appointed Catholic (Priest) Exorcist. I read how some believe that a 'cleansing' and 'blessing and other deliverance prayers are considered by some, as an 'Exorcism', which to the Catholic Church, is not necessarily true. Even though by some dictionary definition it might be defined as such. Grant it, one might use 'other' prayers to effectively remove spirits, but when the word "exorcism" is used in the Catholic Church it refers mainly to the "Roman ritual" being performed by a true Ordained Catholic Priest.

Alternately, as I have found some Catholic prayer groups most often led by a Priest , may take on some '*deliverance*' tasks, but the '*Roman Ritual*' itself is not performed. The Saint Michael prayer, rosaries, and other prayers of intercession may be said, and even done so "AWAY" from the home or person(s) in need of the deliverance. These can be quite effective, except in more extreme cases. Never underestimate the power of such things and solely seek the BIG GUNS in an exorcism. Often the solution is not so far away, and should be started immediately if justified.

'EXORCISM'

I often advise those who seek help through the Catholic Church never use the word 'exorcism' and to use the words "deliverance' counseling, help or 'ministries', when seeking help with any clergy. Don't come out of the gate requesting an 'exorcism' that will not get you too far, merely request an investigation and let the church make that call. You can always ask for prayers, even contacting a convent or monastery to ask if they will offer a mass(es) for you or your friends, or client's intentions, but please consider a donation, even if it is small one.

If you are able to get the process going for an exorcism there begins a process many refer to as the *"red tape nightmare"*. A lengthy process of going from investigation to exorcism can take six months, to a couple of years. Most don't have that time to wait. You can say this is another reason for writing this book, to help get solutions out there beyond such drastic measures that entail such a long wait. Then we also find that sadly, some Priests just use the 'red tape' to purposely avoid these extraordinary task. Which at times can truly frighten them. They find it safer behind the podium as a 'Minister' of the people, and will be very reluctant to show up to "check out" a supposed haunted location, as it is not what they are used to dealing with. Which is why all Priests are NOT sanctioned 'Exorcists', partly because their knowledge and faith can vary so. This makes them not qualified for such an extraordinary job, which requires one of more piety. And not everyone is cut out for the work by nature. I have recently met more Monks who are armed with the knowledge, more than the many priests I have met. So a Priest with a weak faith is not only a less effective in 'deliverance', they can often stir-up more trouble after ineffectively cleansing a home. (*As you will read in more detail later in this book*)

So levels of faith, and piety, even for clergy, are important factors.
Lately we find because of all of the 'ghost hunting' groups out there, we see the negative results of too much media on 'ghost hunting' in itself. When these would-be ghost groups are making it more difficult by running to clergy for an 'exorcism' every time something goes 'bump in the night'. The Catholic Church can get so many requests for exorcisms now, that they had to further close the doors to filter out the many percent of cases which are not in need of an <u>actua</u>l exorcism. So yes folks! The "**red tape"** has lengthened!

Myself and others are attempting to open channels to the church, as so we can help to open the aid of the church to true demonic cases. This through organizations such as the Swords of Saint Michael (www.SwordsOfSaintMichael.org), and similar groups that are primarily Catholic, and will be more effective in networking with the church to act as an intermediary for those who seek the much needed help of clergy within it's walls.
We must realize that we CAN get good clergy and laity to help with prayers, etc and without the 'red tape' process in seeking a full blown EXORCISM. It can often be considered an unnecessary measure, even a drastic measure, as 'self help' can so often be enough to solve an "infestation" and other personal afflictions. So in saying 'free will' can be the source of our trouble in bad choices, the same can be said of the opposite in making good choices and taking proper measures in removing the problem.
Prayer and other measures can be just as effective in the deliverance process or 'healing' as some refer to it as. But this is called 'deliverance' help; keep that word in mind when looking for assistance in the final steps. So again, I advise you to avoid the word 'exorcism' and first seek out say a local 'prayer group' through your client's own church, or your own church might have such a group. In the least, prayer requests for deliverance will get help!

WHAT IS DELIVERANCE?

A term more popularized in the last century. A better recognized word might be *"Exorcism"*; however we as Catholics more so reserved this word in reference to the *"Roman ritual"*. While, *"Deliverance"* - is often the term used to describe lesser methods of removing the spirits from a person, place or even an object.

Sadly because of TV evangelism some avoid these words as to not be associated with some of these 'negative light', stereotype "Fundamentalist" kind of preachers. Who are shown in action with a microphone in their hand, casting out the "demon of smoking". Which, in my opinion, is almost a mockery of what entails a true possession. Especially when it is on public display, it provides a huge misconception as to what the real work is about. Many suspect even, that much of that is to merely fill the collection plates and to sell books and videos, and commercial ad space on their TV shows.

We find the Scientific *"cause and effect"* to prove many theories that are considered by some as primarily "faith based". When they are not only theologically sound, they are tried and tested true by many in all walks of life. Consider when reading that I have seen how the name of Jesus recoiled spirits when spoken by even people who consider him to be a mere prophet a mortal. The non-believer. We can't always expect to get the right help when someone is attacked nightly, so when these people are open to anything they are often instructed in ways to help themselves until another can intervene in person.

It never surprises me how we can still pray remotely and get results, that supposed Atheist can say there first prayers and have a more quiet, uninterrupted night sleep for the first time in months.

It is not simply a placebo effect or the person's confidence in saying his name that drove the spirit, the name itself is a holy and positive power. As in *"His name we do drive out evil"*. You have to understand this alone isn't enough.

The more you realize this, and set aside any prejudices against Christian faith, the better understanding of the reality of demons and their very nature. To better understand them fully and do battle we must know what does affect them, and what also appeases them. Hopefully this book will help you understand more of both.

A TRAINED EXORCIST IN A FEW WEEKS

As Gabriele Amorth's classes began in the 90's, they were designed to get Priests up to speed on topics that are no longer common to the seminary teachings. This is merely to arm them with enough knowledge to successfully exorcise the spirits, and to prepare for the battle. As more of a "refresher" course it was offered over a span of a few weeks, rather than years to months. The Priest is taught mainly just what he needs to know, nothing more.

An "Exorcist" is the recon man; he doesn't do the initial work, that is investigative, with research, interviews and so forth. All of the "leg work" is done prior to bringing them in. Therefore their knowledge doesn't need to be as deep as the "Demonologist", who precedes the "Exorcist" in the work. The need for these classes were to take select ordained Priests and bring them up to speed on things that relate to the task of performing exorcism. I mention this because we might find an Exorcist doesn't have the knowledge, someone like even Ed Warren used to have on these topics. So, there was a need to get Exorcists trained quickly, however, it was at the expense of years of study. But as the analogy applies, an 'Exorcist' is the repair man and the 'Demonologist' is the technician. He only needs to know how to remove the spirits, and proper spiritual preparation before the exorcism and after. Again, it is often like a "recon mission" for them, as another will proceed the ongoing task before and after the success of the 'exorcism'.

"GHOST HUNTERS"

People need to know, client based help is to provide a *'solution'* as this is apart from what *'**Ghost hunting**'* teams offer. These adventurers are more like 'Tourists' are to the Zoo, as 'big game hunters' looking for a trophy kill, or students who are there merely to observe and gather data. Hopefully they won't try to be something they are not, in carelessly waving around a vile of holy water or smoldering sage like a magic wand. So merely looking for evidence of 'spirits' is quite a different thing from, seeking their removal. That is looking for the source of the problem and not a solution. As we find to be a *"Ghost Hunter"*, can be better compared to one trying to prove the computer crashes, or to actually witness the software 'lock up' or crash occurring. While "Ghost busters", these are the technicians. (*Although I don't like that term "Ghost Busters", however, it does fit better than a reference to a "hunter"*) So people need to be clear as to what type of team they are and do not cross over to 'client help', if you are primarily an 'investigation team.' One is more so 'spiritualism' (client help), while the other more so 'science'. (Of course you can be both)

WHAT IS SPIRITUAL WARFARE?

We can call it a 'war' and often we do in this terminology, even though it is more so just a 'spiritual battle' that can be internal. It is still a battle at that. Of forces 'positive' against 'negative', 'flesh' versus the 'spirit'. Choices we make can tip the scales of the war to the 'other side'; we can become a pawn for the dark enemy and not know it. Our daily struggles involve attacks of temptation, as our own actions, words and deeds carried out, can begin as a seed of thought implanted into our hearts and minds. That they can build upon, well knowing our unhealthy desires, and curiosities. And as we carry them out, and give into such thoughts, it can take the war to another level that will 'open doors' and allow a demon for example to manifest physically. As with demonic "infestation", "oppression" and yes, even "possession".

The *'war of the spirit'* even when we still use spiritual solutions and defenses to counter the effects of what has manifested. We never can counter attack or defend with 'physical' methods directly. So set aside any notion you can use a sword or Kung-Fu kicks like "Buffy" to battle true demons. A "Spiritual Warrior" is not a glamorous or adventurous one, it is more closely to that of a Priest as I mentioned earlier. And if you don't take a higher path of spirituality with God, you won't last long. You can be financially hit, your marriage can fall apart; you might yourself find that you have excelled into self-destructive bad habits, suicidal, dead!

Again, you can not expect to be a 'lukewarm' Catholic for example, and survive in this field of work. We must always remember we alone are not doing this work; we are merely intermediaries to Heaven, as we ask for intercession from the angels and saints. Our words mean little in telling an evil entity to "begone", but by the authority of Jesus, we use his name and Paul in Ephesians 6:

```
"...Be strong in the Lord and in his
mighty power. Put on the full armor of God
so that you can take your stand against
the devil's schemes. For our struggle is
not against flesh and blood, but against
the rulers, against the authorities,
against the powers of this dark world and
against the spiritual forces of evil in
the heavenly realms. Therefore put on the
full armor of God, so that when the day of
evil comes, you may be able to stand your
ground, and after you have done
everything, to stand.
```

Stand firm then, with the belt of truth buckled around your waist, with the breastplate of righteousness in place, and with your feet fitted with the readiness that comes from the gospel of peace. In addition to all this, take up the shield of faith, with which you can extinguish all the flaming arrows of the evil one. Take the helmet of salvation and the sword of the Spirit, which is the word of God. And pray in the Spirit on all occasions with all kinds of prayers and requests. With this in mind, be alert and always keep on praying for all the saints." *(Ephesians 6:10-18, NIV)*

PRAYER SAID BEFORE YOU BEGIN

Say this daily before you read this text, so that you may better understand and remember to better use this knowledge to serve the Lord in this great battle.

May this holy prayer, made in the most Holy Name of Jesus Christ our Lord and Savior, cover all who visit this site. May you be covered with the Precious Blood of our Lord Jesus Christ. In the name of our Lord Jesus Christ, and by the power of His sovereign authority, together with the intercession of St. Michael the Archangel and the Blessed Virgin Mary, may you be protected from all the snares, influences, lies, attacks, temptations, approaches, manifestations, diversions, powers, deceptions, and tricks of the Ancient Serpent, who is also called Satan or the Devil. May you be clothed with the

Full Armor of God and aided by the strength of St. Michael the Archangel together with a legion of large, fierce, and powerful Warrior Angels. May the Lord grant you the gifts of the Holy Spirit, particularly the discernment of spirits, in order to overcome all of the activities of the powers of darkness through the power of the Spirit. May God's blessing be upon you and cast far from you any curse, hex, spell, incantation, and, in short, all sources of spiritual bondage from which it is necessary to be delivered in order to grow in grace and spiritual freedom. In the name of Jesus Christ, may any such sources of spiritual bondage be broken and utterly destroyed and replaced by God's blessing. May the Lord bless you so that you walk always in His freedom and accomplish all things with His power and for the sake of His greater glory. We ask this in the name of Jesus Christ, our Lord and Savior, Amen.

PRAYERS OF PROTECTION and BINDING

When you begin studies in these topics you will often be affected in some way, now that you have decide to cross that line and become more knowledge, learning these topics is an act of war against them

Spiritual Warfare prayer of intercession to Saint Michael the Archangel:

Saint Michael, we claim you as our patron saint, o benevolent Prince of the heavenly

Host! Be near to us, we pray, and protect us from the wickedness, lies, and snares of the Devil and all his fallen angels! We pray, O good Saint Michael, that you would prevent, in the name of Jesus Christ, our Lord and Savior, any lies of the Devil from being made manifest in this group. We pray that only the truth would be heard in this group and that the truth would lead us to freedom through, with, and in Jesus Christ, our Lord and Savior. Protect this group and all its members from the wicked attacks of the evil one, the Devil, our enemy. Through your gracious intercession, may we be covered with the Precious Blood of Jesus Christ to wash our souls clean of all sin and impurity. Intercede for us, we pray, before the Most Holy Trinity, before whose throne you are always present like a vigilant warrior and obedient prince. Intercede for us with Christ Our Lord together with your queen, Mary, Queen of Angels, and all the saints, blesseds, angels, and holy souls, that the will of God would be fulfilled in our lives. We pray that we would remain free from the grasp and control of our adversaries, the evil spirits, demons, and fallen angels who prowl throughout the world seeking to ruin and destroy the lives and souls of all people who have been created in the image and likeness of the Lord God Almighty. All this we ask of your benevolent intercession from heaven, O good and holy Saint Michael, in the name of Jesus Christ, Our Lord and Savior. **AMEN.**

As the 'effects' can vary by the individual, (*based on the spiritual life of the person for example*), if you feel a need to add more prayer, turn to the last pages in the book and I recommend that you say the "**Hedge Prayer of Protection**" in this book. (see index)

IDENTIFYING THE BASIC TYPES OF SPIRITS:

We should all forget trying to "label" spirits with other "titles" based on their behavior, based on varied appearances, and so forth. For too long it has been <u>over complicated</u> by others needlessly. When it is not necessary in our line of work in removing the spirits. (*i.e. deliverance, Exorcisms or' ghost busting'*)
We should be concerned with ONLY two categories, properly pairing them to identify the **type** of spirit:

```
Category One:   Good or Evil
Category Two:   Human or Inhuman
```

Good, spirits are either between this world and Heaven, in a phase of existence called 'Purgatory', or they are from Heaven, angels and saints for example.

Evil, would be in reference to the 'other' spirits, I refer through-out this book as "Dark Spirits", they are also called the "Lost Souls", "Condemned" "The Damned". Regardless of their various names their new masters are demonic, and we should never expect them to stray from demonic control to do any 'good' for example. They can work with the demons, yet be a slave to them, as the puppet is to the puppeteer.
So, concerning yourselves with the heritage, age or gender of the spirit for example, is not necessary. As labeling a shadowy being "Hat Man" for example, just because it looks like it has a "hat". It is still a 'dark spirit' and likely a minion with demons, human or inhuman it isn't 'good'.

Most often.

Ask yourself *what type of spirit does it fall under?* While using the above *"types"*. That is how we derive the proper solution.

So don't try to over analyze with an array of *spirit types*, it is unnecessary to over complicate these things like this. To narrow it down further, it is not the nature of "Good" angelic beings to haunt a home so we can almost entirely eliminate TYPE: GOOD-INHUMAN from the typical haunting scenario. So this mainly leaves:

TYPES:
"GOOD-HUMAN"
"EVIL HUMAN" or **"EVIL INHUMAN"**

So in detail, I will help to outline ways to first determine the nature of the ghost as "evil" or "good".

Most often the solution for a 'ghost' is to pray for it's deliverance. Part of the penance may be that they are unable to simply move onto the 'next life' entirely until they learn something, or in the form of some other 'penance'. Such as to let go of their worldly possessions, to let go of their life, or to do one specific act of charity. *Evil* or *demonic*, pray for deliverance. As I say often, as you are discerning good or bad, start prayers now, don't wait, as they are never wasted. (**See the section on 'Purgatory'*)

NOTES ON 'DIAGNOSING' A HAUNTING

Often in this, we find it is a 'play by ear', in accessing the type of haunting, the severity, and so forth. All needed to provide an adequate solution. Just as diagnosing a PC Windows problem, knowing the symptoms is key to finding a solution. As understanding the severity of the problem as well, will entail a need for 'drastic measures'. For Example. I ran into some 'computer guys' who solve things by wiping the hard drive clean and reinstalling everything. A bit extreme when you can fix it without taking such drastic steps. But this is a panic step that a lesser knowledged technician will use. The problem here is in another person calling themselves a "technician" when they are only a 'one trick pony' or a "repair guy" at best. Consider a "repair guy" can be anyone who can fix it, but not necessarily using the best way, or the repair might not hold. He is more or less a "hack", yanking boards, here and there, rather than to recognize symptoms and going right for a proper solution. So a technician is a good mix of both an 'engineer' and 'repair guy'. The engineer can understand the inner workings on the computer well. But it does not alone arm one to recognize and solve problems. An engineer is to design, prototype and build. A software engineer (programmer) is often not the one who debugs it, (troubleshoots the crash, etc.) That often requires a 'specialist', more so in larger companies, where you'll find an 'engineer' is not trained to improvise and troubleshoot well. Although such task is part of the design process.

People who attain a healthy understanding of the common problems and solutions from experience with such an engineered device will know more at some point in how to fix it when it fails.

"*How to repair your PC*" is a good book, but does it make you an experienced repair guy? Do you have a well understanding of the inner working of the computer now? Or will you always revert to a reformatting/restore on the local hard drive when a Windows crash reoccurs?

Wrong solutions for problems not correctly identified…

Both 'science' and 'spiritual' are considered, just as we don't want to assume witness testimony is always accurate in telling what is really going on. The occurrences can be completely 'normal' and 'natural'. In field investigations, a qualified team will professionally help to gather physical evidence as needed of the haunting.

Where a second team will handle an effective solution if one is justified. As I said, all the time we might suggest prayers and offer help solutions immediately, rather than to await results of investigations. Because there is no harm that comes from offering prayers for a family that seems to be truly affected by an evil presence in their home. We want to give them the benefit of the doubt, especially when it costs NOTHING to do so, and there is literally nothing to lose in doing so.

"Better safe than sorry. "

INDICATIONS OF A TRUE HAUNTING

You might be reading this book with the thought you already are sure you have a haunting on your hands or perhaps it is a friend of yours. Now as I outline some information to help you discern the difference between a *'demonic spirit'* and a *'poor (human) soul'* for example. I need to mention that it is not the scope of this book to help you determine you are having something paranormal occurring in general; it is more so designed to help you remove the spirits that might be there, and to better understand why they are here to begin with in any given case. It is assumed that you do indeed have something paranormal going on, and this is about identifying the type of spirits, then help to provide proper solutions.

Pay close attention to the patterns of the haunting itself, the times of the apparition(s), paranormal occurrence. It is not common for someone who has a 'good' spirit, to call upon people like myself for help. So the contents of this book will deal more with:

TYPE: Demonic or Human / Evil.

HAUNTED 'HOT SPOTS' VERSUS 'RESIDENTIAL'.

We have to remember the haunting in an old 500 year old castle, is not the same as one that is involving people living in there home. When people are living in it, the haunting can be very different, it revolves around those who live there, what they do, how and what they speak, and even their frame of mind and mental health. The reason for the ghost being there in a residence where people actually live. This more often has to do with the people themselves, rather than the building they dwell in. Making themselves known is projected to the living not just a show in an empty theater with no one to watch. This is where we say: **"if a tree falls when no one's there to hear it, does it make a sound?"**
Do these 'ghosts' stay dormant until people come around? Or do they carry out their activity and 'business' regardless. Even a camera or similar recording device is a human presence. Later in this book I will go over "Purgatory ghosts", which might be the only exception to this notion in those cases where the spirit lingers at a location regardless of human occupants or visitors. A tie to the place means a holding pattern of some sort between this world and Heaven. Note: I don't subscribe to ghostly apparitions not having some sort of intelligence behind it some how, even if it is merely "projected" to give witness to some past events. Some entity is behind the source of what we see. Also note as I describe as:
"Type: EVIL",
 it is another matter however as I outline as you read onward.

One might visit an old landmark, just for the fun of it, or research, they are there by choice, and they might have even paid for this "haunted tour" hoping to see ghosts. While a haunting taking place at one's home, the others are simply trying to live their lives and they actually live on the site day to day. They are more so the unwilling victims of the haunting. And we find that behavior and patterns of the noted paranormal occurrences play around the people.

It might be harder to capture on video, film, and audio any evidence when people are involved. The entities seem to 'duck' the evidence captures more, this is more evident when it is a 'demonic' haunting. At an old prison the strategy is somewhat different; however some might customize the experience based on each individual. There will always be a certain 'strategy' played by these spirits in who they want to witness their presence. We have to remember some experience can turn an atheist into a Christian, believer into a non-believer. The "dark spirits" prefer you better as a "non-believer" or an "Agnostic" across the board. And they will try to avoid helping you grow spiritually to a more positive life towards God where they can help it. So this is considered by them in the strategies, as far as "dark spirits" go.
God may use the dark spirits in his own strategies to help push people towards him.
"There are no Atheists in fox holes or in haunted houses" is a catch phrase I use, as some experience might drive a man to Sunday services for the first time in years. So it can be said as soon as even visitors show in an otherwise empty building, the haunting itself changes to the individuals who will tour the location. So as it can be part of the strategy to not want to be detected by third party onlookers, and the outside world. If a 'ghost' wants itself to be known it will do it at anytime, day or night. Not just 3AM in the morning that would be day or not if it is able to. In short expect the haunting to have almost a strategy in its pattern of occurrences when it is centered around the living. Versus something that might be experienced spending the night in an old empty castle.

We know how dark spirits are not going to be anxious to reveal themselves in the presence of a team that is there to more or less rebuke them from the premises. So note it a common thing for these types of spirits to duck detection, expect this. This is one of the reasons a "religious provocation" might be in order to force the dark spirits to reveal themselves so they don't get away with purposely hiding to hinder progress in a deliverance. Especially as the Catholic Church will want to be presented with tangible evidence before proceeding towards a church sanctioned exorcism.

Lastly, evil spirits might linger for several reasons in an empty building, but as I stated they might be dormant until people show up. It is hard to say exactly.
Please read on below to the section: `why are you haunted'` where I list some reasons why they might linger at any given location.

THE OWNERS <u>CAN</u> HELP THEMSELVES.

I read an internet blog once, where the writer was criticizing a team for instructing the home owners on how to do a 'cleansing' themselves. To a certain extent, if the methods entailed were correct, this is a good idea in some cases. More severe hauntings will require home owners to more discreetly do battle saying prayers away from the 'HOT SPOTS' where the activity seems to be the most strong. This is under the consideration that one or more family members don't have an attachment where the activity
might follow them everywhere they go.

As we find in the main dwelling, they seem to have more of a foot-hold on the home, and activity is usually not as severe when they pack up and spend the night elsewhere. At least for a few days. Essentially, what is bound on Earth can be bound in Heaven, you own the home in God's eyes, you have more authority as the 'home owners', than some would-be ghost hunter waving sage sticks. There are times where the home owners in a firm voice, tells it to `"leave!"` and it does. And this without invoking the name of 'Jesus' or sporting a religious artifact or holy symbol for example. Obviously in these cases, the manifestation was not too strong, likely just a human entity at best. It left far too easy.

I will say it is important to carefully note that it is also possible that it didn't leave at all. In this case it may have just chose to simply "lie low" and behind the scenes in its ongoing stage of 'infestation'.

Part of this as I later outline is a 'strategy'. It can work on the people in the home psychologically, and spiritually even, without making anything "*go bump in the night*". Just be aware of this fact. So you don't assume it is all over too soon and let down your guard and go on with your life. It isn't as easy as using a 'roach motel'. As they might appear to "check out" when they really have not.

BACK DOOR METHODS

Please note that with true possession, this is not what I typically consider a "self help case", these individuals can barely say one word in a prayer, let alone it is dangerous in advanced stages of demonic influence to take 'lower level' solutions. However, remotely, we begin prayers for the afflicted still. Just not on site, as we are not forcing the suspected possessed person to help themselves. After all, we are not talking about "possession" here, and through out this book it is more about 'haunting stages' that occur before possession as far as 'SELF HELP' goes.

A "**Back door**" to computer networks is a second entry point where a programmer can access more easily or even 'hacker' can exploit to bypass security as to enter into the system as an 'administrator' to make changes to the system configuration and so forth. In this I refer to a **back door method**, is to not directly approach the 'infestation' head on, to say prayers remotely to weaken the entities before going in with "all guns blazing".

(*Note: we don't have to use a back door method if we are certain the spirit is 'Good'.*)

In what some refer to as "violent haunting"; saying prayers on site before a planned exorcism or deliverance can be dangerous (*See also the section "With all guns blazing"*). Therefore to avoid *"kicking the mean dog's fence"* with the gate open, we work externally. These prayers can also in effect 'TEST' the presence; if activity declines from these prayers we have a better understanding of the severity of the haunting. A **"Cause and effect"** has been noted, and if we see external prayers do help, we better understand what we might deal with internally, inside the supposed "haunted location".

Just as a precaution if you are not sure about a haunting begin prayer immediately to help discern the level of manifestation, or 'type' of spirit. It is *"better to be safe, than sorry"*. Never rush in and get hasty in how we deal with these things as they can profoundly affect people's lives, and place them in grave danger. Granted, the back door mentality differs from a sort of 'Cowboy' method we might have been exposed to on TV. But this comes from actual field research and application and has a great deal of success.

BOUND BY RULES

When a ghost is trying to tell you something, or so you believe, never try to contact it. You should not try to contact it directly. Now simply asking **"what do you want."** or **"why you are here"** is harmless, but don't try to engage in conversation with it. Somehow movies like the *'Sixth Sense'* give the impression that we can help these spirits by finding out what they want. Sort of a Hollywood movie rule, in horror movies, that ghosts have a sort of 'unfinished business' which is actually true to a point as I discuss in this book. However, so few are here to try to point out to you 'their murderer', as this isn't a game of 'charades' for you to guess what they are trying to 'tell you' and solve their problems. Often you are being lied to and manipulated.

THE LAW OF INVITATION

A ghost will not go simply where it wants, it is all God's will, as they are bound by rules that they can not break. Spirits do not possess a "free-will" as humans, they are limited and in part by our own thoughts words and actions. As we can affect their limitations I refer to such rules as "mortal law". That is rules that we break that give invitation to these spirits. But in this I am referring to **TYPE: Evil Human or Inhuman** If you read in the bible, the story of King Saul and the 'Witch of Endor', how the King with his weak faith, called upon a local Witch to summon the spirit of the '*King* as to ask his advice'. *(In a way this is what many do with 'Ouija boards' and other forms of spirit communication)* To do so broke a rule between the dead and the living. This mortal law I mention, when humans do this, they open the door, a Pandora's Box. Because if you try to contact the spirit it is suddenly allowed more freedom. These spirits are bound by the actions of man as well as the Will of God.

Remember the old vampire movies, where Dracula could not enter the home unless, he was 'invited' in by some means? As usual there again is truth in a so-called myth. If you really looked into it, you would find that most all myths are based on truth somewhat.

In the same way, you have to cross the line in that manner and invite the spirit(s) in. This is why many advise to ignore the presence and don't try to engage. It is safer that way. It would be better to pray for that soul. Prayers would either ward it off if evil, or aid the soul if it is in the middle world. With this suggestion as opposed to telling it to 'go into the light'.

OUR WORDS ARE BINDING

The apostles drove out demons commanding them to in the name of 'Jesus'. Though the layman is not as one of the original apostles, we can effectively use the name of 'Jesus' to drive away evil when we see it necessary. So in the same manner the opposite is true that there is a certain power in a select few words that can open the door to the spirit world.

So whether you pray, curse, or directly try to engage in the occult and cast spells, you are changing the playfield between your life and that realm of the spirit world. This is why you should be very careful in life to not 'curse' as a Christian especially; they are called 'curse words' for a good reason. Because in saying them we can indeed infuse a curse onto a person place or thing as you shout these certain words, say in a rage.

Keep in mind a 'curse' is the opposite of a 'blessing', it's the 'negative' to say a 'positive' such as with prayers we recite. Not to mention, one can counter affect the other. So under the rules or 'Mortal Law', a man's words can bind or change the playfield. God leaves it up to us, and again we see it is our choice to bring chaos into our lives, as it is to try to follow the commandments. Or to reject it. *"Free will."*

So in this I say to take responsibility, and don't let curiosity or ignorance tempt you to try to contact spirits. Be careful what you speak, your words hold more power than you think. We can bring what seems to be 'bad luck' to an otherwise prosperous household or business, simply by cursing inside the premises. What this does quite simply, is it invites demons in to affect your life. Yes, "invitation" again here, as our 'free will' can take us in small steps to side with Dark/Evil or the 'Light side' with God.

Our choice in what we do or say, gives a little to take away from God's grace and favor the darker side. Or visa-versa as you tried to be good in all you say and do. <u>"Choose your words carefully."</u>

WHY ARE YOU HAUNTED?

Sometimes to solve a haunting you need to understand "why" you are haunted. As it more often plays a huge part. How it all started, might indicate it is partly a matter of 'closing' that door they 'opened', reconciliation with God, and then not making that same mistake again. Other times, people dig too deep out of curiosity; they are drawn into the drama of what might be the history of the residence and the reason for the haunting.

Then we find that often the case is, that the "more dramatic", the less likely what we are lead to believe is "NOT TRUE". And it was a 'demonic' behind the scenes all along waiting to snare the unsuspecting curious 'ghost hunters'. Some of these will use methods considered by the church as 'necromancy' which is to only make matters much worse. All to try to learn more about the assumed *"troubled human spirits"*, and what they might have to say. In some cases, especially nowadays it is more about a "trophy" than anything, I suppose the term "Ghost Hunters" is suitable. Get your gear, gather with your pals, drive to the location, do your haunt hunt, get some evidence, go home tired yet gloating, flaunt your experience and so-called evidence like a 'big fish story' from then on. Nothing gained really. Maybe just elevated levels of pride and self-esteem, it is all "self" serving.

I can tell you there is a good reason why the bible forbids the practice of trying to communicate with the dead. Not so much a theological one even. Call it a father's warning to his naive children. Your own dad might tell you to stay off the icy pond, and until you fall through the ice, you might think he is being 'overboard' and a sort of 'fuddy-duddy' who wants to intrude on your 'fun-time'. When the ice breaks you wished you listen to dad. Children go over these experiences over the course of their lives. Some are the wiser and take note of dad's warnings, rather than to always find out for themselves he was right all along. While others, continue to have to find out for themselves the 'hard way' in this business that will kill you, so set aside your childish side and listen to these words of warning I and others speak of.

The warning to "not communicate with the dead" can be sound as we truly don't know if the spirit is what it might pretend to be. Demons are liars, we can expect a mix of truth and lies to manipulate and snare us. They can know more about your

'Uncle Fred', than well... your Uncle Fred even knew about himself. So specific information passed on isn't an indication it is really your deceased 'Uncle'. Again we know not what we are contacting. And it will most often NOT be a good spirit. We don't want to swim with the fish if sharks might infest the waters, so our heavenly father says to "stay out". It is a matter of the dangerous curves on the road, and you are driving with a blind fold. As you read on you will read of other means of necromancy, not just séance's and Ouija boards, always revert back to the 'Mortal Law', to avoid communicating with the dead 'period'. Regardless how appealing the oracle or device might be, or how cool some new electronic gadget could be. (*i.e. the 'Ghost Box'*)

It is best to stay away from it 'period'. We don't need to contact these spirits directly to solve a haunting. In other words there is no information that must be attained from the spirit themselves, that will help to solve the haunting. Very rare times is a spirit trying to point you to their shallow grave site in a basement, hidden property deed or lost fortune. This is more for 'spinning yarns', again the 'drama' that might lure you in but it is farthest from the real truth. A ploy and deception to better snare you in. As I said ignore the 'drama' that isn't how it generally works. The methods in removing the spirits from a haunting outlined here do not require you directly communicate with them in such matters. No one ever needs to do so. Keep that in mind and set aside that foolish and dangerous notion. Some rare exceptions are "*seer's*" such as Maria Simma and Lorraine Warren, where direct intervention is done, but these people have God's true gift of discernment, and they spend a great deal of time with daily prayer, and are very close knit with their faith. In other words, don't try this at home! (*See also the section on Psychic-Mediums*)

I am finding most often there is more to it, than a mere innocent victim when it comes to a demonic haunting. <u>Something that is not being revealed.</u>

Some books on the market want to portray the people who experienced the haunting in their story as mere 'victims', unwillingly and undeservedly being attacked by demonic entities. When this is not the case.

Look behind the scenes, often than not they lured it there or empowered by their words, actions or even thoughts. In books, TV and movies it is more for the drama to believe they "didn't" somehow have it 'coming to them'. So they may turn a blind eye to indications of such truths to better sell this published media. So more often than not something is NOT being revealed by the client(s) that more so explains the "why" and this includes why it might start up again after a successful deliverance.

GHOST HUNTERS BEWARE!

"Ghost hunting" is more often than not, crossing a 'dangerous line'. This goes beyond people who try to do séances to contact the spirit to curiously find out why it is there. That is part of the typical snare. Draw in the curious, get them to open the doorways with these things.

Remember as I said most often the drama the spirit tries to portray isn't often the reality. And who says this spirit is what it says it is? Best choice avoid contact period. We really won't approach the haunting any different anyways regardless if the spirit is telling the truth or not. Again we either seek to rebuke the spirit(s) or pray for the souls to help them move onto the next phase closer to Heaven.

You'll see people walk around with Digital Audio Recorders as though it is some oracle of communication. One provokes a spirit to talk, insulting it, calling it [names] and cursing at it, all to try to gather evidence of the paranormal. Certainly, the Big Fish" stories must be accompanied by your paranormal evidence in EVPs and ghostly picture captures.

But this is used more so for entertainment purposes and a feather in one's cap. And like a "Hunter" these 'trophies' are much like displaying your kill on a plaque in your den. And accompanying it with a story while you sit in your den smoking a pipe in your monogrammed robe. Except many of these people do this at a lecture hall or on stage. Now when we try to gather such evidence for the church to help a case to move to a church authorized 'exorcism', that is one thing, but when we are in it for the 'glory', and looking for your own "proof" as to exploit in the media that is another. The intentions can make a difference. Although mere curiosity can be enough to get you in trouble. It varies from site to site, and person to person individually. But note, even Vatican Exorcist Fr. Gabriele Amorth says *"unholy places can get you cursed"*, and can bring home an unwanted attachment in a demonic spirit. And from this, it was all for the fun of touring an old cemetery, or historical mansion. Consider that it is not fair to your family to have your kid awake screaming at night because a shadow being scared him/her. If you must do it, for whatever reason, do the proper protection prayers before and after. Wear the appropriate armor (Saint Benedict medal), and stay in the state of grace.

It may sound a bit cliché for a Ghost Buster to say *"stay away from the Ouija boards"*. But <u>ANY</u> form of communication with the spirit world can be a Pandora's Box. This includes pendulums, provoking a response when recording for "EVPs" *(i.e. 'Electronic Voice phenomenon')*, including also the recent usage of the electronic radio scanner or "Ghost box". When you become haunted it is time to end the *"leisure haunted tours"* and "ghost hunting" fun. You are now 'allergic' to the supernatural, as a diabetic is to sugar.

I will say that often we find that <u>many of us</u> have to back away from this work, to give ourselves a break, or it can be too taxing on one's psychological/spiritual frame of mind. That is to be expected. An 'Exorcist' will pray and prepare for days prior to the Rite, to build their strength for the battle, and afterwards, a recoup might be needed in the form of a 'mini vacation'. We are all human after all, and we might need a second wind before re-entering the 'ring of battle'.

AN UNHEALTHY INTEREST

"There are two equal and opposite errors into which our race can fall about the devils. The first is to disbelieve in their existence. The other is to believe, and to feel an excessive and unhealthy interest in them" – C. S. Lewis, The Screw tape letters

An unhealthy interest in them is crossing the line from reading to learn how to 'battle', to a sort of "fanatic". Even in the studies for the right reasons we may need to take a break from the path to offset our minds for a bit from these topics. If we do not, that can be unhealthy in itself. There was a time I found that when I listen too much to political 'talk radio', I would get to where all I can talk about are political issues I heard on the news and these shows being discussed. It started to make me bitter, cynical, as we often feel helpless in world news events that we can not, as an individual, do a thing about to bring resolve. Perhaps it is more so, just in me, to want to fix problems. But needless to say I limit my exposure to these things, which are negative in their own right. The same thing can happen with any topic of interest, as it can become an obsession.

While just as reading of demons, while with good intentions or not, we may need to 'clear our head' to give our mind and spirit a break from reading about these dark entities.

Unhealthy, for some is to start to admire and glorify demons, as they are 'angels', in contrast to humans some might look on them as 'gods'. Sure, we can have a certain respect for them, but that is not the same. We realize as they may be superior over us in many ways, in age, intelligence and wisdom, this is true. But we don't honor or venerate them as we should do the Angels and Saints of the one true God. So it is a 'healthy' respect, in that you can respect your enemy in any war, but still not support them in any way.

It probably isn't the first time that it is heard that you shouldn't purposely '*disrespect*' other worldly spirits. And that the fine line is drawn, say between including words in prayers of deliverance that might include a reference to them as "*unclean*" or "*impure*" spirits for example, things we might consider as "disrespectful". They don't take offense as such references actually in that they are 'true'. And almost have a certain level of pride in their 'negative' nature, so in a strange way it to them is almost a compliment. However, when in fact you call them something they are not, is quite another matter and might prove to provoke them. If you call them weak, stupid, or challenge it:
"*I can take you, where are you?*"

That is disrespectful and foolish to say the least and might invite a retaliation that can even result in an attack or even your death.
Remember we don't fight these spirits directly on any level; it is all through 'intercession'. Alone we are no match to these spirits, even the lesser/lower ranks that might appear as small animals.
Approach these matters with such a certain humility that you are only a 'servant of God' and being used as a tool of 'deliverance' for his greater glory.

THE NAMES OF DEMONS

First, I will NOT write of demon names specifically, because they are often irrelevant to 'spiritual warfare', except during an 'exorcism'. These types of 'guides' are a rarely used reference, essentially only of use to an Exorcist during the deliverance. If the exorcism is done in it's entirety, and it was at first attempt, ineffective, sometimes the Exorcist will demand the demon reveal it's name.

This is often for two reasons:

(Note: this information is only reliable as the Exorcist will force the truth from the demon using religious provocation and prayers of intercession. As we know the demons will lie, and say they are 'Satan' himself, or lost loves ones.)

1. To reference the name, is it a higher demon in rank? If this is true the exorcism maybe a longer haul, as 'devil' the higher order demons are more powerful and harder to rebuke.

2. The demon does not want to be known, and to be successful in provoking the demon for example to cite his identity, tells the Priest he was able to force the demon to reveal itself by name. Was he able to do in 'the name of Jesus'? Or did it take more to get the truth to be told. The Priest notes at what level it was necessary before the demon told it's name. This can indicate also what he is up against in the exorcism.

Many online websites and some other publications will showcase a list of Demon names, their designation, and their ranks. Not only is this unnecessary information, it can be dangerous. We do not want to give demons recognition, especially by speaking their names. It can be like a beacon to say their name, a summoning, as some words should not be said because they are 'evil', in itself as a 'curse' word. This is merely another example of that. Now as an accurate list will be of use to reference the demons names to more details, this when it is a valid list, is a valued reference of it's potential power, to the Exorcist. Again, I say since we can't trust information we might receive from the 'father of lies' and his minions, forcing a demon to reveal it's name is not for laity.

So note this word of caution, especially in saying a demon's name aloud, as even in thought it can lure them to your side. It is also best we do not try to get to know demons or angels on a 'name' basis.

If one seeks to 'look it up', they may run across many 'lists' out there, have a mix of faiths and belief systems, mythology, and so forth, which contain 'inaccurate' information. As I cited in another chapter, this includes a confusion of the 'fallen angels' (demons) and the 'Angels of God'. Citing one name as an Angel of God, when it is in fact a known name of a demonic spirit. This includes so-called "Angelology" resources as well, and visa-versa.

Grant it the lists are also very short, and therefore not of much use in that alone. And I find many are most often just a *'copy and paste'* from another website article. (*This happens far too often in my opinion).* So this misinformation is being distributed as 'fact' out there among these many internet sites, and through various published media. And can not serve us in this field as one might think, as we seldom need this information, and as the data is skewed at best, we find the information is useless.

This is an overall note of caution for any so-called internet resources on "Demonology". To further your studies visit: www.catholicdemonologist.com , where I will provide links to point you to good resources and reading material.

THE MASQUE of 'ANGELOLOGY'

The study of angels is interesting but is more considered *"extra-curricular"* in this field. So as when we study 'demons', who are also 'angels', this is also the basis of knowledge in any area of so-called "Angelology". In what we need to understand that is covered under these topics of "Demonology". So we won't be dealing with angels in true hauntings, and will only call upon them for 'intercession'. It is more a topic for the curious to read of the glorious beings that serve God and mankind on a separate study. As there are many resources out there, and I am trying to cover ones that apply to this area of work. We are not "Preachers" after all and knowing such information is indeed supplemental, and not a necessary study. A 'Demonologist', is essentially both an *'Angelologist'* and a *'Demonologist'* as we understand God's Angels in the study of demons.

In short many books are <u>not</u> a good resource to read if you are interested in learning about the real 'Angels of God'. Where I would recommend say a book such as:
"All About the Angel's by Fr. Paul O'Sullivan", as a 'good' resource. Others such as the Dictionary of Angels are not recommended for the same reason I mention earlier.

THE 'ANGEL BOARD'

What some seem to be unwittingly promoting, what is in fact an unhealthy interest in angels. One client spoke of an 'Angel Board' a few years ago, and I replied: **"Angel Board?"** At first it didn't ring a bell, and I thought what could this be? As I was unable to picture what it might look like. Then clearly, upon seeing it, there I saw what is really an 'Ouija board' dressed up with colorful depictions of angels. With the usual numbers, letters and a "Yes" and "No" text printed on it. It is all simply a 'sugar coat' on the board's overall appearance, with a lure of artistic beauty in its design. A "wolf in sheep's clothing" is what it is here, that can indeed open doors that should remain 'locked'. As for calling it an 'Angel Board', well, demons and devils are after all 'angels', although they are 'fallen' angels. So when they answer and therefore identify themselves as "angels', this is in fact the truth. So you might say a case can be made in calling it an "Angel Board"… Or rather a "Fallen Angel Board" after all, the 'shoe fits'. However the demonic spirits play along with the 'masquerade,' just as when UFO themed boards are used, there the entity cleverly pretends to be some 'Alien' from another planet. Whatever masks it may need to wear to perpetrate the lie that will help to lure in the unsuspecting user. Whatever it can say to trick the person into using the board more and inviting it into one's life.

Honestly, we don't need to know our guardian angel's name, or history, just know that your angel helps you more often than you think. And is there to help and protect you. It is a voice of truth and reason that arrives into your sub-conscious thought in a sea of temptation and desires. It is the hand that diverts you from serious accidents, and even death, when you have no idea they have in fact intervened.

Overall I think for many, Angelology has turned into an unhealthy interest in angels. Often crossing the line into an 'obsession'. If you find them fascinating, a good study of them may be simply to read of stories of how they save lives, appear in a timely matter to scare off attackers, manifest as a radiant light to scare off demons.

ANGEL DIVINATION

Some people believe they are in contact with their guardian angels, when it's a demon all along. The angel, might tell them things to gain their trust, might speak philosophically, spiritually, and very poetic in their words. It should be no surprise that some demons can even quote scripture flawlessly, and speak the truth on many occasions. Even as to portray themselves as an 'angel of light'. When only one seed of falsehood is suddenly presented it can grow to be that person's undoing. The initial impressions are to gain trust and a sort of bond. Look at the way some of these cult leaders can lead their group to a suicide pact, so many people, that is the sprung trap we might await for as it isn't so clear and obvious. Just note it is not the norm to be carrying on two way conversations with your guardian angel for example, especially as it might be more than on one occasion. Angels will interact more discreetly, and often intercede without us knowing.

On an extremely rare occasion we might be warned by an angel as with a "crisis apparition", something so urgent that it was necessary to reveal itself. Then it may just be through a dream. So we more consider some psychological reason for one who claims to receive messages from an "angel" or an "extra-terrestrial" being, either this, or it is demonic in nature. This is where I would assume first. Again, "better safe than sorry". As we should completely remove doubt that it is neither of these two reasons first, regardless, the more you understand how demonic spirits work, the easier it will be to make such a call.

MASQUE: THE LESSER SPELL OF BANISHMENT

Beware of 'occult spells' and 'rituals' bearing the names of 'angels' to mask the nature of the beast. You'll not see 'Jesus' name mentioned, just the names of Archangels, Michael, Raphael, Gabriel, Uriel. While the ear markings can often clearly show this is the same as the 'Angel Board' in a 'cleaver guise' of angels replacing certain "gods and goddesses" by name, in a newly reformed version of an old spell.

In the below example it notes the references of: "East, West, North, South", and four "elements" in a part of the ritual:

```
Raphael - East  - Air
Michael - South - Fire
Gabriel - West  - Water
Uriel   - North - Earth
```

Essentially, you can pick the names of the four Beatles; Ringo, John, Paul, and George, and it will work. This is partly to do with the difference between prayers of 'adoration and worship' as we do with God and Jesus, versus prayers of 'intercession' designed to request help from the angels and saints whom we merely 'honor and venerate'.

There are plenty of prayers around from the last 2000 years of Christian history that do the job. There are no 'new' magical rituals that will do better than these older tried and true ones. Stick with the traditional ones.

READING BOOKS ON SATANISM, AND THE 'BLACK ARTS'

Merely having occult books in your home IS in fact enough to invite a dark spirit(s). As a younger man, I read a text about Satanism from a minister's newsletter one night, it contains excerpts from the Satanic bible, educating on what that book and religion entails. The problem is even excerpts from that UNHOLY book proved to have an effect. I was awoken later that night to find a 'dark shadowy being' in my room. This is typical. So even portions of the unholy text can bring with them certain evil that may or may not reveal itself, but it is there. So, we have learned that, by default, simply reading a book on the occult will mean you have one or more demons sent to you to further tempt you into an unhealthy interest or into the 'practice' of what you are reading.

It is true that even having these books in your home is a lure, especially pre-owned books that might have been used for rituals already. As we consider the Bible a 'Holy Object' in itself, these books are considered 'Unholy Objects' and for good reason.

We can educate in these things without the author providing proof in the pudding, there is no need to go for a shock value in what these texts can hold, but to tell us in their own words the things that might better help us recognize Satanism when we see it. And better understand some aspects of it, as to better help clients who were once of that faith.

God bless that minister, I am sure his intentions were good in getting out the word that this type of thing even exists. But we should learn from his mistakes, this direct method isn't so much of a great way to educate. Also, and I say this again, that we should <u>always</u> say prayers of protection when we study these things in the least.

As I outline elsewhere in this book, let us remember that "Demonology" and 'Demonologist' were more popular terms and tile for a 'Necromancer'. One who appeases demons through spells and rituals to bend them to their bidding. What you might learn from this is near useless. Does a necromancer learn anything more than how to appease and manipulate demons as we seek to rebuke them? How will this information apply to spiritual warfare? This is the point I am trying to make, don't read that information, it will not help you in understanding demons. And at best will skew the facts, and might draw an unhealthy interest in them.

WHAT IS A "CURSE"?

It is essentially a demonic attachment that may have a specific task. A sort of 'Henchman', a 'Pawn' or 'Hit Man' as it is considered by some. Where rituals, spells or even mere 'evil wishes' or thoughts through desires, can send the demon to the person they seek revenge against. The result may not be exactly what they sent it to do, as it may have been instructed to kill you, but may find it cannot for any number of reasons, so it will target your family or mess with your car to create financial hardships for example. Consider the variety of ways a curse can be bestowed upon you. As a curse can result in a "demonic companion", it doesn't have to come from an individual directing it to you; it can be from being near a cursed place or person, buying an object from a yard sale, a used car. Most often people do not know they have a curse on them or when it occurred. Or they pick up objects that have been cursed and they are affected just as the previous owner. I bought a car much cheaper than it should have been, the instrument cluster was dead, and the owner would often run out of gas being blind as to the level of gas that was in the car. None of the electric windows would roll down. And a second new exhaust system "flex hose" began to leak seeping into the car interior. So he would have to open the door to let in fresh air on occasion, such as at a stop light.

The man seemed down on his luck as I met with him at a budget hotel, where he was living. As it turns out he was a musician, granted, it is not uncommon for musicians to live out of a suitcase. But I can attest often as a musician the lifestyle of wine, women and song can be a lure for a demonic to take hold on your life and financial matters. (*i.e. what some consider as 'bad luck' indications*)

You might cut off someone at an intersection, and they curse you, some black witches I have met in the past are so advanced in their cult, they only have to simply look at you to place a 'hex' on you.

Some of you know what I am talking about. A Magician might brag that he/she had advanced from the need of a wand, words, to only directed thoughts with their supposed 'magic' and spells.

We always want to be better safe than sorry, in doing a 'breaking curses prayer' to sever ANY attachments you might have, and to bind the spirits that mind try to linger. We also have to consider 'generational curses' that might come through your family line.

As reciting breaking curses prayer is a recommend thing in <u>any</u> potential dark spirit haunting. We <u>never</u> want to waste time in doing nothing while we try to determine the 'nature' of the spirits, in not allowing time for it to 'gel' and get a stronger foothold. The longer you go with an "attachment" the more it will weave into your spirit and psychology. Imagine how long this span can go if you play with an OUIJA board as a child and now are a "haunted" still as an adult. We don't wait until we are 100% sure there is indeed an attachment. As we can pray the whole while and really have nothing to lose in that. Again, prayers are never wasted.

MYTH:
YOU HAVE TO BELIEVE IN CURSES FOR THEM TO WORK

False, most people don't even know they have such an evil wish bestowed upon them, yet they still are affected. The way this 'Myth' can seem to play a part is in one of two ways:

1. The placebo effect. You might believe you are cursed more than you are, could merely be psychological.

2. Having 'faith' in superstitions and not God, just as faith is the opposite of fear, giving credo to anything of a mere superstition even can be as having 'faith' in that. And can actually give power to it as a demon will do their best to mislead you to think something in superstition is true. To better confuse you and further weaken your faith.

3. Having fear of the curse is the opposite of having faith in God, so that might further strengthen the supposed curse.

WHEN IT IS HARD TO BREAK A CURSE

Hand drawn symbols under your bed on the floor, a certain set of objects which might include your hair, and photo, brought together in a small burlap sack. Unless these things are uncovered, and removed or properly destroyed, one might be still continually afflicted with the curse therefore, and not be "healed" entirely. Demon possession is harder to exorcize, and we have to remember the individual might have someone swallow something that is part of the cursed object. No doubt living near the person who might steal some of your personal belongings will play into this more. Or someone you trust, who can easier slip something into your drink. I have to say, luckily the cases I worked on, the objects were found. However, we often don't know when someone is "haunted", it might be the result of such a curse, and we take the usual road to solve the problem, not realizing there is more that lies beneath the eye. So the effects might weaken, but may not diminish entirely.

Now this CAN vary, as many things can. Just be aware that such methods of Black Magic can be an obstacle to a successful deliverance. Especially when it concerns the "possessed".

REINCARNATION

Catholic and Orthodox Christians do not support the belief of 're-incarnation', as well as most of the other denominations. This notion is more from an eastern religion based belief that accompanies a 'No Heaven or Hell', as the late John Lennon envisioned things. So enter an alternate view to the 'afterlife' in a cycle of 're-incarnation'.

I can safely say I have not run into, or read of a case that can't be explained as an 'attachment', or some other lingering spirit providing information through the person as sort of 'divination'. Some in my field won't take this stance openly as to be politically correct. People will do those *'past life regressions'* in therapy sessions, and suddenly it is revealed, a supposed hidden *'past life memory'*. When in reality, they are vulnerable in this 'semi-consciousness' state, (*as I mention elsewhere in this book*), and they are simply having an entity communicate through them. Furthermore I can even say by this action that it is more likely going to be an 'evil' or 'demonic spirit'. As we know how these types of spirits work.

When you allow yourself to be hypnotized, or in some cases 'drugged', you then allow yourself to be an unwilling host for 'spirits', who might communicate through you or even step in for a 'possession'. (*Yes it has happened!*) When you open yourself up like this, you therefore allow yourself to become a vessel for ANY spirit to enter and communicate through, as a sort of 'Trace Medium" when they purposely 'channel spirits'. Except you are <u>not</u> in control, as you are not often even aware of what you speak while these 'sessions' are in progress. Even dreams will also come randomly and out of your control. You are in effect 'channeling' spirits, so in this, hypnosis alone can be dangerous.

Knowing this, it suddenly is no mystery in how it can reveal something accurate of the past, and provide true details of a person's life from long ago. It is obvious as the spirit may have simply lived back then, or as the case with a 'demon', it of course has a superior knowledge of people and places of any point in human history. It can simply be baiting you into this 'reincarnation' idea, by pretending to be some 'past memory' of you as a 'Nobel King'. And consider how the more elaborate your so-called past life is revealed to be, the bigger the play with 'pride' and 'ego'. People too often say they were "royalty" in the past, nothing mundane or lower level, which should make people think they are being told by someone or something.   Only what they want to hear, in something exciting for a past life personality. After all, what are the odds so many were Napoleon or an Egyptian King? How many would be disappointed in hearing that they were merely a 'buck-private' from world war one'.

All the better to stroke the ego with a much more significant past life story, or a more recognizable person from history. Not to mention it will generate more money for added sessions, as your curiosity peaks. All to better line the pockets of the hypnotherapist, or whoever is providing the information. There might even be a deception there, to keep you coming back for more, shelling out yet more money.

A last note in these studies of demonology, is that your personal demon might have themselves been one to accompany a great many people throughout the history of human existence. You are not the first one your 'personal demon' has been assigned to. They could have very well been a personal demon to a well know person from past history. And thus, more of an up close and personal source of information. So as a demon might even relay the information for firsthand knowledge.

A Word about WITCHCRAFT and OCCULT PRACTICES.

It amazes me the way people will brag about being a 'Witch' in wielding 'invisible forces' to their bidding, bringing them 'good luck', and 'love'. However, these same dark forces are quick to punish you if you perform a ritual with a broken salt circle, using the wrong candles, or leave out a phrase in a spell… In other words, if everything is not perfect as the spells requires, you'll likely pay dearly becoming "haunted" by these spirits that you (tried) to called upon to HELP you. Not surprising to me often people who dabble in these practices find they need help in removing what they have conjured up or unwittingly lure in through these rituals. To "Clean up the mess".

I picture how a dabbler in chemistry might have noxious smells in their makeshift home laboratory. You might see acid burns on the table and floor from spills, charred surfaces from explosive reactions. The less experienced they are, the more mistakes and therefore, the more dangerous the 'dabble' is. Beyond the novice trying to dabble in dangerous occult practices, far too often these practices result in a problem haunting or worse. They are indeed dangerous, who can deny this? It is not a matter of opinion or Christian Theology only. It is fact, and it has revealed itself as such, like as compared to playing with a loaded gun. Perhaps this is better stated as a game of "Russian Roulette" to the novice in the least.

Thus, more serious consequences for the "inexperienced".
Some witches I met brag about wielding these forces with a certain pride, all without thinking of what they are dealing with. I consider these forces that are the power behind witchcraft as a more of a psychotic, jealous and abusive relationship. One slip up and you are punished! Any signs of Christian faith about your home and you will often see a retaliation as though it is a 'jealous' rampage. And in many ways it is. Anytime a choice is made in a belief system/religion on a certain level we more than merely befriend the deities we chose to honor and worship. We commune with those entities, it is a personal bond. So the question becomes a choice of bad judgment, when considering the true nature of the 'Deity', where as it has a dangerous and dark side. Question: Why get involved in such an abusive relationship? An Alcoholic can be quite the 'friendly' guy, when off the bottle; a 'Bipolar' can be stable during their 'high' point. Always remember the darker side is who we really are. We work to remove the darker side entirely in ourselves and certainly don't want to turn a blind eye to the dark side of people and... so-called "gods" that can turn on you like an ill tempered pit bull. Again, the darker side is the revealing true side.

Now as some might make an absurd argument of this with the 'Christian-Judeo' faith, I can say that if I am saying the 'Our Father', and I stumble in my words; I will not be punished with the visit of a malicious and dark spirit later that night. I often hear of stories how 'dabblers', mere amateurs get a book from a library or fresh off of the shelf of a local bookstore, start to do a spell, and simply because they do it 'incorrectly', they pay certain consequences in it turning sour towards them. If these spirits are really 'good' there would be <u>NOTHING</u> to worry about. What level of patience with the newbie is this a display of, in NOT allowing new practitioners to safely grow into this religion? That alone says 'negative' as well. But the idea of 'witchcraft' is these spirits can be used to do 'good' or 'evil'.

The problem with that is again in my philosophy, the 'evil' side more so defines who or what you are. (*This concept is what we use in trying to first identify if a haunting is demonic or not, as you will read*).

For whatever reason the 'spell' may backfire, this makes it "dangerous" - plain and simple. As is handling explosives that are more unstable in handling as with nitro-glycerin or plutonium. Remember, that the word 'backfire' in it's origin of meaning, is a reference to a gun that blows up in your face. And that is what this can be. It is as playing with a gun.
These spirits have an evil side and that dictates their true natures. You might have a pit-bull that is trained to kill if you or a family member is attacked. Do you really trust such an animal around your young children? Something quick tempered, and vicious as they can be is not an animal I want around our kids.
Their history and 'track record' says you shouldn't. Let's face it; 'witchcraft' doesn't itself have a good historical reputation either, to indicate it is 'safe' or 'good' in nature any more than it is now. Christian ministries don't talk about the dangers of the occult because of petty 'prejudice', or to purposely be 'politically' incorrect or some other petty reason. It is in part from experience and in understanding as to how such practices can open doorways to 'dark forces'.

You will find that there are plenty who were once practitioners of the dark arts, and later became Ministers, Priests, Nuns, and Monks. In part as they sought help when this faith began to affect them profoundly, in a very negative way. Then they work to help others who are afflicted as they were, and having been through it they are more so well aware of what these people are going through.

Harry Potter is a concern to these organizations for the same reason as it promotes these practices. There is reason for concern because of the results of practicing without "proper guidance". This is what a *High Priestess* said once when asked why some do rituals and spells and it goes terribly wrong.

"They did the spells without proper guidance"

Why doesn't it alarm even those in the *Wiccan* communities, in how practicing without **"proper guidance"** can bring danger upon you? Having occult books on the store shelves is the same as selling loaded guns to all ages. A preteen can buy a book on witchcraft **"without proper guidance";** single mothers with small children at home invite these beings into their homes because of a lack of *"Proper guidance"*. For me I can say as to the fact they are not pure 'good', and have such an evil side, should alone be a red flag. Again, just look at the nature of these beings, I need not to label them here.

One should ask themselves as to **"how long can I trust this relationship of getting 'something for nothing' -?"** They always want something in return now don't they?

A good analogy is how a 'Mob Boss' might take you aside to call in the favor, **"I need you to take this package for me to 13th street..."** You feel you don't have a choice as you feel you 'owe them', and you also fear them. You may or may not realize you are transporting illegal 'drugs' or 'stolen merchandise', and this begins to become a regular thing.

As in this example, I say to just be ready for your new 'metaphysical friends' to call you in on the so-called favors they do for you soon enough. It won't go on for long, getting without returning the favors, with you giving something back they truly want.

TESTING FOR "CAUSE AND EFFECT"

As I mention in this book more than once, we can test for the true nature of these would be spirits, using 'positive' elements such as holy symbols, holy water, words, the name of Jesus, and so forth. This is no different of a matter as when you are trying to discern if a haunting has a **TYPE: Good-Human**, spirit or a **"TYPE: Evil Inhuman Spirit"** (*dark spirits*). As I made mention before, the entities that are the powers behind witchcraft, already have in the least a sort of 'jealous' side. So in this, I will go further and question why these entities react just as demons to these things? Food for thought. This alone tells me their true nature, as in the least, being a 'negative' one, as even human spirits will not react in the same manner as the demonic do in such 'tests'.

Sort of in all you have to do to test for a 'carnivore' who is supposed to be a 'vegetarian', is pass some meat in front of it's nose, and if they take it, well there you go! Truth is revealed!

The logical mind can see through the dark veil that clouds some minds...

I have known many people who practice these forms of the occult; thank God I didn't get lured in and would have to be another to learn the hard way.

We should realize that even people can be deceptive as to their true 'nature' as well. As Ted Bundy might have been a model neighbor, the way he conducted a spree of mass murders is more tell tale of his 'true nature', more so than how he was known to kindly return a neighbor's lawn mower refilled with gas after borrowing it. Again, I stress, the dark side defines who we really are. And often this will contradict and nullify the good, and make it seem like an "act".

OUIJA BOARDS

Someone once said:
"There is nothing to the board itself, than a pressed piece of wood, with letters printed on a sticker."
But it is <u>more</u> than that.
These boards are created to be used as an "Occult item".
It leaves the factory as a "profane object", as it is "tainted" by what it is designed to do beyond being a mere 'pressed and

printed board' of wood. What few know or understand is that a demon is assigned to each board by default, waiting for someone to buy it and use it. As it will be the first to answer your curious questions, and it IS all too willing to do so, that is, if it truly can. Consider it a 'booby trap'. Your teenage girl will have the demon play to her as a *'teenage boy who died tragically in a car crash'* to try to lure a school girl crush. Or a small child that is saying it "misses her mommy". All lies, and tricks to get you to use it more, and give it more a foothold in your life. Be warned!

Communication with the dead, necromancy, again, as we all know with séance's and so forth, can wedge open a 'door' that can be a very hard one to close. One can bring in evil through a life of sin, but it is at least by 'two fold', to bring it in by such 'occult means'. True, even while playing with these things as a toy or in curiosity, doesn't take away from dangers, because of mere 'intent'. This is just a reminder how these so-called harmless toys and beliefs can be a danger to our lives and spirit. We find these are so often part of the life of one or more family members, as every household has a computer; they typically had an Ouija board in the house at some point. Even if it was only brought for 'fun' to a teenager's slumber party.

Bottom line, is in that "no good spirits will communicate through the board". Period! Good spirits are tightly governed by God's laws, and would not be allowed to communicate through the board, simply because this is tempting one to use the board further.

Only 'dark spirits' will be talking through such an apparatus. And this also includes pendulums, and other methods which use a sort of mechanical sensitivity (or electronic, as you will soon read of), to allow the spirits to affect the movement. So there is not much of a difference really in using a 'pendulum', 'table tipping', or some of the new electronics introduced in the last 5 years, such as The 'Ghost Box', and the "K-2 meter". Granted, people report getting better results from the Ouija board.

Plus it has more of a notoriety and history, as it is more popular, therefore more horror stories are associated with the use of it now, than over the last 100 or so years.

Plus it is a more 'intimate' communication, in touching a pointer, and closing your eyes for example. People are closer to opening themselves up than with 'other' devices. With the "K-2 meter" and even the older 'pendulum', they don't take some approach as though they are "channeling" "concentrating", as the K-2 will even often be sitting on a chair, and not held in the hand. So it doesn't entail one or more people to be so 'focused' and all physically connected to this 'one' device. I think that will make a difference there alone to make the Ouija board seem more to fit the taboo. Keep in mind also, that we can be infected by dark forces in so many ways we don't realize, and we may not even think of as 'paranormal'. So we have to be aware of 'other' signs that such spirits have taken a foothold in our lives especially after using such devices. To more accurately report the "cause and effect' of these communication devices. So as you will read further in this book, I mention how even these new electronic devices, and not just the 'mechanical' ones, are essentially the same thing.

DEMONS CAN'T SPELL?

By some opinions, what seems as a rather silly bit of a debate was going on behind the scenes. One that began as I was reading an article from a website of a supposed "Religious Demonologist". I realize the topic doesn't seem all that important to some of you, but you have to realize this is basic "Christian-Judeo Demonology 101", rookies might learn of this fact through a keen observation from their first few cases through experience, apart from personal study.

To be honest this is the first time I heard that 'theory', I even conferred with others I respect in this field such as *Lorraine Warren* to further validate what I have already known for years and years.

Where she said: "**All I need to say is that demons have the knowledge and wisdom of the ages**", that sums it up.

Most answers in Demonology are a matter of knowing the nature of demons, as well as their origins, and so forth. It's not a matter of memorizing some facts like their 'names' and 'ranks' as I have discussed earlier. But just knowing their level of intellect, knowledge and wisdom and how it far exceeds man. (*Which can vary by rank*) That alone can answer the big question "*Can demons spell*"?

So it is easy to say, less any experience even, that "demons <u>can</u> spell" is a fact. However, to the contrary, I will cite some cases where one or more of the following may be true to say why they may <u>not</u> spell correctly:

- Some, especially as they pretend to be "children" misspelling is assumed, as they are expected to make spelling like a child part of the masquerade.
- A demonic preying on a teenage girl for example, might try masquerading as a teenage boy who was killed tragically. Might better respond to the savvy spelling that is more of a "chatroom lingo", or chat shorthand. All to better snare them into believing it is a teen. So miss spelling could be "cool".
- Some demons, are mute, some can't spell, lower level/rank demons are of a lesser intelligence, and wisdom, and might even appear to write like children. We suspect that when a person uses the Ouija board, a lower level demon will more than likely not be interacting on the board. As to have a demon (or human) who can better spell as to spin the web of deceit to better catch the unsuspecting user(s). Unless the bad spelling is <u>part of</u> the deceit.
- We get some that might erratically move the pointer, to spell nothing.

- The demonic might spell in another language we don't easily recognize, spell backwards, for whatever reason. They speak Latin when no one in the room knows Latin for example. So a need to communicate and be understood isn't always the goal.

   Also assuming someone isn't moving the pointer themselves, or it isn't a HUMAN spirit. I am referring to DEMONIC communication as it were. In short, saying "demons can't spell" is not true.

ORACLES OF COMMUNICATION:
THE 'NEW' ELECTRONIC MEDIUMS

An old rumor was in circulation for years in how Thomas Edison tried to create a 'mechanical medium' before he passed away. But it was never completed. In the past, people have reported messages printed on their 'type writers', that could not be explained. This includes more recently with MS 'Word documents' in having supposed messages 'from beyond'. They might return from lunch to resume on an open document and find a sentence or word has been added. *(Consequently, we should never rule out a prankster, which is likely the most common reason.)*
So now we see that Edison's idea of a sensitive device wasn't that far fetched. That primitive scribbling of text in automatic writing or blasphemies in red lipstick on walls and mirrors isn't the only way to get a 'text' message. It can transcend and make use of the current technology, just as it has the old in a type-writer, or staring at a snowy TV screen, some reported effects on cell phones, or through the more common Ouija board's pointer.

You can figure if people can get to where the spirit moves the pointer without anyone touching it, it certainly will not be that hard for it to text message from the 'spirit dimension' when one is so 'haunted'. Keep in mind the Ouija board rarely, if it ever has, has had good human spirits talk through it. As many suspect it is most always going to be the 'dark spirits', that will 'talk' through that board and other devices as well. Fortunately, this has become common knowledge now, and now as they need a new way to dupe those of us who avoid the obvious lettered board from 'Parker brothers'. So enter the new 'gizmos' and electronic oracles of communications that again expedite from simple curiosity, to a full blown demonic 'infestation'. It is like I mentioned before, when they merely reface the Ouija board with angelic art and suddenly call it an 'Angel board' to cater to those with an unhealthy 'Angelology' obsession. Same thing - different look, just as it can be the same thing, but using different 'technology'. So the same goes for using electronics instead of the Ouija, so you might want to keep this in mind.

Again as with any 'otherworldly' communications, we have to take the proper steps in investigation. YES so many of us are duped by a demonic looking for an opportunity to exploit in the least our 'curiosity'. The pretending to be some poor child or a teen that died tragically. Playing on our empathy and emotions, we fall for it. And we are suckered into the carefully laid out 'snare', as we are trying to communicate with this spirit. The idea is to lure you into taking steps that will open doors and allow the demon to manifest. Sometimes it is sadly taking advantage of a mourning friend or family member, pretending to be a 'lost loved one', just as with other times when it is simply appealing to the curiosity of the human mind.

We should note that if a deceased loved one wants to indeed communicate, they will do so without provocation for an interaction. You should seek comfort from the living in your friends and family. And pray for the deceased, so that they will truly rest in peace, and pass on to Heaven soon enough. The key is we don't have to look for it, it finds us. And we shouldn't have to look, if there is a message it will reveal itself to us somehow. If we follow this idea, we will not be susceptible to treading in dangerous waters, and therefore, no doors will be opened. The demon is all too willing to pretend to be the lost love one, and do quite a convincing job of it.

The ghost in the machine is more so a term metaphorically describing that our body is a ghost controlled organic robot of a sort. So don't be surprised in those who like to possess our 'machines' to try to exploit newer technology to manipulate you from the outside with the same goal in mind:
"*Your destruction and eventual death*"

"THE GHOST BOX": (i.e. *Electronic spirit communication)*

A Brief History:
A technician named "Frank S.", is the supposed inventor of the box, how it came to be alone sounds demonic. Are we to believe 'Aliens' or some other otherworldly beings gave him the instructions on how to build and use this device? We should always consider that technology that is 'inspired' by paranormal means is automatically highly suspicious by default. As 'diabolical' in it's origins. Now, the first time I really heard about the box in detail was in 2007 via a convention speaker. He said that "*only one of the 30 chosen people in the world*" can use the box. That is, some small number of pre-selected "chosen" people in the world. This was March 2007. Later that summer at the Stanley Hotel, the box announced that *[another]* was now one of the few who could use the it. (*Yes, I said the BOX announced this*). So now the number was over thirty, clearly the limited number of '30' was set by the spirit of the box. (As we are to believe)Granted, regardless if this was fact or not, I thought that "thirty" people seemed like a low number, and in 30 years, I can say, that it is really nothing new for a person with an 'attachment' of some sort, to simply detune any AM radio to a blank spot on the dial and hear 'voices' on it. As

opposed to this choppy, garbled mess we hear on the electronic box.

But lately, you don't hear of any such limitations, and many have built their own box or purchased one pre-built. The buzz from the 'Ghost Box' camp isn't going with that 'only thirty' notion, perhaps because now it has become profitable to sell the box, not just perform a demonstration, or a ghost hunter convention "side show" attraction.

HOW IT IS SUPPOSED TO WORK

The box is supposed to 'scan' radio broadcast frequencies, and pick out small samples, and build words from these fragmented portions of various broadcasts. The end result is often garbled and not intelligible, and takes some imagination to hear it. Sort of like gazing into the clouds and seeing 'animal shapes' from random cloud formations. Some have hard answers to intimate questions, more clearly I will say, just that often I think maybe only 30 in the world could make sense of the garbled mess of so-called words coming through the device. They might be trained as some EVP's do, in a form of sensitivity training, where they can better hear something from what others describe as 'nothing'.

Let's say this is in fact how it works and it is NOT simply a hype as to how the electronics really works. (*I'll soon look at the schematics again, but my point here is NOT if the box works the way they say or not, it is about the moral issues of using the box.*)

What does it entail for the 'spirits', who communicate through the box. What will they have to do to 'nudge' it to get it to work in their favor as a device of communication? As we realize it doesn't take much to move an Ouija board's pointer, we should ask what a spirit has to do to manipulate the electronics internally.

I extend on this with these points:
- First, in the 'scan', they will have to tell the box where to randomly scan to, which broadcasts to sample from. In other words induce a control over an otherwise 'random' scan, therefore manipulating the internal electronics, in 'nudging' the scan over to specific radio frequency at just the right time.

- Second, they will have to preconceive what is going to be said on what frequency, to best assemble an intelligible word.

- Third, they will have to do all of this at lightening speed.
  Now this is an extraordinary feat, even for a spirit, and from my experience and understanding - *"extraordinary"* = *"demonic"* typically.

While people may 'shy away from' the OUIJA board, the same ones are clinging to this 'Ghost box' as though it is somehow 'safe', where the Ouija board is not. When the two devices are essentially the same thing, just that each is using different technology to 'interact'. It also doesn't take much to nudge an Ouija board pointer and of course it isn't so complex, and is a 'mechanical' versus an 'electronic' device at that.
I can say that in my opinion the BOX leans more to 100% demonic, where it is possible for the board to have a mix of different types of spirits. Human or inhuman. At least in theory, however we suspect the demon will always be the one to answer the questions through the board. *As* the demonic is always looking for ways to get in. As it will push it's way passed any spirit to get a shot at you. They rule their domain and any human spirit will be bullied away from any such communication. So that they alone will best capitalize on the moment where the curious dabbler is seeking a 'response' from any spirit.

THE MASQUERADE STILL APPLIES

I spoke before of the 'masquerade' the demonic can do, quite often portraying itself as a 'child spirit' to pull on one's heart strings, to better manipulate the people it seeks to oppress. A trick to get them to take certain actions that will ultimately 'open doors' as they try to help the *"poor lost little girl's spirit, who misses her mommy"*. And yes you *"Psychic-Mediums"* *"Sensitives"*, all 'six' senses are fooled by these spirits. With the box I have already heard stories of one using the box talking with *Thomas Edison and Nicola Tesla* of all people. Remember a demonic can even know Tesla liked to where green socks, or name his favorite Adult beverage. Again with the '*masquerade*' here, don't be fooled!

CHRISTIANS TAKE NOTE!

Lastly, with all the indications pointing to this device and others like it as *"DEMONIC"*, I will mention this lastly, as I was not merely basing my opinions on this biblical/Christian perspective. I made my point without using 'bible' sources once.
But I'll need to remind you professed 'Christians', that it should be no surprise that I can find this box to be 'demonic'. For in the least, the Christian/Judeo faith, Necromancy is forbidden. This is NOT necessarily 'ghost hunting', what I am referring to is attempting to communicate with the spirits, by any means.
 Using devices for EVP, this 'K-2 meter, or other apparatus in trying to 'establish communication' with other worldly spirits is forbidden by church teachings. Look it up!

EVP (Electronic Voice phenomenon)

You use the Ouija board, speculum mirror, or even stare into a snowy TV screen. Eventually you will start to see things that others do not. If you read some books and articles on EVPs, the author will often tell you that you need to listen deeper, to pick out the voices. What they are doing here is teaching you a form of 'sensitivity training', in this you open yourself up, as though 'channeling' with a desire to make contact. Again here, *"be careful in what you wish for"*. At some point you can pick out voices from radio, as where no one else can even hear so much as a whisper in it. Your sensitivity training has opened you up, but at the same time it has also made you vulnerable to potential demonic influence and oppression.

Again, with the 'Ghost box' there is no exception, the more you use it the more it might be easier to understand what the sound is. But to others it would be garbled as the TV will still look blank and snowy to other onlookers. Just consider that.

Now I know of people who use Ouija so much they don't even need to touch the pointer to have it move. You might think that is a good thing, but it is not. You are not simply getting better at it from practice. They are solidifying their foothold with you! This is not a video game!

WHEN IT IS 'OK' FOR CHRISTIANS?

Since this comes up often, I thought I would mention when it is 'OK' for a practicing Catholic to do 'EVP sessions' under the following conditions:

Intention:
To gather evidence to validate a "haunting" is one thing, doing so for the glory of the 'hunt' is quite another. If we do it to 'help' people, the evidence is needed. Good 'intention' doesn't directly violate church doctrine or biblical teachings, but having the wrong intentions can affect you on many levels regardless.

Method:
To hold it and ask questions is provoking to get a response. To have the recorder run without trying to force the EVP, is 'OK'. In this you can hold it or set it down stationary.

SINFUL SEXUALITY

Likely, one of the top three reasons a person may become "haunted' by a dark spirit, is "sinful sexuality". Going back to the poltergeist phenomenon, and how these new emotions and "urges" can lure these dark spirits in for a fest. We have to consider, how much acting on perversion will go even further in empowering something that might have began as an "attachment". Read the later section where I describe physical encounters with demons, particularly, "Spectrophelia" encounters with the Incubus and Succubus, a.k.a., "The demons of lust" / "sex demons". The demons you appease with your actions of mortal sin(s), are the very ones who will 'haunt' you as soon as the opportunity is there.

For example, as soon as you give it 'invitation', it will come in and affect you more. Helping to push it to more of a 'sexual addiction', and more of a 'perversion' to a level of self destruction. Extra marital affairs can literally tear a family apart; and we should never consider in that which some believe to be merely a 'harmless recreational activity', is in anyway somehow different today, than it was historically. The demons haven't changed in six-thousand years, so the same thing that lured them in prior to the 'sexual revolution', will lure them in now. As we talk about the basics of 'positive' versus 'negative' in combating these spirits. Keep in mind immorality is a 'negative' not a 'positive'. No matter how liberal your thinking is of this matter, it does indeed play a huge part. As in anything we choose to engage in with our 'free will' can and will affect our lives.

ALTERED STATES OF CONCIOUSNESS:

George Lutz revealed that he believed that *Transcendental Meditation* or "TM", had very likely contributed to the Amityville haunting. As we understand how 'dark spirits' are always looking for a 'way in'. When we are in such an altered state, we are in effect leaving control of our body, as leaving your keys in the ignition of your 'valued sports car', that is your body. I mentioned this prior to this a bit, as in the topic of 'reincarnation'. But I simply cannot stress it enough, in that when we are in such a state of 'semi-consciousness', a demonic spirit just 'might' take it out for a 'joy ride'. I have also heard how there are countless stories from doctors who find some patients with behavior that mimics something like 'possession', as they are coming out from under a dose of 'anesthesia'.

The truth is, until such a drug wears off, and the person is able to completely connect and control themselves entirely, the *"joy ride"*, or in the least, the demonic effect, may not be over. Partly as the will of the person makes for only a part of the complexity that is *"possession"*, it does indeed come down to a battle of wills. For the person to fully *"come to"* (awake), it is like the hoodlums who make a run for it after the sleeping security guard starts to wake up from his nap. This too can vary.

"PSYCHIC-MEDIUMS" / "SENSITIVES"

Many '*Sensitives*' as some like to be called, have at some point had physical trauma, or even *flat-lined on an operating table. (**Electrocardiogram showed no heartbeat, died*), while undergoing surgery, and then surviving the ordeal. Then finding they suddenly: *"Have a gift"*, and they assumed by default it is from *"God"*, or completely 'natural'. There are indications, however, that the part of the brain is damaged that would be otherwise suppressed with a specific 'drug' by the necromancer. In order that they may "see" into the netherworld, and better view the very spirits they seek to 'manipulate'. LSD had some of the same effects for some, where seeing demonic beings was merely consider by the "psychedelic drug culture" as a "bad trip". Some might experience this effect somewhat while coming out of a deep sleep. As this "dreaming while awake", or as it is commonly referred to as 'night terrors', can be very realistic. But at the same time, this condition can be somewhat of a cross between some 'other world reality' and mere 'imagination'. In the way the before mentioned 'hallucinogens' affect the mind. This condition however, is temporary and usually only lasts for less than one minute. But can last up to 'five'. *(As it varies to the individual)* Even so, it can be quite disturbing, the things one might see, and all of it is not imagination. As we can see into their world to a certain extent, but it is not a look into a 'positive' world, but a 'negative' demonic world, no matter how pleasant it might seem at first. Such positive experiences are merely a lure to draw in further your fascination, the sheep skin over the wolf hide, as it helps to excel towards a curious experimentation. Again we are talking about 'altered states of consciousness' when it is a drug, and the demonic can cease the opportunity to take advantage of this state of mind, where your defenses are weak.

So as it can be through the divination of a demonic spirit, where these abilities originate from which can also be the result from 'occult practices', in this it is certain. As even something as mild as an Ouija board session when resulting in a successful spirit contact. If you begin to have abilities afterwards, you can bet this is not a good thing. But what they don't realize is the demon has a foothold more than they think. Look at the person, their very personality, appearance; it might entail some "demonization" in itself to reveal this is not a gift from God.

FOR CHARITY, NOT PROFIT

So as we find such said abilities can be induced by drugs, and by trauma to the head, near death experience, demonic divination, now where they go with these new abilities is another matter entirely. And some then charge money for readings etc. at some point. If your gift is truly from God, you are not to charge money; it must be used for charity only, for the greater glory of God. That is- "To help your fellow man", nothing for personal gain or notoriety. If it is God's gift, as soon as you lose sight of a 'charitable' aspect, you will lose the gifts! Now as you may not actually lose the gifts, in some cases a demon will seamlessly step in, and suddenly this 'other' type of spirit will be working with you to provide the "gifts", as the divine spirit mentioned in the New Testament - **Acts 16:16.**

People don't understand how a demon can co-exist without turning you into a head spinning, split pea soup spitting, possession case.
Yes, and apparently in helping you do good, but we cannot rely on the information we might get from this source, as it is expected to be 'skewed'. Also, remember, that accompanied 'warm and fuzzy feelings' don't always entail an encounter with 'good'. Remember Satan can appear as an "angel of light". Even emit a warm, good loving feeling, so you can't trust your feelings when in the presence of true evil. They can be a master of disguise! (*See 'Discernment'*)

So as some might feel this peaceful 'co-existence', seems
relatively harmless.
Think again!
What they don't realize is the demon has a foothold more than they think. Again, just look at the person, their very
personality, appearance; it might entail some telltale
"demonization" in itself to reveal this is not a gift from God.
The Demon(s) will certainly want to have a hold on you, so self-destructive bad habits will often be present even if they are not notable clearly to others at first. They will eventually begin to affect enough to show clearly. Just as with levels of 'oppression'
One can fall to bad habits fast as they no longer are a 'moderate drinker', as 'alcoholism' may begin to take hold. Their lifestyle might become more perverted, into an addiction to sex. Recreational drug use could turn to a 'drug addict'.

Eating begins to turn towards 'over-eating' and an 'unhealthy obesity'. In other words, 'self control' slips to an all time low, and this is what the demon(s) will give you in exchange for these so-called 'gifts'.

So in the company of a chain smoking medium, you might suspect one who doesn't have a real gift, just an attachment of a possible 'divine (demonic) spirit'.

(Again as Acts 16:16 tells.)

When *Lorraine Warren* was attending a Catholic grade school around the age of nine, it became clear to the Reverend Mother that she had 'abilities'. Lorraine is a 'clairvoyant', and she has notably used these gift as some 'seers' such as *Maria Simma* has. That is to help discern 'human' from 'demonic', and to help the 'poor souls'. Reverend Mother's concern is clearly with reason, as we know that such gifts can come from either side, so they put her through a sort of filtering through weekend 'retreats', and so forth. To help weed out any possible demonic origins, by using the 'positive power' of prayer and the Catholic sacraments.

As television has really set a stage for this circus of "Psychic-Mediums", almost making them into 'super heroes', exploiting these supposed "Gifted" individuals to the max. It won't win any popularity contest in saying that we should really be leery of all of them, even if they sport the word "Catholic" in their profiles.

A 'REBIRTH' After 'NEAR DEATH'

Little known fact, if you flat-line and die, you need to be re-baptized, partly because of the simple exorcism built into it. You want to remove attachments you might return to life with. Second, to re-anoint you a Christian, this is based on the idea that in coming back after "no heartbeat", this is a physical 'rebirth'. You could very well require a renewal of baptism. Regardless we should play it safe and follow through with these. If you find that your Priest / Preacher/ Pastor tries to tell you this is not necessary, then I suggest that you should go to someone else. Don't take ANY chances. There is so much today's clergy do not know!

So this is in saying that regardless if you do not die, 'last rights' (*The sacrament of 'Extreme Unction'*), should be performed, even if you're unsure the person will pass on. Also, to break 'attachments', in the least one should consider as a 'Christian' to get baptized again. This will not only act as to 'reaffirm' your Christian faith, lest we forget the Catholic Orthodox Baptism is more than a mere christening, it can be a help to 'detach' any spirits that might try to make the trip back. With it's built in '**simple exorcism**'. As you have been in a way 'reborn', in how you were dead and now have returned to the living, you might consider what you may have brought back.

I will say, it is merely a precaution more so, and that these 'new abilities' that were a result of 'flat-lining' or a 'head injury', are more than likely with a medical explanation, as taking certain drugs can apparently give some similar abilities. We have to consider a medical reason for this new function is in a 'permanent state', because when our heart stops certain areas of our brain will start to 'die' as we lose brain cells. A condition that is otherwise temporary under the influence of certain drugs. But would be permanent, as we might sustain brain damage in and around that same portion of the brain.

ASTRAL PROJECTION

Is a dangerous '**altered state of consciousness**', (*refer again to earlier mention of this*), again, would you purposely leave your keys in the ignition in a bad neighborhood? Don't give a dark spirit opportunity to take you out for a 'joy ride'. This so-called "silver cord", if it exists is there for a reason. People are taught to 'stretch it' or 'sever it' to more freely float and

"travel". *(The theology states however the chord cannot be broken until you pass on in death. I wonder if those who have an NDE experience return with a broken silver chord?)*
I can cite one case where the mother was teaching her son to do supposed "safe" astral traveling, of course it resulted in a need of '6 exorcisms' since he was nine years old. There are good and clear reasons why we avoid occult practices, the demonic is always waiting to capitalize on thoughts words and actions where it may. All I can say is what a "dangerous playground" and it isn't safe! Now this child I speak of would often get 'lost' in "astral travel", sort of like being drugged, or in a catatonic state or a coma. Unresponsive, as though asleep and cannot awaken. Be assured that holy water and touching crucifixes to the forehead will still be a TEST to see if a demonic spirit is present. If the child doesn't react, the spirit is NOT present, and the child might be merely unconscious, or in this case disconnected from his/her body, sort of like a comatose patient. The 'Ghost' that is our spirit or soul, isn't there to man the machine. The body lays still and dormant, while the spirit is wandering away from the body.

Today as the boy has had his 21st birthday; he is still affected, and can't control how he travels. There are many occult practices that might be tempting such as this but it is better to avoid these as you heard on one case, there are thousands of others. As to make a case why you shouldn't dabble with these things.

BABY BIRTH AND BABY BLUES

People will say that the **"activity didn't start until the baby was born"** -and this most often has absolutely nothing to do with the baby's presence by those in the house hold. Consider our negative emotions can draw in evil spirits, and empower them to step it up a notch. Just as with a child going through 'puberty':

1. Mother: Baby blues is depression plain and simple, now pregnant mothers have even noted activity starting or increasing while pregnant. Again this applies as to the emotional state of the mother.
2. Resentment. This can be from siblings or even the mother herself. A new baby sister or brother can draw some resentment, more so from those ages 7 and up. Jealousy is common, but deep seeded negative emotions are again what we are talking about here, that indeed can lure and feed 'dark spirits'.
3. Increased stress levels. From the newborn, could be the father taking up the slack with extra work, while mom recovers from the pregnancy and birth. Money matters might increase due to the addition to the family as well. Paying for doctor bills, another 'mouth to feed', daycare expenses, and so forth.
4. Curses. The child might have been cursed by a relative, (has happened), people will have crib death occur and don't realize it was a demonic spirit that was sent as a curse of a sort of revenge on the family. Sad but true, as these things have revealed themselves as fact over the years. We cannot ignore this possibility, even as it might be from a 'generational curse'.

Remember we are talking about problem hauntings, not a supposed "good" spirit who is somehow lingering in the afterlife and finds itself attached to the child, for whatever reason. Although we won't rule that out. And most certainly problem hauntings don't result for a spirit that is prone to maternal instincts' in the presence of a baby. People assume such melodrama before the more likely truth.

A RECENT DEATH
...of friend, family member, co-worker, or an acquaintance.

If you think they might not come back to haunt you, think again. Did you attain things they used to own? There is even a sad scenario where a family member, who cared about you in life, passes on to become a "condemned soul" because of the way they treat others. They might be a pawn of the demonic in the house they used to live, forced to torment their surviving loved ones, against their will, at the control of the demonic.

It should be noted human spirits are quite often used as pawns to help the demonic get 'invitation' taking part in the 'snare' that ultimately triggers our own actions that will begin a demonic 'infestation'. Also keep in mind it may not even be the spirit of the one you knew, it might just be a demonic pretending to be that person. As to create a certain 'curiosity' in the least, this might go to taking actions that might 'open doors' to a demonic manifestation. Always consider a demonic master is holding the leash to any human spirit, especially when their characteristics are pointing to a "lost soul". This is one reason I have no trouble with labeling them as **"TYPE: HUMAN-EVIL",** because of the company they keep. And I refer to them as 'dark spirits', which is beyond how they might appear as a 'shadowy being'- it is to better classify them in the same minion as the demonic.

Apart from their 'apparent' current mood or behavior in the haunting, we have to pay attention to the bigger picture or what is going on behind the scenes and note the "puppet masters", the ones manipulating and calling the shots of these human spirits. As they never act entirely alone in these cases. The demon itself does not have to have been manifested, and it can lend a certain level of power to the human spirit as well.

There might be some confusion between **'TYPE: Human-EVIL'** and **'Demonic'**, because the human spirit might appear to have some 'traits' that are clearly known more so to indicate a 'demonic' presence. Never expect malicious activity to be a **TYPE: Good-human** spirit.

SPECIFIC TO HOUSE HISTORY:

DEATH: MURDER and SUICIDE
Often the demonization that is behind the acts of murder and suicide linger on the site where these atrocities happen. For example, a Saint Louis area Hotel where a suicide had occurred, residents report black figures in the room and in the hall near by. They were reports that people who would stay in that room for a few days, almost felt stronger temptations and ill feelings, depression setting in without apparent reason. They check in happy and healthy and check out, sometimes with their own thoughts of suicide. And worse it may 'linger', as they might have left with an 'attachment'. So living in a place or even just 'visiting' for a short time can be enough to pick up an 'attachment'. What Gabriele Amorth says is to refrain from visiting evil places, as the 'proximity effect' takes place. And we should consider prayers to break such curses if we note anything in changes in oneself, after a significant visit to a certain place or person. Specifically, a demon specializing in suicide has a foothold in that room, which can result in strong temptations into such similar thoughts of self destruction. As 'murder' also would be the same manner.

GRAVE SITES known and unknown
Building a home over a gravesite, can be a 'desecration', there are enough indications that disturbing the burial site, can stir things up.
Improper burials can result in a haunting as well. Having a loved one's ashes in your home can be taken as a sign of disrespect, and I would expect that the spirit might linger near their remains more often than we think.

BURIAL GROUNDS IN GENERAL
Some people will have you believe an Indian burial ground is under the property of every haunted home. If you do a little

reach these aren't so plentiful and many, as we are led to believe by some TV "Psychic-Mediums". Sure some people love the drama associated with such a foretelling, however, I feel it is more often far from the truth. Consider where the Native Americans chose to bury their dead. They would travel miles to special places to bury those who have passed away. And consider how vast the states are and how few of them in population there really were in comparison to the total population of people now. If there is proof of a burial site, you might have a grave desecration on your hand and might have to rebury the bones and offer a funeral complete with prayers.

Would-be "haunted properties" are sometimes more difficult as we pay more attention to the dwelling places therein.

Note: The boundaries prayers (which entail a Saint Benedict medal and so on) can help to dissolve a foothold these spirits might have from the past rituals and history of the property. Referred to later in the book as I begin to outline the steps for removing spirits.

CHANGING PROPERTY LANDSCAPE

I heard of a story where a local Native American tells a family they're "haunted" because they cut down a cedar tree recently. Can this be true?

Some possible reasons why:
- The property itself might be cursed under circumstances such as to protect the trees, a preserved the area.
- The tree itself can even be cursed; it could mark an area of satanic worship. This depends on the tree, how old it is, who might have lived on or near the property in the past, or had access to it.
- Some might argue that the "Feng Sui" of the property was skewed when the tree was cut down. I am not one who believes some simple act such as this can get you

"tormented" by spirits based on something like "Feng Sui".
- Grave marker - We have to consider also that cutting down the tree might have even disturbed a grave; the practice of burying next to a tree was quite common to mark a gravesite and other reasons.
- As different (Pagan) faiths might initiate ways to bind certain spirits with their spells and rituals. Say if you move an arrangement of rocks, this can unbind the spell and in affect curse you. You might open a 'Pandora's box' in such simple actions. However, this applies as a curse, even if it wasn't intended to be a sort of "booby trap" as some can be purposely set to be. The results are the same. And in a sort, so can the solutions for these soon mentioned 'curses' such as I detail in this book.

I realize we can't explain all of these things, matching exact "reasons' with the 'occurrence'. We must keep somewhat of an open mind on these matters of course. But we should also understand there are a variety of ways a curse might affect us and the places in which we live, dwell, work or even travel upon.

"PORTALS"

Again as some areas of land might have been the site of occult practices could have 'open doorways' still, or portals if you will that were a result from such rituals that might have stemmed back as far as the Native-Americans. Satanic rituals might have their tell tale landscapes, but more so if indoors, a former Catholic church is often the place of choice, as part of a desecration, and sacrilege to Jesus. A portal doesn't necessarily mean 'active' since it was first torn open. It might become active again if those in proximity are active in mortal sins, or themselves dabblers, in the least, in occult practices.
Which is also the scenario as to why a known 'haunted house' might become active again, when it seemed dormant over the years. *(See a later section related on this topic)*

The fact that a point in our space is in the least 'corrupted', also makes it a 'hotspot' for potential evil spirit activity. In other words this portal doesn't cross into a 'generic spirit world'. It is a gateway to the realm of the demonic, which will include human spirits as well who are merely their servants and minions.

It would be foolish to assume that you could have a 'Warlock' close the portal in the way they had opened it through rites and incantations. Instead stick with that 'positive' versus 'negative', as in how water douses a fire. As to always use a 'positive' GOD solution to deal with these 'negatives'. I am not sure to what extent specific Catholic prayers have been composed specially to 'close them'.

I will assume that a rite of exorcism would close all doors and rebuke evil. But for laity, since these things were done as 'curses' and are imposed on someone or some-thing's, breaking curses prayers directed specifically to this might be a part of the best solution. As 'negative; opened it, close it with 'positives'. For example, some Priests have been known to celebrate mass in homes that have infestations to counter the effects. I would recommend that you don't have a bedroom in a suspected 'area' of say a residence. Except to further witness a measure of future activity, it is better to not be in proximity of such things.

When a demonic is invited in directly by a means of some occult practice, this is more difficult to deal with. We lure them here through our choices, but in directly bringing them here, the metaphysical door which they came in through is harder to close.

We consider that "portals" are more a point in space where an occult ritual, in some past or recent point in time, have opened the gates to their realm. Sometimes it may simply need the right conditions or the right people to have more spirits cross in and back.

Sometimes the work to 'cleanse' a home and close such 'doorways' are too much to deal with and the people taking residence in the home or on the property, decide it is better yet to maybe move from the home to another place. Sometimes we can't so easily locate a source of a haunting in a buried artifact, undiscovered corpse. I agree at times, that it might indeed be better for peace of mind in the least to move. I would prefer that the family is sure it won't follow and resume with equal strength. Then it will feel as though the move wasn't worth all of the trouble. So this is why it isn't by default a good thing to vacate the premises until you have 'diagnosed' the haunting better. And there should always be measures taken to ensure there aren't any spirit 'attachments', and have the new place blessed.

HOME/BUILDING RENOVATIONS

In 2006, a common question came up again which I address in an e-mail. Which has helped to conclude that there is more to it than simply 'remodeling' a part of the house as being the cause. There is most often something that the owners are not saying that would better explain the reason for a start of such activity. So the actual remodeling is likely not connected.

I wanted to go over this a bit more closely, and maybe ponder on the idea that maybe they are _already there_ to begin with, and that the spirits(s) who have now made themselves known were just dormant until these recent changes. And the home's renovation in the least awakes the sleeping giant.

Here is a short description of the 'why', thus indicating that one or more of the following may be true of renovations that seem to stir-up activity:

1. It can unbind a 'blessing' done to a room or area of the house. People should always have a house blessed (again) after renovations. The idea here is that a blessing can bind or ward off evil spirits, so somehow removing the blessing can do the reverse in releasing them.

2. Uncovering 'dark places' by tearing down walls to open closets for example, shed some 'light' on what used to be 'dark' confined places. It in a way can 'run out' evil spirits from the seclusion of a dark area, (*like an old concealed closet or crawl space*), as to let in 'light' even, as with some 'lower demons' for example, can provoke like a blessed crucifix. This is maybe like waking a grizzly bear from hibernation by destroying its habitat. And where is it to go? Elsewhere in the house you don't want it to go.
3. If the house has been built over a burial site, doing renovation can be the same as desecrating a mausoleum or grave site, in disturbing the dead. There are surely some houses out there with bodies buried 'onsite'. But not just from historical gravesites, we should consider the possibility of a more crude burial, hidden in the confines of the home's basement and crawl-spaces that were placed there to hide a murder or accidental death. Or in some cases, just a 'lazily' dug out grave, made for a 'loved one' who has passed on.
4. Some people brought in to do the construction themselves may actually be the start of the activity. We know very little about the people we hire to help remodel our homes. For example, one person might unknowingly bring in spirit 'attachments' that stir things up.
5. Uncovering a 'secret'. On occasion reconstruction uncovers a dark secret of a former occupant. Photos tucked away, personal belongings, unholy objects.
6. The 'common' old theory of the spirits not liking it when people remodel their once owned home can be true. As we know human spirits often work with demonic spirits so if an evil spirit is suddenly perturbed over renovations to their former home, the collaboration may bring a stir up of demonic levels of activity. Something beyond mere simple low key grey lady apparitions and old Civil War soldiers suddenly making themselves known. We won't simply unrest a former owner from changing their former home, and draw what some consider 'malicious' behavior, that seems to more parallel 'demonic' activity. It could also be the home renovation is

totally unrelated. As I mentioned earlier, the home owners may 'not' be telling us the full story. Which is more common, and reason why we need to have 'people skills' to get to the heart of the matter more so. Human actions, words and even thoughts will always play a part in a 'haunting'. Regardless if these relevant things are not fully revealed in the first interview. They still apply to affect the haunting in general.

7. Lastly, I won't rule out 'Feng Shui' theories, especially since I discovered by accident years ago rearranging furniture puts a damper on some ghostly activity. But it is important to note, will all of my theories say <u>the spirits were already there to begin with</u>, and that the 'renovations', for one or more reasons can stir them up? From research and experience, to me this appears to be more so a fact. Ignore the religious beliefs of such a concept and consider it more of a "Metaphysical science. "Reflexology" and "Acupuncture" have their Asian belief system that accompany them, however affecting nerve endings in one's body to control pain, through pressure points and key locations on your body, is something scientific in nature. Feng Shui I believe is explained by a sort of 'energy weave'. As a spider will weave a web over time to an area, it becomes it's domain; it cannot catch insects if you move about items and objects that the web is attached to. The web gives it a certain extended level of freedom that is limited after the web is destroyed. Consider relocating or rearranging furniture, breaking this web for the spirits. For at least a few nights it seems to weaken the activity, this was once discovered unexpectedly, so you can rule out a sort of placebo effect. As I find the term "Cleanliness is next to Godliness" to be true in a way, a messy room cleaned up can greatly reduce the activity and occurrences in the same manner, without moving about furniture. Even simply doing the laundry to remove a pile of dirty clothes, and putting away books and magazines back on the shelf can affect the area. Thus is yet another great example of how a 'positive' can affect the 'negative' -but to what extent is this merely a disrupted energy weave as I described? It is hard to say. Remember that is only a theory from observation and study of 1000's of cases.

WHY WILL SOME BE "HAUNTED" AT A LOCATION AND OTHERS NOT?

The history of the house is one thing, as it can be built upon a combination of one or more of the before mentioned scenarios that can indeed play a part in the ' if' one will notably experience what they believe is a 'haunting'. Since we are dealing with people in these cases, yes more than one, which entails a profile of their spiritual and psychological make-up individually, and of everyone who resides at the residence. These extra 'variables' can play a huge part, and be the 'key' in 'why' a haunting might vary from family to family, or person to person.

Here are some examples of why one might become haunted, when prior and future occupants may not report anything out of the ordinary:

- **Previous owners or occupants are not in truth.** For whatever reason, they may not want to be bothered with such questions. Consider also that they might be frightened to speak of the occurrences for whatever reasons, don't assume they all will be forthcoming in speaking about their experiences, as some are who seem to delight in telling their story to the public. It is typical how in this field we have to be leery of the words spoken from 'witnesses' and try to read deeper in to the supposed phenomenon.
- **Unintentional Religious provocation.** A Catholic family might move in, and hang holy symbols all over, including crosses, pictures of the Scared Heart of Jesus, (*A divinely inspired portrait see also Sister Faustina*), a Priest may come and bless the place. Certainly enough to light a fire under the foot of a demonic to in the least bring him out of hiding. As we know these spirits aren't always going to make

themselves known like the 'noisy ghost', unless it is part of their strategy. At times better lay low and work on the household spiritually and psychologically, sometimes that is all they can do, as they haven't manifested enough to display certain levels of physical activity. (Sights, sounds, smell, etc.) So a previous occupant might move in and find at some point their recreational drug use on the weekends has evolved into being hooked on heroin. Personal destruction was on the rise while living there and that was the result, not some stereo typical 'demonic' haunting.

- **IGNORES activity.** Depending on the person they might rationalize all things they experience and not give it a second thought as it being "supernatural". Sometimes the divide is within the house, one tells another it is their imagination.
- **Personal "Attachments"** come and go with the person. Some house and homes might have a certain attribute we can not see that allows more for a demonic to have more strength in that environment, the household might allow for a better foothold. Then when one enters who has an attachment already the spirit might more thrive in a place where evil has energized the home with a certain negative energy it can better manifest in that room or property as a whole.
- **Haunted Items brought in".** As with #4, however instead of a person it is an object, refer to the text earlier where I mention OBJECTS.
- **The Battle of Free wills.** When you have a place that is "tainted" with evil for whatever reason from the past. New home owners move in, it might restart itself around these new occupants and revert to an early stage of "Temptation" the less these planted thoughts are heeded to, and self control is exorcised the less the demons will have a certain

control over you and the environment, this is true regardless of how bad a haunting might have seemed to the previous occupants. It really comes down to our choices in a certain extent, I can't tell you how many times I hear of what people were 'practicing' in a supposed 'extreme haunting' environment, and my response is **"No wonder why they were haunted"**. Remember our words, our deeds, and even our thoughts we harbor, can attract and empower these entities. 'Who' is in the house plays a huge part, so there is no surprise as to how customized the experience can be from case to case or how one family might be haunted and another not.

Bottom line: The truth is each case is unique to who occupies the home, the history of the home, including the previous owners, and the overall environment. If one family isn't afflicted that is certainly no case to say previous owners/renters were not afflicted, and those who follow will not be affected.

SCIENCE – NATURAL

Parapsychology: The Pseudo Science

A pure scientific approach is blind when it comes to matters of the supernatural. This is why many consider parapsychology a 'pseudo-science', and some still do not take it seriously. I wondered how one can attain a science degree in something as wide open and inconclusive as this topic? How can you be sure of anything through scientific analysis, that can't be easily tested, or measured, and through conditions that can't be recreated in a lab. Or easily captured on film and other media. In these things that defy what we call 'science' in it's very essence. So just take what you can learn from them and then move on to a more spiritual approach. Machines can't outright capture ghosts, electronic gadgets don't clear houses of poltergeist. Because if it is indeed a haunting, science alone can not be trusted to offer a reasonable explanation, nor offer an adequate solution. As we have recently come to a time where we come to rely too much on science and humanism to solve all of our problems.

LESSONS LEARNED THROUGH HISTORY –
WHEN IT WAS ONCE ALWAYS CONSIDERED AS 'DEMONS'

Now on the other side, in the past, we have the age-old view of a 'religion only' perspective. That is all things were considered as 'supernatural' at one time. Blaming so many things 'natural' on the 'devil', 'witchcraft', as we can go back to an even more primitive culture, and see storms and volcanic eruptions meant that the *'gods were angry'* and it demanded a 'human sacrifice'. Common to the middle ages, 'mental' and 'medical' illness was cited as 'demonic', such as in the case of 'rabies', when they did not recognize it was related to an animal disease. At times they made the connection to an animal bite and formed a sort of werewolf explanation to explain the animal like behavior of the person. 'Ignorance is bliss'. By the same token however, turning a blind eye, in a 'science only' approach is not only foolish, it can be dangerous in this field. Just as a more extreme fundamentalist religious view can be far from true as well.

As 'humanism' slithered into existence, with Freud and psychoanalysis, advances in medicine, Darwin and 'evolution'. 'Humanism' and 'socialism' came to be to where the evils of communism and other forms of socialistic forms of government resulted in a 'Godless' mentality. The problem is the swing began to go too far to the left, when it is better in the middle to 'moderately consider all avenues as far as science versus spiritualism. You can't expect to explain the spiritual realm with science alone, as the paranormal in general is merely beyond much of what we recognize as science. And for the most part, we don't explain 'true' science with religion either. We also have to remember that science in general, is the study of the 'physical and natural realm', of things that can be measured, tested and often seen, even on a microscopic level. They will try to explain 'supernatural things', with a 'natural' explanation, and the result is often a conclusion that borderlines the truly 'absurd'. Especially to those of us who know better. On the other hand, we should keep in mind also, that we also have to consider a 'science only' approach useful in that they are in a way the 'skeptics' who can help to expose 'fraud', correctly weeding through claims of demonic possession and conclude the condition as definitely 'mental' and 'medical', and help to discern some things as actually 'natural', although inconclusive at times.

To me a man or woman in this profession who also understands the true affect demons have on the human condition, is worth their weight in gold in this field. And I seek them out to continue to build our network of able bodied individuals through the http://www.swordsofsaintmichael.org website.

SCIENCE DEBUNKING WHAT IS CONSIDERED PARANORMAL

To the credit of science, information about certain phenomenon such as the Bermuda triangle, with one theory proving how methane gases from deep ocean volcanic activity can sink ships, disrupt aircraft engines. As this 'can' explain all of the missing craft in the area over the years. Which actually to me is a better explanation than UFOs, or a vortex to another dimension. And this 'does' well to provide some 'food for thought' and a credible 'what if' to something for a long time labeled as the 'unexplained'. Once it would be inconceivable to think we could harness the power of electrons or atoms, traveling through wire conductors from one location to another. And without a Wizard's 'magic' or a 'spell'. So I have to say, where would we be without science?

SCIENCE IS TAINTED WITH FRAUD AND BIAS

But when it comes to the paranormal, science has lost me in it's arrogance, and too carries that often 'atheistic' bias on many levels. However, as cited above, one can't ignore the fact that things can indeed have a rational explanation for them. We never forget that notion as well, so we have to know when to give credo to a science-only spin on something that is supernatural in origin on occasion. While science has scorned itself with fabricated evidence, and they overlook hard evidence suppressing the contrary to what they are researching. Anthropologists for example, sticking with some old outdated theory's ignoring the contrary which are more so the 'facts'.

For example, as it was discovered how 'fossils' do not take *'millions of years'*, as it was initially thought through the years by Paleontologists. How *'radio carbon 14 dating'* is not accurate as they thought and can be off significantly by thousands of years.

I am reminded of the blatant fabrication of evidence in trying to find a 'missing link' to support the theory of evolution. Yet nothing has proven any animals have evolved from one species to another. And especially humans.

The problem is, in Paranormal research, what is known as 'Parapsychology' does little to try bringing anything to the table that isn't very outdated, all too common knowledge or absolute untruth.

So take your EVP recorders, measure some magnetic and electrical energy, try to snap a picture of an orb, or video tape a ghost by chance.

The late *Ed Warren* was very quotable and had a very diverse understanding of science and spirituality as it applies in this field. He has had his battle with these 'science types'. In the book by author *Gerald Brittle*, *"The Demonologist"* which chronicled the extraordinary life of *Ed* and his wife *Lorraine* in this work, he mentions the following of these so called "Parapsychologists"; that he has often had the displeasure of knowing:

"In general, the parapsychologist is looking for one thing and one thing only: A link between the unusual phenomenon and the latent abilities of the human mind. However, when a parapsychologist comes against inhuman spirit phenomenon, he tends to refer to it as poltergeist activity... the term is poor bookkeeping though, because it doesn't specify or come to grips with the true cause of the disturbance. Parapsychologist give no credence to the supernatural; whereas demonology is concerned only with supernatural events. Although both Parapsychologist and demonologist may investigate the same case, each tend to look at the phenomenon entirely different from perspectives."
-*Ed Warren* (**"The Demonologist"** *by Gerald Brittle*)

I also mention *Ed Warren* because of his public battle with these 'skeptics" such as the late *Steven Kaplan*. Ed was a seasoned debater towards these self-proclaimed "*Parapsychologist*", and so-called "Scientists". Who tried to argue cases such as the Amityville haunting and other cases that the Warrens personally dealt with, as "fraud".
So this fits my discussion of the topic at hand.

Here is another great quote, as I couldn't have said it better myself:

"A dozen investigators can go through a demonically infested dwelling, and come up with 'zero'. Because for the most part the scientific investigator is fishing without a hook. The scientist, coming at this problem with his stopwatch and litmus paper, poses no threat to the infesting entity. Certainly the entity is not going to voluntarily tip it's hand to it's presence. But go in with a religious object and the inhuman spirit will respond to the challenge." - Ed Warren

Ed passed away in the summer of 2006, it never hurts to say a prayer for the souls of the departed, especially people who had done much in their charitable works of deliverance as Ed had in life. May God rest his soul, thank you for all of those you have helped Ed.

THIS DAY AND AGE

It is a mix of science and religion, however even today, the shift can dangerously lean to 'science only' when it may be a 'spiritual' problem. But beyond that, we do not wish to look to science after this initial stage of investigation. Although we keep an open mind to it, the hope is to close the door as to a 'natural' reason during the first sweeps of field investigations. To the contrary I will say that with 'demonic possession' for example, we are thorough in determining first it is not 'medical' and it is a 'spiritual' problem, which requires a 'spiritual solution'. This can be an ongoing process as it is very deeply rooted into one person, and we can spend considerable time discerning 'if' or 'not' they are in fact suffering from true spiritual affliction (demonic) or not. (*Although we take precautions in having prayers said for them regardless all the while*) Some are not lucky enough to have a knowledgeable 'Priest' or even an experienced 'Paranormal Investigator' such as I mentioned in *Ed and Lorraine Warren*, who has dealt with demonic possessions many times over the past 50 years.

I shutter when I think of someone getting a 'science only' perspective analysis, and soon they are committed and placed in a straight jacket, never relieved of the torment and control of the possessing 'dark angel'. But consider that, such a 'barbaric' science solution of being restrained and drugged for the rest of your life? The "dark ages" indeed!

Thankfully many doctors in the least will go along with an exorcism, believing it has a 'placebo effect' where psycho-somatically the person believes they are cured and therefore they are. But, this is only if someone makes such a suggestion, rather than to stay with some medical solution which only involves 'sedating' the person.

Today <u>all things</u> need to be considered:

```
[ ] The 'physical' and the 'metaphysical'.
[ ] The 'normal' and the 'paranormal'
[ ] The 'spiritual' and the
'physical/mental health'.
```

And so forth...

Today these so-called 'Parapsychologists' fall short of topics such as the true origins of 'poltergeists', and that notion of *sleep paralysis* as the only explanation, as they stay biased more contrary to anything of a 'paranormal' explanation of these 'night terrors'. To these individuals I say to again look closely at the evidence, listen to your client's story, accounts and description of the events surrounding their supposed sleep paralysis episode. The answer is there, and that will help determine a medical 'sleep paralysis' versus a 'demonic' night terror attack. Just the same as we can tell 'rabies' from 'demon possession' now. Again, I cannot stress this enough, in how we as field investigators need to consider <u>both</u> science and religion, and not make the mistakes of the past. Or as some still do in the present. As I am not quick to call some behavior and 'addictions' being directly related to a condition of demonic possession. You can say in some ways I am a healthy skeptic to my own field of study and practice. The psychology aspect most certainly does play a part. Some people simply make up things just for attention. Or they grossly exaggerate events.

Now in truth, a new device that no paranormal investigator or deliverance team should be without, that would be called a **'Lie Detector'**. Unfortunately we don't have access to such a device of accuracy. So we have to use our judgment, our interpersonal skills, a bit of discernment, praying that anything of the truth is revealed that we need to know to help them help themselves.

PARAPSYCHOLOGY: THOUGHTS CONTRARY TO POPULAR BELIEF.

New research is shedding more light on some older beliefs Parapsychologists have clung to for so long:

COLD SPOTS

One being in how COLD spots are believed to be from the ghosts "drawing energy" from the room. On the contrary, they are apparently generating the cold, not simply drawing the heat from the area. This also explains why the cold spots are more localized, like the entity is made of ice. And that thermal imaging cameras picking up the shapes of human forms in BLUE signifying a lower temp of the being. (*Based on the FLIR color scale settings*) But not so much a larger area around it, as though it is really absorbing the heat from the room. Theoretically, if the using of the room's energy is true, then the temp would stay lower after the entity is no longer there. This can also be noted when more closely analyzing recorded video from a thermal imaging camera.

As we can see the color noting a clear outline of a lower temp entity, while it doesn't affect the room as something "drawing energy" in the form of "heat". We have to remember some demonic spirits are so cold it has an 'ice cube in a glass of water' effect in the room. Not to mention a demon's size can vary enough to where it can encompass the whole room with it's massive size. They are not restricted to the size of humans after all. Saint Michael for example, had been shown in apparitions to be a giant compared to a standard six foot tall male. We must remember that they are 'angelic beings' and not 'humans'. Thus they are not restricted to human limitations even by their actual size. As some can be much smaller than a human has ever been, the opposite is also true.

RESIDUAL HAUNTS and APPARITIONS

Residual haunts I feel are more an outdated description of what is assumed as a phenomenon that somehow occurred where the person's energy was recorded in space and time, even as they did mundane things such as daily cleaning of certain rooms. Part of this conclusion is because the apparition or sounds pay no mind to who is there, there is no response, they simply do their thing like robots or a mere 'projection' as the event often reoccurs at the same times, sometimes almost nightly.

To the contrary, first I will say that it is clear that all entities are not able to see and interact with us, as we are not always able to interact with all entities. Even those who call themselves "Psychic-Mediums". When these apparitions pass through a person there isn't that feeling of 'cold' or other changes that says *'something 'metaphysical' has passed through me.'*
Those who cite residual hauntings as a mere 'recording' always bring up how experiments have shown that a sort of 'aura' of energy remains in an area where some tragic occurrence has taken place. Some had been able to measure and view with a Kirlian camera, say an aura of a person lingers

for a bit, after they scream in pain for example.

There are primarily 3 reasons why residual hauntings are not related to these experiments and they don't prove a thing:

- The auras are 'static', not in the least animated, at least as they retain their original shape. Even the experiments where the Kirlian camera could see a holy man has blessed an object. The halos don't move from one spot to another they stay put. Nor do they change from the silhouette of a man sitting to one standing. It is constant and doesn't move beyond a variance of it's radiating effect it may have.
- They are simply 'auras', or only 'outlines' of the person, not a detailed image of the person or even near a ghost image of the person.
- They didn't last long. The test showed them to not last but for a few hours at most, and then the anomaly dissipates as it loses it energy. So as they try to explain a civil war ghost as being simply a recording, as these 'aura like images' that the Kirlian camera shows. Then how are there 'animated, and moving images' with a clear likeness of the deceased person, and are still repeating after hundreds of years? We know how stored energy will diminish over time, a 'shelf life' for rechargeable batteries even. If the same energy isn't there to re-energize the scene, it will get weak and no longer be visible, even with special cameras.

  Which brings me to point #4-
- These experiments did not result in something that was 'visible' with the human eye, say in a dark room. And required a Kirlian Camera or similar device.

In conclusion, there is some intelligence always behind these types of apparitions, the spirit might be a soul in the phase of existence we call "Purgatory" serving some time served doing some task, or unfinished business. We might also be seeing a replay of actual events of the past, but 'for a real reason'. This is projected for reasons unknown, but I highly doubt, a maid walking through a kitchen diner with a feather duster, falls into this category. Whereas the replay of a 'suicide' and other tragic events, would better fit this scenario.

Consider the source of this old theory as well. Science types who have difficulty in believing in an afterlife, or the existence of 'God'. I find many of these theories are to explain it from another perspective, in the way Darwin tried to provide thoughts alternative to creationism' (i.e. Adam and Eve). I say always pay attention to the source of the information if it came from science types who are so biased in such ways. We can't give these thoughts much credit. Especially as they have 'holes' in these theories.

'BLACK SHADOWY BEINGS'

As some people state that these are spirits that "have not manifested", in other words, these entities are said to not have 'physically manifested' visually where they would otherwise show a specific appearance. We know that a ball of energy might grow into the shape and appearance of a recognizable apparition. This should be considered a case of a witness to the spirit manifesting into a human form. However to say that black shadowy entities are just your 'typical ghosts' that haven't 'manifested', it is too general of a statement that doesn't always apply. Human spirits that are **TYPE: GOOD-HUMAN** will not appear this way. This is what some shadow people are, they are 'lost souls', void of the light of God, their own positive light has been extinguish, so they are now cold, dark entities, versus a warmer, brighter soul.

PURGATORY

This is a theology, not regarding science, but while I was discussing outdated 'myths', I thought this might fit in as well. The middle place Catholic's call "Purgatory" is not actually a place, but it is a 'phase' of existence in the afterlife, between this world and a final stop at Heaven. The 'purge' is described as metaphysical purification, often a final stage one needs to go through before entering Heaven. As so there is another place besides a mere Heaven or Hell, so now what?

Realize Purgatory goes back to the first century A.D. Realize also that spirits believe in such a place. (See section on 'Purgatory' for more information) The problem here is that we get a bias from those who say it "isn't in the bible", and one from Catholics who are stuck on the "hell fire and brimstone" definition of Purgatory. And it is overlooked how this 'phase of existence' explains the great many ghostly encounters and mild hauntings that involve clearly 'good' human spirits.

EMF EFFECTS

It is said if you live near an electrical source of high EMFs, even your fuse box, that the result may be hallucinations, uneasy feelings, nausea even. As science can often get it backwards, the "*cause and effect*" can be that these forms of energy can indeed attract spirits, and/or they might draw power from them. This, rather than to assume the presence of higher EMFs are somehow always going to affect you mentally or physically. And not be a lure for certain types of spirits. It is also interesting to ponder on the idea that these EMFs might affect our minds in the way I stated some drugs can. Suppressing one part of the brain, even 'activating' or enhancing another portion that enables us to see a glimpse of these other dimensions better. SO as we will say often, consider both. The research on this is still open to debate. But again I see that the alternative to the 'medical' actually might hold more truth under more circumstances.

EMF METERS

I fail to understand why 'Ghost hunters' go in so blindly with EMF meters, that can't tell the difference between radio and electrical, and something an entity might give off that is in the EMF ranges. Now if they would go through with something not so primitive and vague, as with an 'oscilloscope' readout, where they can see it is not a 60 Hz. signal, not a sine wave. Maybe we can see what sort of characteristics these spirits actually have. And it will put an end to using an EMF meter as a sort of 'ghost detector'.

POLTERGEIST

Those aged 'Parapsychologists' out there, often use this term in referring to the activity that is centered on a child going through 'adolescence'. This is their 'label' for this sort of phenomenon. The thought here is that the psychokinetic energy from a child going through puberty is so strong at times; it is enough to affect surrounding objects. As to mimic a 'haunted' environment. So in parapsychology, you often hear the association of 'poltergeist' and 'adolescence', as a common duet, a 'mind over matter thing'. But the evidence suggests the activity has a mind of it's own.
It could involve the movement of small objects, the phone or the doorbell rings with no one on the other side. I am one to believe that these paranormal occurrences are definitively controlled by an 'intelligent entity'. And I will go as far as to say, that it is absurd to assume a child with this stray, uncontrolled chaotic 'PK energy'- could ring a phone perfectly, when I know to ring a phone would require a set of pulses on the phone lines @40v AC. Such a directed task would not result from chaotic PK energy. But would in the least require a moiré focused attention on the action of the phone ringing. Which I am sure in that alone will never be proved as conclusive to be possible for a mere human child to do. Being so 'focused' as to move a glass of water from the

kitchen counter to a table top so carefully as it had not even spilled the contents. All the while, the child was not in the same room. I don't think a twelve year old can do that with an RC controller having a toy helicopter carrying the cup that easy, if they can't even see into the next room. So we are also to believe the child can make the 'phone ring', which takes even them by surprise? Use your logical mind here, it doesn't add up. So in saying, it is clear that some of the reported activity often has the child not even paying attention to what is happening, they may be totally preoccupied, with video games, reading and even sleeping. Or not even in the same room.

So 'PK' would be more random and chaotic and not as precise as these 'science only' explanations seem to believe. We should ask how should an eleven year old kid gain a mastery of telekinesis suddenly and control things as if by magic. This is absurd, and maybe one reason why parapsychology as a science remains considered a 'pseudo-science' by many, it is likely because of conclusions like this. It is reasonable to assume that the child wouldn't be able to control the chaotic energy of PK so well, it would be new to him/her, and it would have to be without a blind fold, involve focus concentration on the object. As it is hard to take such claims seriously, and it is really easier to believe a spirit is controlling these objects and sounds, while the child is unaware of the activity. But precise actions by an otherwise spread of chaotic energy are quite impossible, without an 'intelligence' to direct the matter.

Another factor is that PK seems to dissipate it's power of the distance from the person. So a close proximity is required for actual PK. This is at least true in the experiment conducted that concluded the human mind without demonic influence, cannot move objects over 5lbs. You see them very close to the object, waving their hand over a pencil, or marble, getting some movement, but it is slight in comparison to what is reported in these supposed 'poltergeist cases'.

We might have to understand, as with Darwinism, this theory also is likely first introduced over 100 years ago, and again as I emphasize, by a 'science only' perspective, and I can safely say it is 'out dated' theory.

The original word in its root meaning is German for "*Noisy Ghost*" – The name is more so tell-tale of the true origin of what has been incorrectly identified as '*PK activity*'. Others in my field of work have agreed with me in saying they have never encountered a case of 'PK' poltergeist in this over 50 years and thousands of cases. A child might at best have moved a pencil on a table, but not the activity witnessed in much of these cases. This is what I discovered as well. So it should be always considered that the explanation of such activity be attributed to an otherworldly origin in an entity. More often negative spirits or demons. These opinions also consider with the investigation concluding that there was a spirit present.

We know how children going through 'puberty' can harvest 'negative emotions', from biological changes as they are 'coming of age'. Some experiencing certain 'feelings' and emotions for the first , as they undergo these stages that are changing the 'child' to an 'adult'. Along with this phase of life, can accompany higher levels of 'stress' and other 'negative energy' that might come from sexual urges. And yes, this 'can' lure demonic spirits. We also have to consider how 'temptation' can play a role in this, as suddenly the child is becoming a man or a woman and will be more susceptible to temptations they were virtually immune to as a younger child. We know in the field of research that, as even 'negative thoughts' can attract demons in like flies to sugar. And since the state of their emotion and spirit is displayed on a band of colors known as the 'aura', these spirits are drawn by color. This is how they know to flock to the child, reading their signature auras. Which convey many things about their current state of mind, body and spirit.

Temptations can blow in like a March wind, and then suddenly back off. And once they have gone unsuccessful, the 'poltergeist activity' will likely soon subside, as they often do if it is indeed merely surrounding the child.

The Catholic/Orthodox saints, in their early writings, talk about how strong these temptations can be, and to stand against and resist, and to not act upon them. And soon they will lose strength and will dissipate. No matter how strong the desire might seem at the time. The thought is they are there to get the child to act on these new feelings and emotions, the 'red flag' is seen, and they are there to capitalize on their heightened state. So it goes beyond merely an invitation and empowerment through 'negative energy'. There is also a motivation here again in taking advantage of the pre-teen child during this time. This may involve a greater number of demons who will join in on a temptation, if you could see their numbers it might look like a sea of small black animals in a frenzy about the floor and even across the ceiling, or encompassing the room. (*Yes, it can grow to that many!*) Which can create some very powerful spiritual struggles against these temptations; this just puts out even more negative energy. The demonic presence is there none the less, with power to manifest. So activity will accompany the 'party' of the 'coming of age'. Similar occurrences surround a suicide, although in this case it is with those harboring moments of suicidal thoughts. Although this case with a child isn't as extreme, it is a time for them to try to affect choices that can have an impact on their life through adulthood. So these smaller stages of growing into adulthood are stages of trial and testing, learning, and personal growth. These decisions, will affect the teen going into adulthood, having appeased these demons. They might have more of a struggle with 'sinful sexuality' throughout their life, more so than if they had ignored these fleeting moments of temptation and triumphed past them without acting on these temptations. As to tempt a child 'coming of age' from their innocence and purity, is a victory for these dark entities. Let us not take lightly what affects the spirit when we begin to lose our innocence and morality.

So, the real source is more due to 'spiritual changes' in the child as they come of age.

Negative emotions, sex, the dark forces have a party.

REAL OR IMAGINATION?

Twilight dream state can result in a sort of *"dreaming while you are awake"*; we can see some unusual things. But are they real? Most often probably not. But we do have to keep in mind these things before calling it 'twilight dream state', or 'imagination'.

First, as a child my parents told me it was this, when many times it was not. As an adult I know the difference, especially when it does affect the environment in the room, to move objects in plain sight, or another witnesses the same phenomenon in a late night 'visitor'. It wasn't until I was eighteen years old, that I had this 'validation' to what I was seeing, when a friend witnessed the same 'dark visitor' one night. This prompted me to rewind and look back at other experiences, the very things I have encountered since I was seven and younger. And in this, when finally another person describes what you saw as a "black shadowy figure" as you have seen it that night as other times before.

Suddenly your perspective changes on your life. But I have to think how many out there also though it could be *"imagination"* or just some *"twilight dream state"*, just as many confuse the *Medical Sleep Paralysis* with an actual paranormal encounter. We have to be clear on 'if' or not it is truly 'paranormal' where it needs our attention and not a therapist or mental health professional.

HOW DO WE DISCERN?

We do have to pray before the investigation to better discern the true nature of the haunting. We never want to get caught up in the drama or the story told to be detoured from true logical investigating. Some people will exaggerate, or even flat out lie for attempts to sell a book or simply because they love the attention. Sad but true…

As I have times where I awake and see certain things, it is true that sometimes it feels like I am experiencing the paranormal. Or a haunting apparition. And sometimes you might be 'dreaming while you are awake'. And as you slowly come to your senses the images fade, and logic starts to say *"that couldn't have happened"*. Sometimes that slow to come logical thought is alone an indication you were dreaming while awake.

A paranormal experience in the presence of evil is hard to shake. As you can feel the 'evil' and a fear for your life might kick in and you react, not just in sitting there watching what you are seeing in awe, or confusion, your sense kick in and that DNA encoded self preservation all humans have, will likely send you running to the nearest exit.

'FOOD' FOR THOUGHT:

In the classic tale "A Christmas Carole", Scrooge says to the ghost of his former partner, *"Philip Marley"*, that he could be simply
a **"figment of his imagination"** or a **"piece of undigested beef",** then the ghost quickly lets him know he is neither.

I mention this for two reasons. One, even back then it is realized that eating dinner later at night before bed can cause this *"dreaming while awake"* scenario. (*Especially sugar snacks*). And second. Scrooge was sure it was indeed Marley's ghost after the spirit displayed a displeased anger over his lack of belief. Then to Scrooge, it was unmistakable that Jacob Marley's ghost was present, as Scrooge huddled in fear and fell to his knees in fear.

As in this for him was *"unmistakable"*, it is key as you will note a difference between your *"undigested beef"*, or *"imagination"*, versus *'reality'*. The other is *'physical evidence'*. I awoke once to a cardboard box lid flying around my room, I got up from bed and had to duck to avoid the movement as it continued to fly back and forth, it made one last pass and went behind my chest of drawers. I ran out of the room into safe refuge in a well lit, small room in the bathroom. *(And I often did during any night terrors such as this.)* When I was fully awake, I went back to my room with lights on full, climbed in bed eyes wide open, eventually fell back asleep. But it wasn't until the next day, I happened to recall the event from the previous night and slide the chest forward to get a look behind it. And there sitting on the floor was a piece of cardboard, just as I had seen. This piece was easy to identify, a corner of a cardboard box, looking as though it was torn off a large box top. Corrugated, and brown, with the same size, look, and shape. I thought: *"How could this be?"* My hair stood up on the back of my neck. I got chills. *(This is Another indication for the list.)* Another point to say it wasn't just my imagination.

So far this experience has us note these things:

- Unmistakably as I am fully awake I still believe in what I saw. Real encounters seer the thought better into your mind where experiences that are merely of your imagination would fade more quickly. Sort of like the way dreams of tragic events might linger through the morning on your psychological. But by midday it is hardly a glimmer of thought.

- Physical evidence. Not common, but certain smells, a handprint, or objects moved, something to verify what you have seen.

- The feeling of fear/evil. Our 'sixth sense' can be reliable. When you get that feeling listen to it. You know yourself better than anyone on this one.

- The fact is I also believe that we may be seeing some things that are actually there, but perhaps not really there 'manifested' in our dimension. What I mean is they are not a part of a haunting or paranormal experience, only that a short time you are seeing the room without the veil to the other side. As we go through the day we carry near us one Angel of God and at least one demon or devil in what people refer to as a *'personal demon'*. The demons/devils hover about us, and day and night they are tempting with subliminal implanted thoughts and images trying to break you down. Yes, even as we sleep they try to affect our dreams.

- Sometimes all of the devils gather to chant when they are pushing for you to commit acts of 'sin'. A personal example here is when I would awake and hear the voices repeating the same thing again and again, like a chant of many people. I can't understand the dialog, but it is more likely reverse language of English. Or possibly Latin. (*This was something also experienced in the story as told in the book "The Devil in Connecticut" by Gerald Brittle, and is a very real phenomenon.*) In this chant they might call upon the higher powers of Satan, it also might be something in repeating the phrase, to 'program' you as you sleep. This is more something that involves lower demons, and their minions in human spirits, calling upon higher powers in their 'generals' in this spiritual war. The higher rank demons we call the 'devils'.

WHAT ARE "ORBS"?

Orbs are considered a spirit in their raw essence, as 'metaphysical balls of energy'. The colors may vary, however dark orbs typically are "dark spirits" plain and simple. (*This is not to say demons may not try to masquerade as an 'Angel of Light ' in this case.*) Some have seen a ghost manifest itself from a small orb, that begins to take shape into a more humanly shape for example.

First, true orbs are not simply specs of dust, insects, or lens flares as they often are in Film and photos. Many have had their fill of people claiming to have captured an "Orb" when the anomaly is anything but supernatural. This includes "rods" on video. When you are witnessing an orb it is unmistakable, and surely you will find it easier to identify one on film, when you have the memory of what a real one looks like as to better to compare it with.
If you talk to some ER doctors, you might be surprised to find many have at least one story where they saw an orb about the size of a 'quarter', exit the patient's chest through the solar plexus, or the open mouth.

Interestingly, demons are said to 'enter' via the solar plexus or the mouth, I think this is because of the same reason in part I mention how they seem to enter through windows or doors of a house, rather than the entity to simply pass through the walls. It might also be that human blood in it's web or network of veins and passages through the body might provide a barrier they cannot pass through. Human blood is special in itself, as the purity of water is a 'positive', blood seems to channel an effective shielded array in blocking access to these 'evil spirits'
.

As these 'orbs' are disembodied spirits, what some have called "pixies" more often a pre-cursor to something 'evil', and not good. If you were able to get a closer look at them you might see that they look to be 'little devils' in appearance, and can be quite frightening.

I heard from my mother that her great grandmother Lettrile believed in 'fairies', as she did 'leprechauns'. Do I think she was nuts? No, more likely she had never personally seen one, but no doubt meant accounts across that part of the globe that are handed down through each legacy. Stories told based on actual accounts.

As a child, before the age of 13, I did see what are known as orbs. (*As so has my 5 year old son*) One encounter began as the size of a 'pin light', near my far bedroom wall, and in a swirling motion it slowly moved towards me. It became bigger and bigger, as it came closer to my bed. When it came close enough, I could see it was a 'man's face' wrapped in flames like a fire ball. I jumped back from the fiery face as it disappeared at what seemed like inches from my face.

More recently, I awoke one night to see a blue toned light spot, what some call a 'ghost light' and it seemed more two dimensional, not as a 'ball' as 'orbs' are described to be. Plus it was moving in space, without the restrictions of a mere light beam which wouldn't be suspended in mid air. It would have to have a surface to light on. It was dancing around like a child playing with a blue beamed flashlight. (Oddly *like one we have*). I rolled over to scold my wife for being playful with a flashlight, and for waking me up. I started to say: **"What are you doing with that flashlight?"** But as I did, I then saw she was fast asleep lying on her stomach. I said **"Oh..."**, then I turned back to see the orb still there, then it swiftly went through our door and down the hall. (*The door was open a crack which is odd in itself because we usually sleep with the door closed.*)
It was odd in itself that she did not awaken from my words; it doesn't take much to wake her up. But for some reason if such

an episode occurs, she doesn't even get so much as stirred from her sleep to change positions in the bed. We realize that many ghostly encounters such as this are not shared, and the spouse next to you, or even the pets, and others in separate rooms, will not wake up until the phenomenon is gone. Keep this in mind as it can be this elusive, and one witness, although it can be one possible indication of a story that is not credible. We have to understand how these things occur so often as a 'show' for just, one person.

I will probably never know in this lifetime what that was doing in my room. Not as clear as helping someone with a dark spirit haunting, and finding a hulking shadowy figure bedside that same night. It is possible such a spirit was a Good-Angelic spirit that simply ran away a dark spirit just before I awoke. This is not to say, <u>all</u> bright colored orbs are 'good' spirits, never 'assume' this.

BI-LOCATION CAN APPEAR AS A "GHOST"

The ability to 'astral travel' to alternate locations and "remotely view" and even interact with the people where you projected yourself is not unheard of, but is rare. This is <u>not</u> a spirit we might believe it to be as a 'deceased human', or 'inhuman' who has never lived in flesh.

Typically, a human spirit will likely not have enough power to physically attack someone for example, without assistance from evil spirits. Just be aware it is possible a person you know might spy on you in the least and you might catch their projected ghost looking at you in the bathroom. This is an occult practice as you will read in the book of the 'dangers of astral travel'.
On the "positive" side, *Saint Padre Pio* was able to 'bi-locate' as such to do his positive works of 'charity', even giving Holy Communion (Eucharist) to a sick person miles from his church. In this case, such a thing is a true 'gift from God', only attained

when on a higher spiritual path; it was not attained by other means of training or practices in 'astral travel'.

DREAMS MIGHT INDICATE A 'PRESENCE' IN YOUR ROOM

I am not sure how relevant this is, but at times I have been in a state where I was vividly dreaming. Then suddenly in the dream scenario, out of nowhere I suddenly get a feeling of an evil presence and the imagery and tone of the dream changes to that of pure evil. I awake and the clock is showing 3:00 AM. Here was a visitor, and around me it was strangely darker, as though there was a black veil encompassing the room. I mention this because it is an example of how it is possible that when you dream you may sense the presence of such 'evil' in your room. And this feeling translates into a drastic change in the theme and setting of the dream. But this visitor will continue with it's business even if you do not awaken when it is present. Also we still might wake up and see nothing. But in these cases we should still take precautions and say prayers to remove any would-be spirits, again as I stress, just to be on the 'safe side'.

Imagine if we could take a '*pill*' that allows us to see into one of the other dimensions where these spirits exist. I believe this "twilight dream state" can be one that we see into this realm until we wake. I can say this because what is seen, doesn't relate to the dream that proceeds the 'vision'. The imagery is of things that parallel actual encounters. Not the typical obscurity we get through dreams. I say as I do with suspected cases of medical 'sleep paralysis' to be aware it may not be elements that discern the difference.

Drugs such as LSD and other drugs again come to mind, as it seems to throw you into an '*awake while dreaming state*' as some other hallucinogens can do. In this also, when are these things we see affected by spirits? This is what we have to ask, as I have mentioned altered states of consciousness are 'highly vulnerable' to spirit influence, especially demonic. So as in a 'night terror' a certain part of the brain is perhaps still partly subdued and you get some of the effects that are similar to the effects that a drug used by a necromancer would take to interact with the spirit realm. It is in my opinion that this dream state is the same that 'Psychic-Mediums' and 'Black Wizards' try to attain contact with the spirit realm. Many know some practitioners of the dark arts will take certain hallucinogenic drugs, to better assist them in their craft. I was told once that they do not use 'LSD', because the demons can 'tear you up' and you can't control them while using that drug. So here even, this is sort of making all that was invisible, suddenly visible. But it doesn't open that veil that separates the physical boundaries. It's more like looking at sharks through a fish tank glass. I realize this is part theory, but I am finding evidence more to support this notion.

Get a hold of *Timothy Leary's* notes if you can and it will chill you to the bone, in describing what they called a "bad trip". I have some stories told by friends, and I find what they see to be too farfetched to be their imagination. And the accounts more seem to be 'demonic' in nature. For example, one could see 'little black beings', which would try to be elusive and quickly hide behind furniture, and when they would look away, they would peek their heads out, and come out of hiding. Then when they would look again, they would try to again duck out of sight. When they would turn their head in another direction, they could see another one elsewhere trying to hide, say behind the TV or a dresser. The descriptions of demons matched those accounts of true encounters. While this person had no clue what they might look like prior to this experience. Also the trait of their nature to try to duck detection is right in line with their behavior.

They said they were about 12 inches high, all black, unclothed, genderless, and had a tail. That is a real quote. This higher state of consciousness is reached and we tap into the other realm. This is why 'self-hypnosis' and 'meditation' can be dangerous. It can leave you 'wide open' and vulnerable to demonic influence and attack. This can depend on your 'state of grace' with God, as you may even become 'possessed'.

As I stated earlier, in the famous Amityville house, the Lutzes were practicing 'Transitional Meditation' [TM]. I also believe as others, that this increased the activity there. As when we allow ourselves to enter this 'altered-state', we are in fact in danger of an entity trying to control our body. While a 'natural sleep' is excluded and we are more protected by our guardian angels.

FIELD INVESTIGATION NOTES:

MORE THAN THE "ONE" WITNESS

We often note that if a second or third person doesn't at first support the claims of the alleged initial witness to 'paranormal activity' in the household, this might be a 'red flag' to note if other elements surface that begin to spell that the claims are in the least NOT authentic. As for example when the husband states that he has 'not' witnessed these occurrences. You might find that if you interview them further, you might be surprised as to what you find. Often men will rationalize something as "normal" or not in the least "strange" when I find that it is "suspiciously" paranormal.
He might have had his own separate experiences that he shrugged off. You can dig deeper and find some experiences he might have to be in line with a 'haunting' as the wife claims. For example, in a demonic infestation, every morning the man of the house was leaving later for work, as he was unable to find his keys. He reveals this in saying:
"I swear, every morning I can't find the keys to my car". And he blames it on others, the kids, his wife and even himself for being so careless. Grant it,

losing one's keys can be a result of living in a 'stressful environment', carelessly dropping the keys while you have your mind on something else. But in hearing the wife's experiences, it seems to fit as a strategy of an 'infestation' or 'oppression' to stir things up between family members and to create such tension. Plus, let us use logic, in that the kids wouldn't place the keys in a draw after the first time when he 'blew his stack' accusing them of placing them there. Yet they turned up there again. Sometimes we can recognize the strategy at work of a demonic spirit if not in rather obvious paranormal experiences. But being as the wife's experiences seemed 'credible' to the level of an 'infestation' this could entail what some call "The borrowers", as I mention elsewhere in this book.
None the less, misplacing one's car keys can create stress that affects the family, also providing more 'negative energy' from these emotions stirred, for these beings to feed on.

We get a little into police work here almost as the human element enters, comparing stories, looking for inconsistencies between stories told, telltale "paranormal signatures" in the events they describe. Better to have two tell the same story as I said, than one alone.

PROFILE THE CLEINT(S)/WITNESS

Always carefully profile the people involved psychologically. Look at their house, is it unkempt? Look at their bookshelf, are they in the least showing an interest in the paranormal or things of the occult? Even a robust amount of DVD Horror movies may indicate something 'telltale'. We are not looking to condemn their story however, only to help validate it. And we 'never' want to hold back helpful action while such meticulous investigations are underway. As I mention before, begin to use lower level solutions in starting prayers and offering some 'generic advice' that might also act to help 'test' the severity of the haunting and the effectiveness of prayers

alone. (*More on 'tests' later in this book*)
This is something police officers and trained psychologists are already familiar with.

LEARNING FROM CATHOLIC CHURCH INVESTIGATIVE PROTOCOLS

One of the problems as you might have often heard with help through the Catholic Church is the 'red tape' reminiscent of a bureaucracy run amok. A lengthy procedure such as they impose on other "less urgent" matters such as marital "annulments". As to not reflect such an over meticulous methodology as it is through the Catholic Church we should learn from two things.
First, it is a dangerous thing to drag on the investigative phases to be more sure that the haunting is indeed "demonic", and justifies a church authorized "exorcism". While the people are in peril and even mortal danger, these cases can't wait for the slow machine to turn its wheels. This is why we should offer help regardless, even of the suspicions you might have. Just that we don't want to spend too much time on cases that are fraudulent, when true cases that need our attention now might be waiting in line behind.
Second, the example of the type of 'filtering' as is the procedure of the church, although it tends to go overboard, is still a good template as to how we should all conduct out investigations. But in doing it more so in an urgent matter. I think it should be clear to all, that if we had easy access to an 'Exorcist' at any occasion, they might very well be exploited and called upon on far too many cases. Even true cases that are notably found later to be merely a 'psychosis' for example. This is something to keep in mind, as we know that it is indeed human nature to want to 'cut corners'. Field investigators might get careless in knowing they can always 'default' to calling the 'Exorcist', and therefore they begin to lean towards lackluster investigative protocols. So we can learn from the church, keep that in mind!

TYPE: DEMONIC-NON-HUMAN
– A MORE INDEPTH STUDY

THE NATURE OF DEMONS

Confusion may come from the notion that we should expect only 'malevolent' behavior and clear evil intent from the demons. We have to know that there are different types of demons; and with each it may not be as clear as to it's true nature. For example, 'sex demons' don't necessarily entail 'violent sexual assaults'. They can be "*gentle as a lover*", and this is often the way such encounters will begin. Consider the types for each of the seven deadly sins. Sloth, being "*laid back*" "*Lazy*" isn't going to ring as true "*EVIL*", demons of gluttony, you might enjoy your food immensely as you add to obesity and move towards an early ending to your life in diabetes, stroke, and other health issues related. Not to mention the financial hits that can come from over eating and a desire for the 'best' food. Still if your house was haunted with a demon of "*sloth*" or "*gluttony*" would we see clear evil in it's presence? We consider it to be a matter of a 'negative' where eating healthy and moderately, over eating is clearly the more negative. Each 'negative', more or less, has its own representing 'demons'. We should note that evil isn't always so clear that we can make such a call without some rare gift of 'discernment'. As we may not detect it's presence at all, yet self destructive habits continue to grow thus indicating to the wise it hints at a form of being 'demonized'. This is just to say even 'possession' won't always necessarily be defiantly evil and reveal itself as such. We need to look at the 'big picture' many times such as in these cases, when there is in the least a form of 'demonic influence', where the end results lead to the goal of the demonic. Regardless if or not it is clear to those who might be affected at some point before the said goals are achieved.

Thus within our five senses, we cannot discern the evil intentions of people often, we are none better at telling 'good' from 'evil' with spirits, relying too much on our limited perceptions. An abused spouse surely dated a "nice man" in the courtship stages, some are very good at concealing their dark side, and the demons are masters of such deceptions. *(See also my article about "Psychic-Mediums", in how demons can fool all "six" senses)*

WHAT'S IN A WORD?
-DEFINITIONS THAT VARY FROM THEIR ORIGINAL MEANING

Here it is a matter of words, words to describe, not being used or understood correctly. But the main point of this is in saying how people get too caught up in the online 'Wikipedia' definitions of the word, and meaning, as opposed to how it is really used today.

Here are some examples that apply to Demonology:

"DARK SPIRITS"
As I define them throughout this book are human condemned souls, or demonic spirits. In other words "The Devil and his minions" to sum them all up. So any reference to a "dark spirit" can both describe the nature, and origin as well as the appearance.
In this Book they would be classified as TYPE: EVIL; HUMAN OR INHUMAN

"DEVIL"
Some refer to Lucifer as "The Devil", while higher rank demons are referred to as "Devils". Being as Lucifer is over all demons he would in fact be 'the' Devil, or boss Devil. So the 'shoe fits'.

"DEMON"
OK we all know some intellectuals always have to try to rationalize what demons really are because of the origins of the word. Copy and paste blogs and articles from researching using a dictionary will make for a misinformed piece on demons.
And by typing in the word "demon" "*The Greek conception of a daemon (< δαίμων >daimōn) appears in the works of Plato…*" and so forth… In short the origin is misleading in this case. Demon is referring to the "fallen angels", as is the meaning in the book, as for those who are in involved in my line of work.

"DEMONOLOGISTS"
Although the dictionary will cite it is one who "studies demons"; in deliverance it has become a buzz word for one who is top in the field in Demonology and deliverance. Especially for laity that are non-clergy members of the Catholic Church who work in Spiritual warfare, (*i.e. demonic hauntings*), this has become a more known term because (a) The need for such individuals, and (b) Because of the notoriety of the late Ed Warren, who was the first who was considered a 'Demonologist'. A Demonologist because of an uncommon knowledge in many aspects, but more so a sound understanding and knowledge of Christian-Judeo Demonology.

"ROMAN CATHOLIC"
It is clear to a few to cite "Roman Catholic": as there are some denominations such as the "Old Catholics" that are not affiliated with the 2000 year old Roman Catholic Church, except by using the name "Catholic".

"EXORCIST"
One who expels demons, when we refer to this title we are generally referring to an ordained Exorcist of the Roman Catholic or Eastern Orthodox faith, other than that, other

denominations would call them "healers" or 'deliverance ministers".

"ANGEL"

We too often equate "Angel" with God's Angels, good spirits, and the word "angelic being" gives us an image of a beautiful winged humanoid, with a bright glowing positive light and aura surrounding it. But we have to remember that demons are angels as well. Such as revealed in the well known story of 'Amityville'. The young child's invisible playmate she called "Jody", said it was an 'angel', and as a 'demonic entity' this would be true. But typically we paint a better picture, thinking perhaps the child was seeing their own 'guardian angel'. While clearly here, as the story is told, it was not.

"POLTERGEIST"

It's origin is 'German' for "*Noisy Ghost*", however the scientific community has used this word apart from the original meaning in association with "PK" (psycho-kinetic energy) which isn't in reference to an 'entity' or spirits at all. But a special ability of the human mind. Typically as it might revolve around a child entering 'puberty.' As Poltergeist is the phenomenon, PK is only one possible cause. However, as you read in this book, myself and most of my colleagues will agree that we have not seen a true case PK poltergeist

"EXORCISMS"

First 'possession' is 'control', we find confusion out there between *'Demonization' and 'Possession'*. As 'temptation' can lead at some point to self-destructive bad habits, such as alcohol or drug abuse, chain smoking, or eating disorders such as anorexia. It is believed as you hinder to these temptations you empower the demon(s) that tempted you initially through that subliminal level of thought. They gain a strong subliminal voice in your mind (so-to-speak) as you "give in" more and more. This is more or less "*demonization.*" It is NOT 'oppression' or 'possession' as some of you might believe. Note that some forms of 'demonization' occur from the stages of 'temptation' through to 'possession' stages. But being "demonized" alone doesn't constitute a "possession" and certainly does not warrant an exorcism.

The problem is with these 'TV Evangelists' treating this condition as though it is in fact 'possession', as they exorcise the "demon of smoking" for example. Now prayers for one who is demonized will help, but portraying it as an "exorcism" on TV is misleading and wrong.

"DEMONIC ATTACHMENTS"
An "Attachment" says more of how it is there and who it is with. It is a sort of personal 'infestation'; however, it may not have advanced to that level of manifestation in our environment. That will depend on the individual for one reason of many. With an attachment, you are essentially "haunted", and you might experience what some consider "bad luck", while your psychological might be affected where it begins to lean "darker" or more "negative" by nature. As your over all personality might overtime reflect this change as well. Self-control will typically diminish, as existing 'self-destructive habits' will increase, while new ones might appear. All of this can happen overtime, slowly or faster. It all depends on the person's spiritual and psychological makeup. Overtime surely it can lead to possession, so this is why I give strong caution of "*ghost hunting*", why you should always take precautions in protection prayers before and after the hunt.

"POSSESSION and OPRESSION"
The second and third stages of a demonic manifestation, in a sense this is a bit vague, sort of saying it has gone from yellow alert. (Infestation) to orange, (oppression), to "red" (possession). Realizing how advanced the level of manifestation is important in deliverance. In a sense think of it as

how advanced the cancer has spread, is it more deeply rooted in the advance stages? That would compare to "possession". You can have an attachment that might tempt you to do things that will invite it to manifest as an infestation or more.

Typically I don't say it is an "exorcism" unless it is the Roman Ritual that is performed. However this will vary to others. Where I call it "deliverance" in other cases where it might be successful. This is where I vary from the origins of the leaning. The problem with this is, what is the common understanding of the word?

If we say it and others don't define it as you do, you are not adequately communicating with them. Wile a client, and colleagues need to understand what we are talking about. "Shop talk" is one thing but if your own personal definitions are not widely accepted in the mainstream, be prepared to not be successful in conveying needed information. We try to avoid "fad" words, so as to better stay on more recognizable words and phrases that are universally understood by everyone.

WHEN 'THEY' CAN BE SEEN

As with the John Carpenter movie 'They Live', a man finds that he could see these alien beings, when he put on special glasses that he had found. Otherwise undetected as they have blended into society with humans, appearing as humans. The glasses sort of filter out the disguise of their true form and appearance. Imagine if we had such an ability, how it would affect us profoundly to see the actions of 'demons' and to witness their lesser levels of activity. Say while engaging in stages of 'temptation' for example.

If you recall the movie the "*Exorcism of Emily Rose*" where she began to see 'demonic faces' in people. This is to be expected when you are affected by demonic spirits, in some stages of oppression onto possession, as suddenly you can better see where they exist as it might be 'merging' their presence into others. This is assuming 'hallucinations' are taking place as they can do, however this is more of a 'third eye' view into their realm.

And it is more likely with this; they are seeing what is really there on a lesser level, un-manifested. These demons do not necessarily always 'possess' the body when they meld so close, they can be inside us, but not as a 'manifested' physical presence. It is a hard concept to grasp. But consider this, as we have at least 'one' demon with us at every moment of our lives. We may not see it, and sense it's presence, it has not manifested to where it can do more than mere temptation. These are called 'personal demons', that is demons empowered by our own actions. An opposite to our Guardian Angel they are there to help tip the scales in our thoughts, words and actions 'away' from God. When we give into temptation to where it becomes something more of something 'unhealthy'; as with a drug addiction or even an eating disorder. Another demon is added for each mortal sin for example. So in this state several might be seen in some people, merged into their human form. During temptation stages, there will be smaller creatures swarming around the person. Flying erratically, floating, some on the ground that resemble toads, larger insects and cats. When the moment has passed, they will dissipate. It is said when a child is undergoing changes associated with puberty, this sort of thing can go on for very long periods of time. Or they might come and go quickly like a thief in the night. Hence the 'Poltergeist' phenomenon that many associate with a child, when in truth it is more likely that these spirits of havoc are creating these 'events' in the household, like a band of 'hoodlums' or teenage pranksters. And when these fleeting moments of temptation also pass, the occurrences cease. (*See the section on 'Poltergeist'*)

There are histories of those who were canonized as "saints", in their writings we are very aware of these abilities as they might also come from God, a "discernment' of a higher level where we are allowed to see where these spirits might be attached to someone on a lesser level evil. Padre Pio is one to mention, the ability to better see the enemy would indeed aid to the charity

of 'hearing' and 'deliverance' ministry and exorcisms.
(*See also the section on "Discernment"*)

TYPES OF DEMONS – REVEALING TRAITS

There are so many types of demons, and these "*Elementals*" as some refer to them as, are just a certain four types of demons, of fire, water, air, and earth. So what was called a "*Water Poltergeist*" is essentially a demon designated by the hierarchy as a "*Demon of Water*". The term "Elemental" is perhaps used in the book GHOST TRACKS because it may be more of a 'universal' term understood by more faiths. But we don't use it in our work as "Demonologists". Relating to that case of the "*Water Poltergeist*", in that land where the noted case occurred, such a type spirit could have been called upon by local tribes that once occupied the land. Thus that spirit has a stronger foothold in that area. For it to manifest would be a matter of those who live in that area, or in this case, a house built upon or near that certain plot. You see the demons we appease with our actions past and present, are indeed the first ones through the gate, when we give that certain 'invitation' and open doors to let them in. They can very much so reveal why they are there. What may be unrevealed, that is NOT revealed in initial interviews. So as we don't understand exactly what function each demon might have, it still might have a 'primary function' and it will often not stray from that assignment. Therefore making its presence telltale to a surrounding circumstance. In other words, the type of demon can reveal things that might have brought it to be manifesting in the residence.

For example, in 30 years I have heard and experienced enough RED EYED Shadow being cases to determine these types are associated with the practicing of "black arts" that is black magic. It has gotten to where I hear a haunting has started in a house they lived in for 20 years, and I can more easily say:

"OK someone in the house is practicing black magic." Now the opposite is true, if I see someone is dabbling in Satanism, I might ask if they have seen a "red eyed dark spirit", and they will more often say "yes".

One can validate the other.

Now as they often reluctantly answer "YES", when it wasn't revealed before. They might have purposely left out such details and yet the fruits of their actions are around them.

I wish some others could seem to be so absolute however, as I have found a sum of cases give hint, as some relational symbolism or types of demons. For example, pig squeals seem to indicate a site of satanic worship, black dogs, dog growling with witchcraft. Small cat like creatures show in houses with much stress, there can be many at one time, with their numbers increasing as the tension grows. These things are with ongoing research...

THE SIX STAGES OF THE DEMONIC

Here I propose that there are 'six' stages we should note, and not 'three' or even 'five' stages as I have taught over the years.

NOTE: I go into detail throughout this book about each, in some instances out of this actual order. But for a brief description, I have provided some information on the next page:

1)-TEMPTATION

See the section on temptation. We must remember that temptation is a stage of demonic activity, one we all are affected by. As far as it being an 'early stage' that can lead to a demonic "infestation", (*The first true stage is then considered a "haunting" or actual "manifestation"*), as temptation might be more in alluring certain people into making choices in words and actions that will open doors, and give "invitation" to the demonic to manifest.

2)-SCOUT AND ROAM

This stage will be confused with an 'infestation' often, when in fact the demonic 'does not' have a foot hold or 'invitation' to manifest in the house. It might be considered part just a 'visit' in some cases, from a military sense. A military occupation has not yet transpired, and the invading army has not yet entered your battle ground. Human spirits will be used in this phase onward. Especially if there is a spirit that is already 'lingering' in the house as a 'ghost', they might be a pawn to help lure in an 'invitation' so a demonic can move to an 'infestation'. As previously discussed in the way it might do this in part a certain curiosity created by the human spirit activity, might bring an Ouija board for example in to try to initiate communication. Then the demon steps in and takes over this phase in communication, to best strategically work against their weaknesses. This stage is one the home owners can safely do their own 'cleanings', and say daily prayers and so forth as outlined in the later pages of this book. To keep it from working at this stage.

3)-INFESTATION

After "invitation" the "infestation" can begin, and it may not be apparent. We might see and hear 'warning signs', as these things don't begin without signatures. But they also might go ignored or unnoticed for some time, that may stray into the next level almost undetected. To the experienced "Demonologist" for example, we can recognize the "hoof prints" "ear marking" the very things others might not recognize to "red flag" a demonic presence. I find that too many times when these signs are recognized fully, and the clients are finally seeking help, it has already moved to an "oppression". Sadly the average person is not going to recognize the early signs as we do in our field. They can find ways to explain the "unexplainable", to think something as imaginary and not real, natural and not supernatural. It is human to do this, and to a certain extent we should not give too much attention to these things, however we must be aware of them and take action immediately.

4)-OPPRESSION

"Oppression" is when it begins to come off of the 'stage' and affect the audience, with infestation it can be more for 'show' and 'intimidation', to wear you down, break your faith. To make you more vulnerable as to move on to the next phase. Where 'infestation' can vary in a 'show' of various activity, a resulting 'fear' can counter your 'faith', all of these negative emotions play into helping the stages progress.

The number three still surfaces in different ways. But this stage is beyond the earlier introductory three knocks that signified a sort of *'admission stage'*, marking the beginning of infestation. Now as the people involved in such a haunting are going to be affected, we might see the number *'three'* show in the form of three scratches, which might have an additional 2-4 more in another direction that are horizontal to the three that are vertical. In the oppression stage the individuals the activity focuses on are in danger of possession. There have been cases where the activity is strong when the one person is alone, until say a parent comes running into the room to answer the screams of their teenage daughter.

And as soon as they enter all is quiet. Might as well be a Priest where you have to ask if it is trying to divide the family ducking detection, where the parent might accuse the teen of making it up. None the less when one witness is mainly experiencing the phenomenon, it is more difficult to arrange for an exorcism to be done in the home, until things have escalated to a level much more severe. Apparent markings on the body could hint to a *'Demonologist'* or such seasoned investigators that a demonic might be present.

5)-DEMONIC_POSSESSION

I don't go deep into possession, this is beyond self help. This book as I have mentioned is more so for the family or individual "haunted" with lesser stages. I recommend Vatican Exorcist *Fr. Gabriele Amorth's* two books. "*An Exorcist Tells His Story*" and "*More Stories*". However I will cover briefly some commonly asked questions:

Confusion is in the answer to the question. When is it a "possession"? Part of the myth is from movies and Hollywood dramatizes TV shows based on a "true story".

First we don't expect to see cases like that portrayed in "Emily Rose" and "The Exorcist", the effects of the possessing spirits are more often not so evident, and can take some time to diagnose. Especially as it might be '*medical*' or '*psychological*' in nature, although the physical and mental health of the individuals are often affected during true cases of possession and even oppression. We should never overlook the possibilities of a scientific reasoning in this work.

MORE ABOUT POSSESSION:
FREQUENTLY ASKED QUESTIONS

WHAT IS POSSESSION?

Stated in a sentence it is anytime the spirit is able to gain partial or full control of the individual. So this might not be a 'full control' as it could just be taking over speech only, or the possessing spirit(s) might only be present as a "*voice in your head*".

Where it has taken over your 'audible' functions, this is still control although there is no physical movement.

HOW DOES ONE BECOME POSSESSED?

We will follow the idea that 'possessions' are merely a late stage of demonic 'oppression', which many believe simply begins as a "haunt', when it is really a matter of bad choices in actions and words that will "open doors" to a demonic infestation, that could stay more on a personal level, where even family members sleeping in the same room, may not experience anything paranormal. It all begins with "free will" acting on temptations.

A degradation in one's habits and lifestyle may result, which can bring one closer to possession, but it isn't that simple. That is only one part of it, of the bigger "check list",

if one truly exists. It more so is a careful assessment of each individual on a case-by-case basis. As it is never a simple diagnosis through to a solution. Especially since there are too often psychological issues involved. And this could solely be the problem, as opposed to any so-called 'otherworldly influence'.

However, as Psychologists have come to learn of the placebo effect of 'exorcisms' on their patients, even the skeptics in the field, (a.k.a. Atheist), have come to respect these 'religion methods' to help, where conventional methods have otherwise failed.

TO NARROW DOWN A FEW DETAILS:

Appeasement/Collaboration
This is where the person, is somehow working in unison with the spirit. Not resisting, means you will not be met with a fight from them. However, in this state they may take your life at anytime they feel you are no longer a use to them. Typically a car wreck that seems to be an accident, or death during the night in your sleep which appears to be heart failure or natural causes. Serial killers are often likely collaborators for example.

On some occasion the demon works at a low level as it makes progress through the person's destructive habits. Drug addictions set in, theft, robbery, gambling becomes part of their lifestyle to support this habit. Once a calm rational person, they have become unreasonable and violent. The demonic is succeeding in destroying this person, and it may not be long before they are dead. These victims may go to full body possession, if confronted to where it threatens the cohabitation of the demonic attachment to this person.

Victim soul –

More so Catholic/Orthodox, but age old 2000 year old belief. A victim soul is one who offers penance to God, in order to help others by intercession. A sort of silent prayer as you offer up your suffering to Jesus as so it may help others. A truly selfless act as with being a true martyr. No doubt possession is an extreme torture to the spirit, so a great penance it is. An example here is in the movie "The Exorcism of Emily Rose".

Full body possession –

Possession can occur when it will be to an advantage of the demonic. Or it may simply lay low as the person continues on a road to self destruction. The goal of every demonic haunt is to bring one or more of the home's occupants down to a final goal of death. Often during the cycles of a demonic haunting, we make conscious, free will choices that weaken our immunity to these spirits and lift the limitation on their powers over us. Yes, and at some point, it may go extreme and become a possession. But it isn't that simple. However, before it reaches that stage we have many warnings of a demonic presence behind the scenes that will help us to see what is happening before it reaches this extreme stage in what I call a **Full body possession.** (This is also referred to as 'perfect possession' by the late *Fr. Malachi Martin)*, sometimes, the demonic realizes it has to act fast and hard, if it is to have a chance in succeeding in its quest. So full possession is sometimes a result, of a last ditch effort to win the spiritual battle within and to take the soul of the victim. Of course the demon cannot predict God's judgment. So even if the victim dies while still under control of the demon, it doesn't mean the soul is doomed as a "lost soul'. But it is a chance they are willing to take as it is truly a desperate attempt to not leave the host empty handed.

While the person is under this level of possession, the demon tries to kill the host. For example, they may vomit all food intake, in attempts to take the life of the host, and at times the life of another through acts of murder. The victim may have to be sedated and IV fed for a time to keep them healthy. (Although during the actual exorcism the victim must NOT be sedated or drugged up in anyway.) But the limitation of the demonic power depends on several factors. A great deal depends on the person's own spirit, and faith. This is one reason why it is about" spiritual warfare" as it is not a physical battle.

MULTIPLE DEMONS: Stripping away the 'layers'

For each mortal sin, a demon representing the sin can be one of the demons possessing. So at times if there is more than one spirit, one exorcism may not be enough. The late Ed Warren compared this "stripping away the layers.", as each spirit is rebuked one-by-one, the symptoms will subside, as the lower rank demons usually are the first to leave.

CAN HUMAN SPIRITS POSSESS SOMEONE?

If they are allowed access, that is the demons let them try them on for size, they will typically not have the knowledge, wisdom and ability to integrate themselves into the human form and take control. The 'interfacing' of connecting to the victim's brain functions and getting 'control' isn't something easy for a human spirit. Typically they may co-inhabit the victim and appear to be 'controlling' parts. But at best they might be able to initiate speech, in the least words projecting from the victim without mouth movement. We have to remember any extraordinary things they can do is power lent to them by the demons. Just as in life with a wizard, who believes it is their power that is getting these results and effects. When it was always the demon that was carrying out these tasks, in part to give an illusion of power to further 'draw in' the practitioner of these dark arts. A result also in building upon their 'pride' and 'confidence', to better lure them in more with an idea that it 'works'.

IS THERE IS TEST TO SEE IF SOMEONE IS POSSESSED?

We can discuss some traits of possession, but again to state, in this book, we do not go too deep into the topic of 'possession'. We touch on it briefly from time to time. Mainly to answer common question that I feel were commonly not answered well enough. That is another book in itself'. As the focus of the book is more so the different stages and types of "hauntings", and how to solve them. We also have to remember this:

1) PRAYERS AND SPOKEN WORDS

A good test would be a test of faith, a possessed, cannot go for much over 10 minutes saying certain words, names and prayers. I would begin with an "Our Father", watch them closely, do they struggle, watch their facial expressions, prayer can be painful for a demon, sometimes you can see a painful look being held back, as oppose to a relaxed peaceful look. Then I would move onto having them say some prayer I would otherwise say for 'spiritual warfare'. Now higher demons can withstand a few minutes, but will soon wear down and reveal themselves. Gabriele Amorth says that is in about "ten minutes" time.

Sometimes demonic attachment is only an advanced stage of 'oppression' but 'possession' has not occurred.
In this case the spirit leaves quietly. But returns that night to

display disapproval of what has been done. As I said throughout this book. Any form of religious provocation, unintentional or otherwise must be done in great care. Unknown to the suspected possessed individual, prior to such a test, be ready with at least 'two helpers' who can restrain the individual, as they may suddenly rise up and attack you! As I said, exercise great caution when trying to get a demon to reveal itself. This is NOT recommended, and should be performed by an ordained Priest only. We find that most bible verses can be spoken without a flaw, and cannot be a hard task for the possessed. That is, until they reach the name of 'Jesus' in the text for example. Then they might pause or stumble over the name when it is spoken. In more severe cases, they can sail over his name as well. But not for long over a period of time, perhaps 10-15 minutes, they can't endure it for long. A prayer of the 'Rosary' is a good example, where the 'Our Father' is said more than once and honoring 'Mary' with the 'Hail Mary', which seems to affect demons and they can't stand for long. That is, if they don't react immediately.

I have heard another notion is that the possessed can string together words such as:

```
"charity, compassion, faith, gentleness,
hope, humility, joy, kindness, light,
love, mercy, modesty, patience, peace,
purity, security, serenity, tranquility,
trust, truth, understanding, and wisdom."
```

Which can be more of a tongue twister, and I have to say that saying these words are one matter while acting on them is quite another. I think this is another misinterpretation of scripture through more of that "reverse engineering" of the good book. So some of these things can be quite ineffective in determining the presence of a demonic spirit, and are not a practice of Catholic and Eastern Orthodox Exorcists that I am aware of.

2) THE 'HOLY WATER' REACTION

Some through the years have tried 'holy water' in a drink to test the possessed. This goes back to even that historical possession of 'Nichole Aubrey' back in the 16th century, where it was a successful test, in placing holy water into a cup of sacramental wine. The result was a reaction of vomiting and violent behavior, as well as personality changes. So in this classic case, the demon 'did' reveal itself, however the test isn't always that reliable, as there are a few variables that need to be understood.

First, the drink itself needs to be pure, as so to note you would have to add it to 'pure water', not lemonade or Pepsi for example, or it won't be as effective.

The prayer test is unmistakable. They sometimes go across the "Our Father" prayer, and get to "Jesus" name and it seems like they suddenly forgot the prayer at this point. When it is the demon confusing them to avoid saying the name of Jesus, which is poison to the demonic. *(Note: This also works for non-Christians to a point, which tends to reveal more so the very nature of demons)*. The revealing of the demonic presence may be a violent one, or simply a change in behavior. Some see the face change more drastic as though an animal spirit, snarling has taken over and morphed the facial expression and bone structure for a moment. More extreme case, but it can happen. Just be prepared for something shocking.

Interestingly, people ask this question of testing themselves. Any adult should be able to say the prescribed prayers, even simply to humor the other members of the family as well as the investigators. To flat out refuse, may not certainly be an indication of possession; however that is a trait, in avoidance of saying prayers that cause the demonic great pain.

Tell the person we can all lay the idea to rest if they would cooperate and say these prayers. Adults go to the dentist and submit themselves to worse, so no one should really have an issue with saying a few prayers.

3) THE "CHURCH TEST"

Being in "proximity" of something evil can have a cause and effect, just as in the presence of something "Positive".
Example, being in the midst of prayer and the Eucharist at a Catholic mass. Even if the attendees do not participate in the mass, and pray themselves, the affect will be there to a certain extent on their spiritual and psychological. Your children are a perfect example of this. This is something I didn't understand as a child, as my son doesn't yet. And reason why we have our kids go to church with us, even when they prefer to stay at home because they believe it is "boring". The test itself is based on this sort of "proximity effect", a form of provocation and it is not commonly discussed as a method of testing for one's possible state of demonic oppression and possession. This 'test' is somewhat concealed and kept secret, as expected. Just as with the holy water in a drink, as you are NOT to reveal that this is a 'test', even at times to the other people involved.
(Of course there can be exceptions in that some knowing the real reason for attending mass)
This needs to go undisclosed to avoid a something 'psychosomatic'. When I set it up, I do so by simply asking the troubled person to **"Go and sit through a Catholic mass, and tell me what you think of it"**. Sounding more as to see if they like the parish, and the Catholic faith, as a sort of "try before you buy". Which in itself might play a part in later counseling I realize, however, as I am pointing them to church, is mainly 'a test' to see if they react to the proximity effect of being around those many people praying, and more so the "Presence" when the Eucharistic prayer begins during mass. Some might go to 'services' of 'other denominations', and typically when/if the *"Our Father"* is spoken, they might start to hear ringing in their ears, feel nausea, some go into convulsions, I have to see if I would expect that I will not send them to a church. That can create quite a stir, and the people's reaction is one of concern of the man's psychical spiritual health not his spiritual.

In emergency situations you don't get to hand pick the one that ultimately takes him to the hospital, anymore than those whom do the initial analysis.

Calling an ambulance is placing that person under the care of people who are likely going to be ones who truly don't know or understand demonic possession. And they will make the wrong call and recommend the wrong treatment. This can profoundly affect their life, and then we go back to placing people in strait jackets, and heavily drugged, stamped "Insane" by the state. Be very careful in this, as so that you don't make matters worse. When possible keep them out of public areas from such a test, and NOT ALONE especially.

In a way placing them in environments of a Catholic mass or amongst those in prayer at a Sunday service is a form of provocation, and as I state this can be dangerous as we might not know how the spirits my react. And should be ready "Just in case" the demon(s) react like an angry hive of bees when we do this test. Having the right people present if the test goes to proving beyond a shadow of a doubt a demon is present and it turns violent.

4) RELIGIOUS PROVOCATION

This is essentially what we are using here in all three examples in these methods of forcing the demon to reveal itself. Please note that 'anytime' we use religious provocation, be ready for a reaction. Take safe measure in people being able to restrain the individual before taking such action. Remember 'oppression' precedes a 'possession' in it's stages. And that stage alone is a dangerous one that can invite a physical retaliation. To not do so is foolish! Prepare before and after any such potential encounters, including prayer that follows a visit or investigation of these types of cases. (*With prayers to break any possible demonic attachments, and so forth*)

A Side note: We always do a careful analysis of the client and the overall 'oppression' that might be surrounding them. This for the seasoned investigator will help to best predict, what the end result would be while the individual undergoes these simple tests. I am typically not going to be surprised at the results, but to validate my suspicions with these test, can play a huge part in expediting the case further to a RCC (Roman Catholic Church) sanctioned 'Exorcism' for example. And also can play a part in the discernment of *"Mental"* versus *"Demonic"*, then we can refer the case entirely over to a medical professional sooner rather than later. Always pray for 'discernment' as soon as these cases come your way, to have God and Heaven better help you make a good call. Watch for any reactions, especially ones that are out of the ordinary. After all, in a logical mind we should ponder the question: **"What are the odds that they become very ill in church under these circumstances?"**

WHAT ARE SOME COMMON SIGNS OF POSSESSION?

Possession symptoms are hard to tell from "oppression", except that the demon <u>CAN</u> possess the person. While only under "oppression stage", they have not yet advanced to that stage or invitation to inhabit and control the person in some way as is with true "possession".

So in saying the above, some of these are signs of OPPRESSION as well. But the more of these things are evident, the better chance the person may be in late stages of oppression and is in danger of full-body possession. These things were not present prior to the noted start of the alleged "haunting" they might have reported some months before. Drastic changes in personality, self control is off the charts, they may lose their jobs, break off engagements, and

interpersonal relationships suffer dearly. Habits may have

changed drastically, as they might sleep 'more', or much even much 'less', for absolutely no clear reason. Old habits will take over and become extreme. If they once quit smoking, drinking and other bad habits, these will resurface again suddenly, and sometimes this is concealed from others in the family. As the possessed will advert to religious things of God we expect their overall attitude to reflect this. For one example, a woman wouldn't hear of having me step foot in their home, even though she was Catholic. Not a red flag in this alone, but in this case it revealed something typical of a 'possession' that we noted from the investigation. A 'Baptist' Minister performed a 'deliverance' ritual on the woman, and when it was all over with she had decided to return to the Catholic Church. The hatred and attitude against the old mother church had dissipated with the demons that were expelled from her. So as the demon affects the personality so, the 'merge' or 'meld' of the two personalities begin to become one in the same collectively united.

These are of course, just a very few of a much larger list.

WHY DO SEEMINGLY GOOD PEOPLE BECOME POSSESSED?

Consider that when full possession has made itself known and the demon has taken full control of the person. (*Think of the movie The Exorcist to some degree*), this is often a "last stand". The demon(s) doesn't want to leave empty handed and will not go down without a fight. This measure would not be as necessary if there was more of a collaboration between the 'demon' and the 'host' they possessed. Such as with some of these clearly evil 'mass murderers', such as Charles Mansion. In other words, when you resist, they will try to force your will and control away from. So essentially, possession is more apparent when you resist, and to a demon it might become necessary to their strategy to do so.

If they have found a way to an 'innocent', it is also a 'prize' to try to corrupt that person in any way they can. After all, when the person is heeding to every sublime temptation they put forth, they are fully cooperating with what the demon wants. No need to 'force a control' when the host is willing. The point here is maybe the more notable case might be with children or seemingly good people. Sadly they often let the demon into their lives, being so naive. One reason why as a parent we should really be aware of who might be 'baby sitting' our kids and what they play with for "toys" that might be an occult item such as an 'Ouija board'.

Also consider the media might exploit such cases more, and these scenarios get more attention by default. Human nature to tell the story of the innocent possessed, rather than an 'evil man' for example.

A CHILD'S IMAGINARY FRIEND

Pay attention to your child, when they have an 'invisible friend'. We should listen and be aware that it might be a 'dark spirit', in these cases where the demonic appears as a child, to gain the trust and friendship of the child it is targeting. Such a 'bond' has a direct influence on the child, as this might begin at an early age. Such as at the age of 3-4 years old, it can get quite a foothold in the child's life as a few years have passed and the so-called 'imaginary friend' is still a part of your child's life. Again, here I say listen to your children when they start to describe things that don't sound like simply a 'child's imagination'. We want to catch these dark strangers and rebuke them before they affect our children.

What is frightening is there is a recognizable 'pattern' of those who have experienced this 'invisible playmate', which could be as early as the age of two or three years old. And if nothing is done to detach the spirits and to break this union of so-called 'friendship', they could very well be in danger of 'possession' by the time they reach the "age of reason", which is between the ages of 7 and 9 years old. Always keep these things in consideration, again here, I stress prayers to protect our children such as the one printed in this book. Christians and especially Catholics might want to be sure the child is baptized "ASAP", to help ensure their possible generational attachments are broken.

CAN A CHILD REALLY BE A "BAD SEED" INHERENTLY EVIL?

I don't think a child is merely born this way without something evil pushing them. Here are some reasons why one child might seem like a 'bad seed'. A bad seed is one who can do ill deeds without conscious, they can steal from the playmates and parents without a concern, and they can kill their pets without regret, or even kill another child for a toy. To me this is not normal no matter who your parents were. And I highly suspect there is something spiritual in the origin of this behavior, although as time goes on the psychological mind is affected, a demonic spirit can in effect raise your child to think and act a certain way towards people. So the personality might be more noted after the age of reason, then the demonic can begin to weave its own personality traits into the child.

Some possible reasons for the Bad seed syndrome are:

- The child may be cursed by a 'generational curse', a relative or other person cursing the child. It is not uncommon to hear from a family an estranged aunt had cursed your family, and such ill wishes in the least is the same as paying a hit-man in a demonic, to come and wreak havoc on your life one way or another. Illnesses, financial ruin, accidental death and so forth. (read the section on Curses and "Demonic Death") Your child can be the direct target in some case, or the family as a whole which can adversely affect the child.

- The parents might not be revealing the whole story. Many times I find that people are not forth coming to their "darker side", which plays a huge role in the WHY they might be 'haunted'. Nothing surprises me. People prefer you believe they are a mere 'innocent victim' of a haunting when most often something they did and still are doing in their life or even as part of a 'daily routine'. Sadly children get caught in the middle far too often.

- Abuse- there might be unknown abuse occurring, perhaps even by a baby sitter, one at a day care facility, a relative, or even the parent(s) themselves. This might entail "satanic ritual abuse". This can attach a dark spirit, and have a profound effect on them from an early age onward throughout their lives.

- The influence of 'imaginary friends'- As I mentioned shortly before. Keep watch of who their friends are as much as their 'imaginary' friends. A demonic can affect the child's psychological and spiritual growth. Programming them toward such evil. Always pray for your children.

I can say that having 'Three Stooges' on isn't going to program a kid to smack another child with a hammer. I know to some that sounds like a silly notion but this is the fear of some parent's in exposing them to these old slap stick comedies. It really doesn't happen that easy. While movies with 'sexual content' will get one aroused, where we don't become violent or killers from watching action movies or even horror movies. Unless, there is something wrong with that person already. Assuming the child isn't mentally challenged, in this I am referring to things that might cause this negative behavior that constitutes a "bad seed", beyond some medical or psychological reason. Especially since too many times spiritual reasons are over looked as with adults!

ABOUT ADOPTED CHILDREN

Consider who might give their child up for adoption, and what sort of lifestyle they might have to revert to such a drastic measure. You have drug addicts, prostitutes, who gave birth to the child, and you can be certain that 'baggage' will play a part on the child. Also those coming from third world countries, we have no idea what might have been done to them or what they have been through. I have heard horror stories from adopted parents who describe symptoms of 'possession' from a 5 year old. Including citing blasphemies against Jesus, and other innate, clearly evil behavior. Get your child baptized regardless if or not they are said to be 'already baptized', as we don't really well know the psychological or the spiritual health of the child so well. Or even if the baptism did occur. (Is there a record of it?) Plus, we want to get a good fresh start with the new parents, with the 'new' parent and their chosen "God-parent", for the child, it is a good way to bind the relationships beyond a legal adoption.

WHY WOULD THE DEMON SEEK TO DESTROY THE HOST?

When the demon reads indications that the host is in a 'grave state of sin', (*un-repented 'mortal sins'*). And it finds it has enough power in it's effect on the individual, where if it can affect to end the life of the person, it may indeed 'try' to follow through as it believes this might help to collect yet another 'condemned soul'. A number of things would be considered, for example, if the person is no longer of use to them. Some consider to spread the seed of 'evil' and 'serve' a purpose. But for those that might begin to resist, and have a change of heart to their ways, hence, the demon(s) might then choose to 'try' to cut their losses, and attempt to claim the soul by killing the host.

It should be noted that only God can clearly judge the fate of a soul, and the demon is limited to what information they might have that indicates the state of the soul, and vulnerability of it's host. It had been said demons can see your 'unconfessed' sins on your soul, this is true, and that plays a part in their judgment. As preparation for an 'exorcism' begins, the demon might begin to take steps to try to "collect", as it is forced to cut and run. This is why it might reveal itself in 'full force' for the first time. The 'possessed' may try to commit suicide, or even be used to kill 'others' in some cases. Suicide might be more common through starvation and dehydration; through vomiting the food and water they are given, as the victim might have to be fed intravenously, while being restrained or drugged, so they don't pull out the I.V. tubes. Again, all as a last ditch effort as to not leave the host 'empty handed'.

DEMONIC DEATH –

There are two types of Death here to consider:
(a) A Physical Death (b) A Spiritual Death
A spiritual death is to become a 'condemned soul', with no chance of Heaven. As I stated prior, it is the plan of the demonic to try to initiate a "physical death" if they predict that person will suffer a "spiritual death". This is their main concern unless it is merely a desire to have one killed who might create trouble for them in life. This is why in our work we always pray for protection, as they will try to seek revenge throughout your whole life. And it is only by God's will you are protected.

INDENTIFYING THE 'DEMONIC'

Determining a human spirit, can at times be a matter of concluding the spirit is not demonic. So we will cover this first.

RELIGIOUS PROVOCATION DURING INVESTIGATIONS

DANGER! Provoking a demonic spirit can draw retaliation that might incur death. This might not even be immediate and it might occur even days later.

Religious provocation can be a 'necessary danger'. In some instances the demonic activity will lie low when the 'recording devices' come in, as outside help has entered with a hope of validating the haunt. They aren't camera shy per-se more that their strategy is best to go undetected for as long as they can play a part. If one family member is the only witness, even siblings, the spouse and friends might start to wonder if they are really experiencing the settings or if 'imagination' is playing more of a part. *"Am I crazy?"* is what you want to answer with for their piece of mind. And having a 'third party' validation is priceless. We realize the demon can 'lie low' and 'play dead' for a few days while investigators try to comb the building for a 'supernatural presence'. It can delay the real help that might be attained, when evidence is seeking is not fruitful, and worse, things might escalate after the investigators have left to a degree where people get hurt. Or should I say "punished", as there is a certain 'retaliation' or revenge on those living through the infestation, for trying to seek help.

Knowing this nature, this is why it is dangerous to try to give them a 'hot foot' to get them to reveal themselves, and in turn force a "retaliation" as well. 'Religious provocation' again, in rare occasions can be necessary to make what could have been a trip across the country not a wasted endeavor.

I personally DO NOT recommend any 'laity' to do it. Directly challenging the demonic is a fool's game for all put the most pious and devout Catholic for example. But I still say it is better for a Priest to do. (Of course the Priests who are qualified for the work are scarce, this is why 'laity' have had to step up to the plate)

Ed Warren was perhaps the first and the last laity to get permission to act as a 'religious demonologist', in provocation and some forms of 'cleansings'. In reality, any such individual today who claims to be a "Roman Catholic Religious Demonologist", and makes a claim to be "sanctioned by the church", is likely misrepresenting that title, and at best is only recognized by his local archdiocese, and might be called upon for certain matter for investigations. But you will not find the church openly approving of laity doing work that a 'Priest' should in fact do.

Getting back to the main topic at hand, we realize that a Catholic Church authorized 'exorcism', will require a detailed report. And it is better yet, to include some 'captured evidence' of clear 'paranormal activity', especially as it might be indicating a 'demonic presence'. While such measures might be necessary for investigators to capture and witness the phenomenon that might spell 'Demonic'. Beyond that, mostly through witness testimony that you will gather to help form an option beyond any clear physical evidence obtained from the field investigations. So, in a sort of a deeper analysis of all the information you can gather before entering the home. Most often I find these things can be properly dealt with by the home owners, and without the 'extreme measures' of the often hard to attain Catholic 'Roman Ritual' being performed by an ordained "Exorcist".

The diagnosis can be more simple than you know, in considering the way you will find that a great deal of the signs of demonic presence are related to extreme opposites. One example being a 'frigid cold' as oppose to 'warm', A 'dark negative blackness' not a radiant 'positive light'. By appearance the 'hideous', versus 'beautiful'. Strong 'putrid smells', as opposed to what we consider as 'pleasant fragrances'. Also 'unnatural' is yet another tell-tale sign, such as things that clearly defy the 'laws of physics'.

As God's 'cosmic law' divides this world from the next, this seems to play a part in how 'demonic spirits' have distinguishable characteristics to help 'discern' from 'good spirits' for example. These may not always be so well defined, as the demonic can do well to 'mimic' any type of spirit. However, we know what other traits to look for that won't let the masquerade fool you entirely.

Part of this can be in the way they seem to be 'limited' in how well they can go to imitate the appearance of humans and animals. Although it can be slight, again, knowing what to look for is the 'key'.

Animals for example in a demonic haunting, investigators may witness strangely formed animals of some unknown origin emerge from undisclosed areas, to go run across the floor behind a chair. Then as when onlookers go to check where it went, they find that it had mysteriously 'vanished'. These animals often look like a mix of different species, like a strange cross between a 'platypus' and an 'opossum'. Another trait is that they are more typically with darker colors such as with 'brown or black fur'. Some say this is a demon's way of mocking God's creations with a distorted version of his designs in animals. Others say that the fact they are obviously distorted versions of animals we recognize, by this they have revealed themselves as what they are. "Demonic manifestations".

As for 'humanoid apparitions', there is always something of a telltale sign the spirit is 'demonic'. I outline these details in part later in this book.

HISTORICAL DESCRIPTIONS OF DEMONS:

In a physical form some are said to have claws for fingers, large eyes often solid black or 'cat like', small noses, almost nonexistent, and large mouths. Over sized heads often on a smaller body, with a 'hunched over' posture, more like a primate. No ears, just an orifice or 'pointed ears' as in the old gothic portrayal. Features might include 'sharp jagged teeth' or 'no teeth', sometimes with two or more horns on the head, with bat like wings. Many are four feet high, while with the more powerful demons by rank, being much larger. This as opposed to these before mentioned, lesser powerful beings which are seen as being 'smaller'. As we see the 'demonic' is a complete 'opposite' of an 'Angel of God', in that it represents dark/black not bright light, foul odors, not sweet smells, and so on.

The demon, when it doesn't portray a 'physical image' or likeness will often appear as an essence of a 'dark black mass.' Their appearance is partly due to an absence of God, they are cold and dark entities. One or more of these may be evident; however a lack of one doesn't mean a 'non-demonic' encounter.

Although they may choose to appear in other forms this is more of their true appearance. And stay with that appearance as I mentioned earlier, as a sort of chosen form to represent themselves as. Where as they may not vary from this appearance by much.

THE 'GRAY VEIL'

There are cases where a demonic spirit can encompass an entire room, as if with a shroud of a huge 'black veil'. At times this can be accompanied by a drastic drop of the temperature of the room, to a feeling of more frigid 'sub zero' temperatures. Sometimes the veil appears as though it is 'gray', and therefore it might be somewhat 'undetected', as the light from the sun coming in the windows will diminish quickly. As though it is being dissipated quicker through this dark layer, filtering out in part, the 'light'. This is one reason after a successful exorcism; the room feels indeed as though the windows suddenly begin to let in more light and warmth from outside.

As 'human entities' are also cold in their temperature, note when they are captured they do not change the room temp like demons. The cold only follows their presence in the shape of their form.
Note that after a successful 'deliverance', the house seems to have such a veil lifted, owners will say "The house seems as though "a darkness has been lifted". This is a good observation, as it could very well have been.

BY SOUNDS

We often learn that a telltale demonic sound can often be isolated to the left ear when directed to a specific individual. You might never have heard of it put quite this way but "sound effects" are the best way to describe it.
Let me explain…
You might be just starting to fall asleep when you hear something like a "crash", that it jars you awake. And if you were to wander the halls through the rooms of your house, not one thing is broken. When at times, clearly, it sounded like 'glass' or 'pottery' breaking on a hard floor that can almost rule out the carpeted areas. You know that all too familiar sound. So the house inspection for the 'phantom noises' doesn't resume for long, before you go back to bed, puzzled as to what the noise was. 'Glass breaking' seems to be a sound they prefer, things breaking certainly will alarm you from fast asleep to being 'fully awake'. Sometimes it is a sound like a cat knocked over something in your room, something smaller if it had really occurred, like a mug of water with ice cubes.

As for other sound effects, George Lutz for example stated that he would hear the sound of a 'band tuning up'. Less often these days are these occurrences called by the original descriptive word – "poltergeist", under the correct definition as to reference a 'noisy ghost'. (*As opposed to the new reference to a "psycho-kinetic" activity, surrounding an adolescent child*) I can't explain this in which I refer to next, except as a sort of '**boom**'. Again, just as you begin to fall asleep, it is like a 'blast sound' but not as 'bassy', more as though it is inside your head. *(A weaker recording of it.)* Or an M-80 firecracker blew up near your face, however, is was not as 'loud' and 'full'. At least this is my account of it.

Some sound effects can be of **people**. In one case the sounds were of a **baby crying** and **sexual sounds** of a man and woman, like a woman's "**moan**". This I immediately went to thinking that there could be 'infidelity', or something of 'sinful sexuality' within that household that would lure this type of spirit there. And my suspicions were right.

The 'baby' in another case, was more a mockery of an abortion the woman had, who was having feelings of guilt over that decision some years earlier. Since this is a psychological game quite often, we should expect them to hit us where it hurts and make light of our shortcoming and even sufferings.

Human Growls This can also be a sound that wakes you up, the *"guttery growl"* sound seems quite common people have reported hearing this on phone lines as well while interviewing clients with would-be 'infestations'. This is more of something inhuman in it's sound, rather than as with 'animals'. **Pig squeals** and "snort" sounds can be quite disturbing, the animals are often sacrificed, along with animals such as 'cats', simply because they cry out in pain when they are slaughtered alive. There are indications that a pig might also be associated with 'Satanism' and 'black magic'. This sound might indicate such practices are partly the reason for the infestation. The sounds and presence of what appear to be 'black dogs', or 'cats' are also associate with forms of 'black magic'. So growling sounds like a dog might be heard as well in these scenarios.

RECOGNIZING 'DEMONIC' BY ACTIONS:

THEY HAVE AN AVERSION TO HOLY SYMBOLS, CERTAIN PRAYERS AND THE NAME OF JESUS.

Demons for the most part have a deep hatred of all things of Heaven and God; they also have an 'aversion and fear' as well. Unlike most human spirits, we find as previously discussed in *'religious provocation'*. In how demons recoil and are affected by these methods, simply being exposed to relics, holy symbols, blessed objects, and the recital of certain prayers, names and words. So this can be a 'test' of sorts against the spirit which will react somewhat even if it is a stronger demon such as a higher ranked devil. These types will often show off their ability to be able to throw a crucifix off the wall, in part to display their level of power and to confuse those living in the infestation with the notion that perhaps these items don't have an effect. Since the demon can toss it around and desecrate these objects so easily. But even this is a farce, as it does take in a certain level of 'metaphysical pain' and they are indeed affected to be in proximity of these objects.

While lower demons will simply not withstand being in the same room as this exposed holy symbol. Often people might move into a house that seemed to not be haunted and stir things up when they start sporting crucifixes and Catholic holy symbols which will act as a sort of 'religious provocation' in itself, although it was not intended to do so, the results might be the same.

EXHIBITING EXTRAORDINARY 'STRENGTH'

Human PK alone has been tested to not be able to move over 5lbs. In other words, refrigerators sliding across the floor is one for the 'demonic' check list. Keep in mind that this wasn't throwing 5 lbs. but budging of an object. Because of the test conditions, quite honestly, we can't even say for certain that this feat wasn't aided by a demonic in some way and NOT merely the lone power of one human's mind and PK. So as a human is a 'ghost' who may successfully tip a vase, open doors, etc, it is the demonic that will move sofa beds, push over big screen TVs, and skid appliances across the floor. All things considered as higher feats of strength. This will also include 'levitations'.

TELEPORTATION

Beyond a more simple movement of say, larger objects, some things may actually **disappear** entirely, and later found to be in strange places or perhaps never found again. However, the teleportation of objects in general is something to note as 'demonic' in nature. Remember. When it is indeed 'extraordinary' even as far as paranormal occurrences go, this will typically mean it is 'demonic'

UNNATURAL PHYSICS

Demonic activity often defies the laws of physics. Such as with the case of Pat Reading where a glass of water had fallen off a table; however it safely lands on the hard floor unbroken and without spilling the contents. (Refer to the case of Pat Reading in John Zaffis book: "Shadows of the Dark".) It made sounds like it hits the floor hard, but does not break, or when it falls to the floor it may entail an unnatural flow in a "Z" shape zigzag motion rather than a Newton straight fall to the floor. In one case mentioned by Lorraine Warren the glass object bounced like rubber and they found it didn't even chip when it came to settle down on the floor. Phenomenon such as with a set of dining room chairs being found stacked on top of the table while the home owner had simply walked out of the room and returned seconds later. (*The scene shown in the movie Poltergeist was based on an actual true life case that Ed and Lorraine Warren worked on.*)

INDICATIONS OF THEIR PRESENCE - OTHER SENSES

"VERY COLD"

It can be said with certainty, that the colder the experience, the more evil the entity. This can also be an indication of how powerful they are, as in a higher ranked demon. Demonic entities don't have a human shape or form, they can be huge or small, and are not typically a 'human size'. As I describe the 'dark veil' earlier in this book, I will make the same case in how a massive encompassing size might overcome any warm temperatures. Plus, I restate the analogy of how "*the colder the ice, the quicker and colder the drink will become*", in describing how these 'very cold entities' can drastically affect a room's climate.

REPUGNANT SMELLS

In one case the home owners spent days trying to find where a smell was originating from that seemed to be of a 'dead animal'. They believe perhaps a rodent died inside the walls or a raccoon. But the smells seemed to move about the house, sometimes right after they go so far as to cut a hole in the wall to search for a dead Rodent carcass. We know from case histories the demons like to bring confusion and frustration. For example, in getting home owners to damage their own property due to their falsely laid clues on a sort of 'scavenger hunt' for a book or a supposed hidden clue of the past. This occurs more often with wild goose chases based on notions of a body being buried in the house. Read in another chapter about this. The simple fact that the smells move about the house, makes it an "unnatural occurrence".

Some describe the smell of burning hair or flesh, human excrements, and sulfur. But keep in mind these smells can go about moving around the house, rather than to be localized. Also in some environments it is very clear they simply cannot exist. Foul stenches, and smells – such as the smells of sulfur, sewer smells, smells of decomposing flesh, burning flesh, all uncommon to the household, it is much easier to 'notice'. In these examples, we are again seeing how the demonic is going to cling to traits that are 'negative' in their true signatures, which fits well the nature of the demonic. As opposed to a complete opposite, in say a scent of "spring time flowers", a "new born baby", and my wife's perfume. We still might keep in mind the exception to this however, in that the demon might be masquerading as a deceased relative, or some 'positive' form to lure you into the trap as they do well. Also consider human spirits that are the 'minions' of the demonic many times might have a 'perfume scent' not just a 'succubus' for example.

One interesting thing to note, is that when these 'repugnant smells' are around, then a demon is indeed present. In it's manifested form, it is usually going to be seen as a more 'grotesque appearance'.
Descriptions of creatures such as with the appearance of 'rotting corpses', with loose hanging bloody tissue, and burned flesh. When thinking about it, all these are consistent 'smells' that might go with these described appearances.

This is not to say all cases will entail such a demon. But rather than the smell being simply a way to present itself, it appears to be more associated with it's overall manifested appearance and characteristics.

YOU'RE 'SIXTH SENSES

Your 'natural reaction'. Do you get a feeling of doom? Dread? Remember as we are dealing with a negative entity negative feelings will be overwhelming when in their presence. But it should also be noted that such 'sensitivity' will increase the more you try to better follow your faith with God in a higher spiritual path. Discernment may also surface, just as pure white can easily be seen to be infected by black or grey. Being in the proximity of evil, the more you are enlightened by God, the stronger the extra ordinary sixth-sense will be. But as we are vessels of the Holy Spirit, we all have a certain level of 'sensitivity' when in proximity of 'true evil'. We might react in a variety of ways, even physical reactions such as a 'tightness in the chest', nausea. Yet those who experience these sensations, might not themselves be considered in the least, as what some refer to as 'Sensitives'. As this is just a more common and natural reaction to these 'dark forces'

BY APPEARANCE

APPARITIONS

Demons are not allowed by some cosmic law to manifest themselves entirely as humans. There is always something missing. We look for flaws in how they might appear in human form, in this I try to outline some characteristics that spell **TYPE: EVIL or DEMONIC.**

THE EYES…

…are indeed the windows to the soul – black eyes, no eyes are a common trait of a **`"TYPE: EVIL HUMAN OR INHUMAN"`** spirit. Far from human eyes, some have reported even eyes like a cat. Or more cold like a reptile. As human spirits can have 'black eyes' also, but not as deep of a pitch black as with a demon, and not over such a wide area of the face. It is a sign of 'true evil' regardless human or inhuman. When it is black in the recesses of the eyes where they set, and not just the eye balls themselves. As though even the cavities and eye sockets in the skull are also deep black. This I will say leans to 'demonic', although as in many cases one trait alone isn't enough to safely label the haunting as "demonic". We see how possession can have what looks like 'solid black eyes', seeing this in an apparition might entail it is human but it is definitely a minion of evil.

White eyes are seldom going to be a something you'll encounter; it is more of a Hollywood portrayal of an evil spirit. I can't say that these have shown up in 1000 cases I have studied, analyzed and personally experienced. Just more so in classic cases of folklore, cases later learned to be 'fraudulent'. I can say that in the least this type of appearance is uncommon, but can be possible. At the same time it might be a 'red flag' when some put together a fabricated story; they often use references from movies that more apply to scenarios and descriptions more common to movies than in real life.

Red eyes as well, but are more often with shadowy figures, and most certainly are an 'occult demon'. So if you ever here such descriptions from a home owner, as in a *'shadow being with red eyes'*, this is definitely an indication, as I find that *black magic* or *Satanism* played a part in the *'infestation'* somehow. This can tell you what might be going on there that may not be revealed at first by the family for example. In one case, as I heard of such an apparition appearing, I was immediately suspicious of one in the household practicing the dark arts. More so because this haunting started up after a few years, rather than immediately which is more the scenario if such a spirit was 'invited' by a former occupant or home owner. In this case I mention too, the fact the house was new, they were the first owners, which drew a suspicion to this notion. So that increases the likelyhood that no former tenant practiced black magic, when there was no one before them on the premises. (*The property itself of course is another matter, which I outline elsewhere in the book*) Don't be afraid to interview clients again when things turn up that seem 'fishy', very often they are NOT telling you everything and answering all questions truthfully.

NOT FULLY FORMED

Is the figure 'fully formed'? Typically the feet are not formed when this spirit has manifested, as 'missing feet' is a common anomaly to demonic spirits who try to masquerade in human form.
Alone it may not be as tell-tale as the eyes as I mentioned, but it is still one to add to a mental check list moving toward suspicion that it is 'demonic'. When they try to deceive us through appearance of a human it won't be shown with missing limbs clearly showing dismemberment, it is more so as though it is an incomplete manifestation. So as the feet are missing just below the knee, it will start to fade out and at times look 'cloudy' as it approaches where the feet would be on a human. Some 'Marian apparitions' the Catholic church have not validated, or are in the least suspected as 'false' in having had this 'missing feet' trait in the apparition of the *'Blessed Mother'*. Some might be missing a head, as though it was 'erased out'. Not something that resembled the victim of a decapitation. We are mainly talking the way they might not fully manifest. There is a case where a spirit is manifesting itself to a child without a head or feet. To me this is more a 'red flag', a likely warning of a demonic spirit, however again, we always like to try to look for more 'signs' of a demonic presence. This should not be confused with spirits that might present themselves with 'missing limbs' as might result from

industrial accidents or injuries sustained on the battlefield of war. We are talking about an incomplete body in it's manifested form or appearance.

ANIMALS

As described earlier, we know that lower demons commonly choose to manifest themselves as 'animals'. And a haunting that includes animal aggression sounds like 'growling', especially are almost always of demonic origins. Black and dark colored are preferred. On some occasion they can't fill in the features on animals either. But I think this is more of some hideous mockery of the animal's true anatomy.
Missing tails, eyes, legs, these manifestations are more so distortions of the animals, as with 'birth defects' or genetic 'mutations'. Then there is seen hybrid creatures that seem to have some cross features of two animals. Imagine what people thought when they first saw a ducked billed platypus? Demons mix in strange combinations, then run this more obscure creation in front of you and behind a chair or into a closet, leaving you scratching your head in wondering what exactly that was you just saw. (*Also see where I talk about "animal spirits"*)

ELECTRICAL ACTIVITY

Very cold, or very hot, manifestations might also include some form of electrostatic ionization. Some have reported when a spirit is manifesting they can see static charges come out of them towards the entity as it takes shape. It also appears to draw from other sources with these same 'electrical traces' seen streaming from electrical outlets, lamps and other sources. This one is hard to detail to where it can be narrowed down to human or inhuman, but you can note, it can be part of when a demonic begins to manifest. It leans more demonic when the activity is more extreme, and we can note if the entity matches the other descriptions as well of a 'demonic'. Such as when it might begin as a dark "orb". Don't wait for it to gain strength fully formed, start your prayers to rebuke the spirit before it has manifested.

The quick one we can all remember is "In the name of our Lord Jesus Christ, and by his authority, I command you to leave this place and go back to where you came from.

Repeat at least three times.

DISEMBODIED FACES

Without a body. The fiery face is in fact a 'dark spirit', but doesn't necessarily mean it is an inhuman. The souls of the damned have been represented this way in some classic tales and even more current cases such as with my account. I can be comfortable in saying these representations are going to be either **"TYPE: HUMAN or INHUMAN"**. So again here, as these spirits are the minions of Satan, they are therefore treated in the same manner, in using methods and prayers of "deliverance"

SHADOW PEOPLE, BLACK FORMS

FLEETING SHADOWS

Just out of your field of view or 'frustum', you might see moments of shadows, fleeting moments of dark silhouettes some refer to as 'Shadow people'. It will often begin this way, seen "out of the corner of your eye", then it might escalate to where you can see them 'head on' unmistakably. 'Infestation' can have in itself many levels or 'phases' of growing activity as it approaches later stages. It might also seem to skip over this stage or 'infestation' as it is defined, and jump right to 'oppression'.

One thing to note. As these moving shadows are caught out of the corner of your eye, they might still be trying to lie low; your mind's eye a sort of sixth sense is seeing them. They move as to not be detected, to keep you scratching your head: **"What did I just see?"**

We have to remember as an infestation phase might just be a level of trying to lie lower to begin oppression on certain individuals in the house. The strategy can vary, with no predefined stages as such are absolute in how they work, as each is customized to the people and the place it affects.

These 'dark spirits' you might also note are more so nighttime occurrences, that occur after 9PM, but will pick up at around the hours of 2 AM to 4 AM. (*See the note on the "significance of 3AM*). As with many hauntings of **"TYPE: EVIL"** spirits, you might find yourself waking up at 3AM often, and you are not quite sure why. When this occurs, if I might mention some early advice, I recommend that you begin to say prayers immediately, even consider a prayer of 'rebuke' using holy water. I honestly believe in these cases we are often awakened by our Guardian Angels so that we are not sleeping while an 'evil presence' goes undetected. These dark spirits never just stand and watch as some will have you believe, they are always "*up to something*" even as we can't detect exactly what it is. It is better to assume, they are never totally 'harmless' or merely 'keeping an eye on us' such as the theory of the 'watchers'. They often affect our dreams; our children might awaken in the other room screaming about "*the dark man*", a baby jarred from a sound sleep begins to cry.

We might be attacked in our sleep to where we don't even realize it.   For example, you might begin to dream a 'nightmare' when you begin to suffocate in this dream, outside your disturbed nightmare, a dark shadow might be over the top of you and apply pressure on your chest. You could awaken to find you are being attacked, and paralyzed and unable to even speak to call to your spouse who is sound asleep next to you. *(See also section on sleep paralysis)* Some might find they begin to have a nightmare of being strangled; they awaken, and later see marks or bruises consistent with strangulation. So we should consider it a 'blessing' that you are awakened by whatever, so you can do something about it before it grows much worse. If those living in the infestation environment do nothing or little to stop it or to in the least weaken it, it will likely move onto focusing on one or more people as an "oppression".

Often only seen just *"out of the corner of your eye"*.   As 'human entities', *(those condemned souls who have passed on after death, only to become a servant of devils.),* May appear as 'shadow human forms', even outlining the silhouette of one wearing a 'hat and suit'. The dark shadowy figures that seem to have no distinct shape or form or most likely demonic in nature. They may appear as a cloud like form, tornado like, animals as previously discussed like cats, dogs, but as a shadowy version of these. And other forms such as with a hooded, caped figure with long arms and no face or legs. These shadows can hide in the natural shapes of your dimly lit room, in a way of being elusive as to its presence.

One woman awoke to a spirit hovering over her bed in a cloudy form with no feet. The spirit pretended to be the spirit of the woman who used to be the owner of some clothing that was purchased in an old cedar chest at a garage sale just days before.

The first thing that gave it away was that it showed up at **3AM**. This time frame that helps to reveal the nature of the spirit as often demonic.

Second, to no surprise I read on to find the spirit said it wanted to 'live again' through this woman. The demon seized an opportunity in the facilitation of the clothes and linen in the old chest as so it could 'pull on her heart strings' and get her to agree in a subtle way, to allowing the spirit to 'possess' her. Yes some people are fooled in ways they don't even realize.

The Warrens hold a 'raggedy Ann doll' in their museum; this doll was found to be moving around the room into different positions and locations. The Two women who lived in the house called for a séance, they contacted a spirit that claimed to be that of a "little girl who died at a young age", and it asked if it could "move into the doll", they agreed and said "yes", thinking this was harmless. Another demonic trick!

The old vampire lore has it; a vampire cannot enter your house unless it is 'invited in'. 'Invitation' is a key word often times in these cases, our own bad choice made to invite these spirit into our lives. They try to trick you into inviting them in masquerading as often children tragically killed, which helps to draw on the emotions of the person listening to the lie. Sort of the 'wolf' dressing as 'grandma' in the old fable. The ways it finds entrance will be more 'discreet' and not so 'direct' and asking straight forwardly for some form of permission or an invitation to manifest itself or enter into someone or something.

When we refer to "Black Shadows" these are those 'shadowy forms', sometimes with recognizable humanoid shapes, or animal shapes such as cats even. Even in a dark room you can see them as they are a deeper pitch black than a room with no light. We refer to them as "Shadows" because they often do not seem to have features and detail, like a silhouette or a "shadow". Sometimes there is almost no 3D dimension as though it is 2D. Although they might move in 3D space and be in the center of your room for example, rather than just a projected silhouette on the wall. As some encounters will appear.

I have seen black forms that I can say were 'human' at least three times I can recall. Keep in mind this likely happened more, since I haven't talked that much about these occurrences with others. In a way hoping they would pass. On the other hand I wondered if it was simply 'dreaming while awake' or 'night terrors'.

As a shadowy ghost could be either human or demonic in origin.
To identify it while looking for such 'telltale signs' doesn't mean it actually is human when these 'ear markings' exist. As we must always keep in mind the demonic can masquerade as a human spirit and often does to hide its true nature.

First, silhouettes of what appears to be an outline of a human can indicate it is a human spirit. However let it be known, that is certain such human spirits are indeed souls that are 'lost' or 'condemned' by their own choices in life. *(They have no chance at Heaven.)* Often they are tormented by the very demons they appeased with their actions in life. These very demons had "tempted" this lost soul into doing things that eventually condemned their soul to this fate. They may not advert to holy symbols, with that certain 'recoil' as is a typical *"cause and effect"* in proximity of the demonic, who have a profound hatred and fear of all things of God. The blackened soul is often 'sad' or 'angry' even, but not affected in such a way as inhuman spirits.

THEORY AND THEOLOGY OF THE "DARK SPIRIT":

Black is an absence of light, the blackness reflects their darkened soul. Note that they are not as deep dark black as demonic spirits even, and can even have a charcoal gray color in comparison to them. It has been suggested perhaps these are souls in a deeper level of purgatory. I do not believe this is true as the shade of color can entail it all, and we would not expect one so cold and so black, to be a soul of one that has a chance at Heaven. So I would say 99.9 percent of the time these dark spirits will be **"TYPE: HUMAN or INHUMAN – EVIL"**. While in their presence we may not have the sense of 'fear' and a 'true presence' of evil as with the demonic.

Because it is not so strong, and they often don't pose a danger for us. So we don't 'sense' the clear evil as with these human spirits, but don't let that make you think they are not evil by nature. As they are in the company of demons they are part of their world now. They cannot do any true 'good' in that existence. Forget what you may have learned from movie and TV shows, you can't simply 'defect' from the company of demons as a lost soul. Your fate is sealed.

THE "SHADE" OF 'PURGATORY' SOULS

Also it should be considered, that there is nothing to merit them from helping you, and they will also not be able to help. So we treat these human spirits as we do evil ones, with prayer to remove them from our homes, property, our lives, as so they will not linger seeking to do ill deeds. So it can be said the darker the color of the spirit in shades of gray the longer they will need to be in purgatory. Having said that it may be possible some spirits which appear as dark human forms, may be souls more so blackened by their sins. And over time they will get more grey and whiter while they serve their penance in Purgatory.

It has come up about the Waverly Hills Sanitarium, and how these shadowy figures about the size of 'children' are said to have been seen there. Likely we are not seeing children's ghost at all, and one has to think what would make the soul appear that black, when it is a supposed child's spirit lingering from a time perhaps eighty years prior when they are said to have died? What evil could they do before the age of eight or nine years old to be so dark and to be in such a state for so long? Or why would they be damned for all eternity?

The theology states that the soul is blackened by the sins, also that the blackness can simply be an absence of an essence of light. It is of course a metaphysical essence in the color. There is likely no soul so black from sin that still has a shot of

Heaven. It is safer to assume all souls that are so dark, are lost. It should be noted over time the spirit will grow in intensity, from grays to brighter shades or in this case, if any dark spirits are indeed in a Purgatory. They would start to grow brighter in warmer shades of gray overtime.

Our human instinct is realizable, that impeding dooms, strong senses of evil, and fear of death in extreme. This is definitely a case of an encounter with a true demonic spirit. "Red eyes" and other tell tale signs (*as I outlined in this book*) are another characteristic.

So let us use the term 'evil' where it applies, evil by nature and works, which means that a lost soul, destined for their own Hell at some point with no chance of Heaven. May not at all be projected as true evil, but seem to be more of a sad and tortured soul, rather than one that works with the demons in the oppression of living humans.

TYPES OF SHADOWS:

Shadow demon

Creeping 'shadows' along the wall, these will look exactly like the 'shadows' of solid shapes or humanoid beings. Without an actual physical presence to justify the resulting shadow. My thought is this may be more a way to blend in more so camouflaged, and they can better move about in the night in darker areas.

Red eyed specter

Very common to see one where one has an interest or practice in black magic as I stated earlier. On investigation if you hear witnesses speak of a 'red eyed shadow' being, likely someone in the house is dabbling in the dark arts, or the previous occupants have. Dig a little and they may tell you upon a second interview. This information is often not forthcoming in the first interviews.

"Hat man" and Human Shadows

Well defined shapes or outlines that truly look like a fully clothed human standing in darkness are going to more typically be human spirits. Always trump that notion as it is believed a demon might be present and simply masquerading as a human even in this case. Just be aware of that. As a "Hat Man', a hat is because you might be looking at a civil war spirit or one from an earlier time when men commonly wore hats as in the nineteen-forties.
From the hat on the head right down to the boot straps, to the feet touching the floor, a complete detail silhouette can most often be a human spirit. But black as it is in it's form.
This is telling of the company they keep. And to say it is to be treated as a **"TYPE EVIL"**.

So now these human souls are full of a certain 'blackness' and frigid ' lost souls', we must remember in this after life existence, that they are either collaborating with their demonic master or tormented by them. So when one is abound, there is always a demonic master puppeteer in the foreground. An overseer, calling the shots, often lending power even to the spirit to do the deeds. Now they might help bring another human down just as they have been. Many times it is a deceased friend or relative also doing this!
Just keep in mind, though the demonic itself hasn't manifested, it still is calling the shots when any sort of negative activity occurs. The organized hierarchy of the hellish netherworld is very precise and fine tuned. It is near a state of perfect to human standards, the armies of darkness have their missions, and you can bet they will stay on it and use anyone and anything they can to bring down more souls.

A FEW OF <u>MY</u> EXPERIENCES WITH 'SHADOWY BEINGS'

One of my first encounters was what some refer to as a 'shadow person', a short story. Where at about 15 years old, in Marthasville Mo, I awoke one night around 3am and saw a figure standing at the doorway of my basement room. A moment later it starting coming at me. Walking towards me, just like a person would appear in the dark. It was so much of a deep black I could never have seen a real person so well in a basement room in the dark night. When I saw it coming at me, I screamed, probably the first and last time I have ever done that as an adult. My first thought was someone was coming to kill me in my bed. I quickly moved to the window, opened it, and jumped through the screen, went around to the front door and knocked on it, afraid to go back in from where I came.
I was embarrassed in explaining why and how I came to be outside in my bare feet and pajamas. I simply told my mother, "I had a nightmare." As I had through the years kept many other experiences to myself as well. Returning to my room, I eventually went back to sleep with the light on.

Today, some 30 years later, writing of this still makes the hair stand on the back of my neck, and it gives me chills.
For some reason to date I have never been attacked physically, that I can remember anyways. Except for one time, in which I will mention that later, which wasn't so much a physical 'assault' as it was 'physical contact'.

Looking back, and thinking, it is in a way odd that somehow a physical being with intent to murder or hurt is most certainly more frightening than an 'unknown' as this 'black ghost' entity was back then to me at age 15. Maybe this is because we don't know what to expect. I also even feel today I would be in physical danger so much with a spirit as a human with a knife or a gun, so vulnerable in the darkness and half awake in bed.

This is why I say prayers and take measures before hand to ensure I am not attacked and hurt or killed as demons can do at times.

Another encounter occurred at another place, my bedroom in Washington Mo, at the age of eighteen. This was a significant time because now I had a witness in my friend Eddy, who was staying over while on leave from the Air Force right after boot camp. We had set up a cot inside my bedroom for him to sleep; I was the last remaining child in the house as my sisters had moved out before we moved into this new place in Washington Missouri.

Again I experienced another dark encounter, as I awoke at about 1:30 am, and saw at the foot of my bed a tall shadowy being. Apparently hooded, cloaked, and very tall perhaps at a height of seven feet. I could not see legs and lower detail as with the silhouette figure I describe earlier. This was one that didn't seem to have a 3 dimensional presence about it's body. But it wasn't a projected shadow as I describe, it was away from the wall, and it's stretched out arm was certainly giving it more dimension.

Back to the story as it goes, as I awoke half asleep at first, I asked it: **"What do you want"**. And these words awoke my friend Ed, who turned over in his cot to face my direction to reply to my words perhaps. There he saw this black figure, as he later stated it was **"hooded, faceless, and had it's disproportionately long arms stretch out as though pointing at me."** A moment had passed enough for me to be wide awake and I realized something was wrong, I had a visitor who didn't belong, and it was now pointing something at me. A shotgun or rifle? I quickly started to climb out of bed, as I came off my bed, according to Eddy, the black mass seemed to be frightened away by my movement and zipped swiftly down the hall. I had followed it by chance, just running out of the room, and as it preceded me. From my friend's perspective, it looked as though I got up to chase it. As I ended up in the hall, I took a moment to gather my senses in the bathroom, which as a child was a sort of 'sanctuary'. Where bright lights, a lockable door, and an easy view of all four walls made me feel safe. At this point I would pray, but after a minute I went back to check on Ed. He was still in his cot, but confused as to what he had just seen. When I returned, I went to turn on the ceiling light with a click of the switch, the bulb blew out. Coincidence?

Ed sat on his cot in disbelief, and then he went fumbling for the desk lamp switch after the ceiling light failed.

"What just happened"? I asked. "I don't know….something was standing hunched over at the end of your bed."
"You saw that??"
"Yeah… I heard you say: 'What do you want' and I looked over thinking 'what the hell'? "

He continued. **"Then I saw this tall black thing hunched over your bed and pointing at you with a long arm"**

"Wait… **It was pointing at me?? When I asked what do you want?"**
I answered a bit disturbed by the details he had said.
"**yeah** " he replied.

"Then as you got up from bed it took off to the hall and knocked me back against the book case"
He then pointed to the book case behind his cot were he slept.
"And then you chased after it…."
"No way!" I replied. "I was getting the heck out of here; I thought it was pointing a gun at me or something"

So as we went back to sleep later, but only as my friend, who was fresh from an Air Force military boot camp, asked to have a "nightlight" on in the room. I would have to agree.

In this and the other, fear took over as instinct when I thought it was moving to point a rifle at me. And also again here, I thought there was an assailant in my room somehow. I don't even remember looking over and remembering my friend Ed was in the room with me. Yet my first words, even if half asleep were a casual calm question: **"What do you want?"**

And at first I wasn't logically thinking: **"How did this person get in here?"** This was before it stretched out its "long arm", to point where I was in bed. Over all, it seemed almost two dimensional. Like a shadow, as when someone stood by the same spot in a test, they appear closer than this thing did. So it was as though it was 'flat'. I had witnessed this with no accompanied sounds, smells, and an instinct of fear didn't kick in until I reacted to what I thought was the 'shotgun' aimed at me. I mention this because later in life, I have encountered some of the black forms; bring with them a sense of doom so bad you can't draw in a breath. And you actually forget the words to prayers to ward them off, and fall back on something more basic like:

"In the name of Jesus... begone!"

As this encounter I mention was not as threatening as other past and future encounters, it was apparently startling as I moved to get up from the bed. I have to say that having a witness puts a different perspective on things. Suddenly I thought back of other encounters, and realized it wasn't all my imagination, it is something very real. Then the research began seriously. There is nothing like the validation of a friend to help you get peace of mind in that. Yet, it was disturbing to think all of those years it wasn't just my imagination.

OTHERS WHO EXPERIENCED SOMETHING SIMILAR:

Rock Guitarist Tommi Iommi, experienced such a visitation after reading a book on Satanism he borrowed from a friend. Later that night he awoke to see a large dark figure standing over his bed.
As the story continues, that same night he awoke to see a cloaked hooded figure at his bed side.
"It was like looking at the eyes of death" He had said. And few know that this actually inspired a song and eventually became also the name of the band in 'Black Sabbath', as this occurred on a "Sunday".

Lyrics:
What is this that stands before me?
Figure in black that points at me
Turn round quick and start to run
Find out you're the chosen one.
Oh No!!! -From the album (1970) "Black Sabbath"

In another story, a man had said while his life was in a 'downward spiral' at some point his oldest daughter, who was only five years old at the time, was seeing a large "monster" standing over her father while he slept. She describes it later as an adult, as 'ugly and 'monstrous'. Over a period of about a year she reported several such events and now as an adult she clearly remembers.

I mention this because of the account in saying that this beast was *"Standing over him as he slept"* it should be a reminder to say your night prayers before bed, and even why this custom is a common practice. When those who typically recite the 'Guardian Angel' prayer will never know what might lurk at night in their bedroom, that some added protection will prevent, especially as they might affect our dreams. Secondly I want to mention how as we grow older we more can easily analyze our experience from when we were a child and better understand what really happened.

Before bed if there was a sort of 'squabbling' in the house, these smaller black forms would make themselves known. Sometimes little uneasy tensions will draw them into our room at night. This is part of the inside look as to how they work in stages of 'temptation' also. As described through the lives of the saints and church forefathers of the Catholic and Orthodox faith.
In thought this makes sense since they prey on negative emotions. These are definitely demonic in nature. We can learn in how demons work in lower levels of spiritual warfare such as behind the scenes trying to feed and egg on 'domestic arguments', as these things draws demons like flies.

WHEN TO CALL A HAUNTING "DEMONIC"
Some things to note, although some out there are "quick on the switch" to call a haunting "Demonic" first consider these facts:

THEY NEVER WORK ALONE

Spirits that seem to have a malicious nature never work alone, so in reports of being choked, or slapped, aggressive words and actions, do we always call it demonic? No, but we have to carefully consider that. Whatever it is, human or inhuman, in this case it likely answers to a 'demonic'. The hierarchy is in the way that a human spirit, which may dwell in a house, can be a puppet to a demonic master. They most often don't act entirely alone. And here is where it confuses some. The demon itself may not have manifested, but just as they can whisper subliminal thoughts and temptations into our minds, they silently call the shots behind the scenes in this manner, more than merely influencing the actions of the human spirit that has manifested. I have found as also others whom are well learned in this field, that "Shadows" fall into this category when they are <u>not</u> demonic. I read someone misquoting me elsewhere, that I said *"all shadows are demons"*. When I never said such a thing and that is not true. I will go as far as to say they are NOT what I considered "good" spirits. But they can be either human or inhuman. If they are human the "They never work alone" scenario often applies.

"I AM LEGION"

When a demon identifies itself as 'Legion' this seems to be an indication not of the number of spirits present in the infestation or possession. But speaking in more military terms, in the way they work, the mention of a 'Legion of demons' would be in reference to the whole 'unit'. Not just a count of the ones 'present' in the human host in a possession case for example. They will also identify themselves as a higher rank demon, when it really means "In the court of" That is the higher ranking demon over the demonic 'troops', they cite the name of their 'general'. I often say how they act and they think in terms as a "collective" as many connected to one central brain. Again as I compare to Star Trek's "Borg". This is why I say a demon can get any information about you or anyone it desires. One information network working together in collaboration like a bee hive.

LOWER DEMONS

A lesser rank and power, as with some demons, are 'lower level' or lower in 'rank', in a reference to the hierarchy of demons. And they don't exhibit as much power and aren't as easy to identify as "Demons", they seem 'weaker' as these are also often easier to rebuke. And we find that they have more of an aversion to basic "positive" things, even Incandescent lamps (artificial lighting) not just 'sunlight'. Darkness is preferred. The inexperienced might incorrectly judged this as a 'human spirit', because it is easier to subdue and rebuke as it seems. A demon might be behind something that is not so severe as we are lead to believe as all demonic haunting will be. Just consider this rather than assuming only the more severe hauntings are the only ones that are 'demonic'. Because also it simply may be the strategy to lay low and work into 'oppression' strategies, for example, helping to push someone towards suicidal thoughts. So we always don't expect access activity in a true demonic haunting. And each case is unique as a finger print, different people, involving different types of demons, in these 'demonic' cases.

WE DO KNOW THEM BY THEIR FRUITS'

We never want to assume some spirit is less than what it is, incorrectly diagnosing a demonic haunt as a simple ghost (human) haunt is when falling short on the true nature and origins of the spirits can be 'dangerous.' This is saying over analyzing a case and coming up with a "demonic" as the culprit, isn't so bad, as assuming it is simply a "ghost of a little girl" when it is in fact, a demonic.

Exorcist Fr. Gabriele Amorth made a case saying that it is **"rather silly"** to scrutinize possible possession cases to be sure it isn't 'mental', when all of this 'red tape' further delays a solution that could be the right one in performing the "Roman Ritual" (exorcism). Saying no real "harm has come from the ritual", so why scrutinize it for several months to be 100% sure?
Good point! Even modern psychology recognizes in the least, what they believe can act as often a successful "placebo effect" as a result from the ritual. *(But remember they are taking an "Atheistic" view, and would never recognize the source as* real demons*)* But we know Fr. Amorth is speaking of the "Roman Ritual", not some half-baked solution that is a careless mix of other belief systems for example. Let us never confuse these other so-called exorcism methods with the one I am referring to.

Other methods can be quite reckless. (Now don't go throw salt all over a house, it corrodes everything!)

An inadequate and incorrect solution can also bring a "retaliation", as it can essentially *"piss them off"*. However, having said that, just keep in mind that it is 'safer to assume the worse', however acting on it is another story. And how you take action is also.

THE MASQUERADE

Another thing to consider is the "Masquerade". The demon doesn't portray itself for what it is. Quite commonly it is not the more melodramatic scenario. (*i.e. the little girl who missed her mommy, or say the spirit of an attractive teenage boy who tragically died in a car crash.*) These however are snares, lures, to pull the heart strings and to manipulate us into making bad decisions. Often custom designed to the person they are presenting themselves to.

In further reading I detail this in more depth below:

"UFO ALIENS"

In the Mid nineteen-eighties, I spoke with a woman who claimed to be visited by *'Grays'* at least once a week. As the scenario was described, she would be woken from sleep to find she was not alone, and then became paralyzed, she couldn't move or speak. A Larger gray alien, with larger black eyes, about 4 feet high, would emerge from the darkness and come to her bedside. Soon followed by additional, smaller ones as the weeks went by.

As expected, she felt terror, no peace even though she was fascinated with the UFO thing. As she went on to describe the encounter I pieced together some curious attributes about the encounter. During our conversation, it sounded too much like a 'night terror' as those who experience a classic encounter with the 'old hag'. Exception is the appearance was not of a hag it was a UFO 'gray' being. I told her it indeed sounded 'evil' in nature, and although she believes them to be 'UFO aliens' to try treating them as something else. Demonic. *(Note she wasn't of a practicing Christian~ Judeo faith)*

I advised her to **"Humor me, and tell it to leave in the name of Jesus"** the next time she wakes with a 'visitor'. Especially as she might be 'paralyzed', to say the words in your head as though you are shouting them at this being.

Long story short, as I instructed upon one of the next encounters she tried to say a prayer. She again could not speak. She had remembered what I had suggested and began to try to say the words. She was able to utter the name on a few tries, and as she did the 'grays' reacted like *'vampires to a crucifix'*. The paralysis was lifted instantly, and they shrieked in their departure from the room.

Regardless if you believe UFO aliens or not as 'extra-terrestrial life forms, and not demons as they were in this case. We have to take note that the demonic likes to pretend to be something other than its true essence and appearance to customize the experience, to better fool you into thinking it is "something else", to lure you in.

A dead relative, a poor child who tragically died of a rare illness, a teenage boy who died in a car crash. Whatever will work it may try. When this woman accepted the encounter as 'aliens' she didn't think to treat it as some 'evil entities', and she was confused about the encounters for some time.

Just as if *'Uncle Fred'* comes to visit, would you grab some 'holy water' if you thought it is indeed your old deceased uncle paying you a visit? Or might you be lured into a repeating occurrence that is a part of a more elaborate demonic trap.

At least the signs are there to help 'I.D.' these dark spirits, as we know they give themselves away with tell-tale signs. And that "cause and effect" with the proximity effect of religious objects and words spoken. So the 'masquerade' isn't always a flawless deception. (*NOTE: The medical condition dubbed as*

'Sleep Paralysis' 'SP' is not the topic here, this is about when it isn't simply a medical condition and it is indeed a paranormal encounter. I discuss paranormal cases of "SP" more later on in this book)

In a discussion of supposed 'close encounters of a forth kind', that is alien abductions. I realize that it isn't popular to say, nor have I said it much publicly, but I have formed an opinion based on strong evidence that many so-called 'forth kind' alien encounters are in fact 'demonic' in nature. This book is not as detailed or as lengthy as I would like, I am not out to prove anything to any of you here. Just take my word, past clients and people I have dealt with in the last 30+ years give many reasons to in the least suspect this, I say 'can be true' and is in some cases as I cited earlier.

Now I will try to keep an open mind as to other types of experiences with strange UFO craft, but with these 'abductions' I will say are mainly 'demonic' in origin.

History shows, that early Catholic/Orthodox church accounts that describe *demon*ic encounters much as in the way we call them 'grays' now a days. As we find in history some of the fore fathers of the Catholic Church have described such encounters with demons. The descriptions also compare. We should learn from the past, in what we identify with a more modern view partly skewed by Sci-Fi movies, books and TV, the Saints recognized for what it really was, true encounters with evil. Think about it, to one who might believe in UFO aliens, what a perfect way to find an acceptable appearance to invade one's bed side late at night. These UFO-ologists wouldn't have recognized the need to use the same methods to release you from their paralysis and ward them off as was the case with demonic beings.

So we need to pay close attention to the *'ear markings'*, *'foot prints'* that might be present that could indicate a 'demonic'. There is a need to rule that out before calling it "*Extra-Terrestrial*".

These similarities already have been noted that a re-similar between 'demonic' and so-called 'alien' encounters as a few are noted below:

- ✓ Alien encounters often at night, noting a time close to 3AM

- ✓ Compared with 'night terrors', which can include 'sleep paralysis'.

- ✓ Victims typically describe the experiences as a 'terror', <u>not</u> a peaceful encounter.

- ✓ Often reports of the feeling of 'evil presence'. Again not a 'friendly' one, or 'good'.

- ✓ Telepathic communication. Just as demons and other types of spirits do.

- ✓ Sexual molestations, similar to Incubus/Succubus.

- ✓ 'Probing' matches descriptions of 'satanic rituals'.

- ✓ During abduction a 'drug induced state' as describe is consistent with drugged state reported by victims of satanic ritual abuse.

- ✓ An utterance of the name of 'Jesus' has an effect. We have to ask ourselves on this alone: **"Why do they often react like demons when such a name is uttered??"** –Red flag!

Also, what we typically hear in up close and personal encounters, involve <u>sheer terror</u>. These people are often <u>traumatized</u>; very much like the ones we work with who are living through a demonic (extreme) haunting. Plus, when you think about it, we really don't have much proof of them being *'interstellar travelers"*, but rather more so 'inter-dimensional' travelers. Which is really what demons are.

Yes- Some oh so want to believe in **'aliens from outer-space'**, hey I love SCI-FI too, it's fun to ponder of other planets and life-forms, but I for one will not allow myself to be a naive fool either. I can separate what is fantasy from reality. The reality might often be the darker gray or black. We cannot simply ignore the information given that spells something other than a *"little gray man from outer-space"*.

THE GHOST OF CHILDREN

What might entail the appearance of a child's ghost? Here I will go over the possible origins:

- As you know, evil spirits very often **masquerade** as 'children'. Note how we prioritize cases involving children as counselors and field investigators? Of course, the deception is to draw the occupants and/or those over-eager sappy 'ghost hunters' into a drama of a supposed 'child' who is some tortured soul who 'needs our help'. For this reason they seem to pretend to be children more, often than say 'adult' humans. One of many tricks to get humans to be curious enough to try to communicate with it through OUIJA boards for example, or by some other similar means.

    When we take the 'bait' in such tactics, we will help to excel the stages from a simple occasional bedside or hallway apparition, to manifest into a complete demonic 'oppression' stage. <u>Watch for the signs that tell it is 'demonic' in nature and not an actual poor child's spirit.</u> The signs are always there! *(Often in the eyes)*

- **God's Angels** have been known to show themselves as 'kids' to children to keep them from being frightened at something not familiar. Remember Mary when Gabriel appear to her, she was at first afraid. A child would most often be as well if it appears as a bright light, etc. More of a tell tale 'true' angel visit from heaven. But the message would be in one visit more likely and an extremely rare event for anyone to experience.

- As with these classic cases we see on TV and movies, where they might involve the child's spirit **pointing to where their supposed body** is hidden from a murder. This is actually rarer than in the scenario where the experience is being falsified by evil spirits, again to note #1.
And it is a manipulation leading owners on a wild goose chase tearing up their house, never finding bones or evidence of a 'body' in the house or on their property. Unfortunately it becomes an unhealthy obsession in finding the body, which has serious effect on the mind and spirit over a longer term. Not to mention financial cost in reconstruction of floors and walls damaged during the search.

- What some consider as **'Classic Poltergeist'** noises, seem to play any audio they want, not reflecting on the past environment of the house hold. *(Which can cross into being defined as some state as a 'residual haunting'.)* The sounds of a marching band tuning up, and old 1940's radio program for example sounding off, do not mean the former occupants played in a band or even owned a radio. Anymore than they had kids if you hear the sound of children 'laughing' or speaking.

- Then we do have those cases where they are 'trapped' souls, as you may define them as typical

ghosts. Somehow it is a 'child in Purgatory', and who needs your help somehow in releasing them. Personally if I would narrow it down to #5, I pray for the soul. We don't need to risk breaking the 'rule' with communication when we can ask God and Heaven to help deliver the soul into Heaven.
(This definition can go deeper in a general topic on what I consider are 'good' ghosts', which are ghosts that will someday go to Heaven)
So in saying these evil spirits very often <u>do</u> masquerade as children, just as you have read previously of that case example where the demon(s) appeared as "UFO Aliens", again this is to hide their <u>true nature</u>.

And to lure you into a 'snare', into thinking you are dealing with something other than a true "demon".

A WORD ON ANIMAL GHOSTS & SPIRITS

There are various sources of folklore, stories, that might seem to more than indicate that animal spirits seem to linger after death somehow. First, I need to state that animals do not have a soul, although I think the essence of a spirit of beloved pets are probably going to rejoin us in Heaven. There really is no afterlife for an animal, or reason for an animal spirit to linger here after death.

So what are we reading about in all of these accounts of apparent animal spirits?

There isn't real evidence that a family pet will in fact linger like a human soul, and I would have to say <u>one of the following is true to the contrary of it in fact being the 'spirit' of a 'deceased animal'</u>:

Demonic: A Pre-chosen form

While on the topic of the 'masquerade' here, instead of putting on disguise to make us think they are 'human spirits', they often choose certain appearances of 'animals' to represent themselves somehow. As in how the common depiction of Lucifer for example, is with a 'goats head', and the before mention of a type that appear as 'small cats'. While black dogs typically are associated with practices of black magic, even the sound of dog growls can be an indication of such activity of those in a recent or past residence. There is a need for a deeper understanding of the reason these spirits chose to represent themselves as certain animals. But it is a better way for some of us, who recognize them, and under what circumstance surrounds the appearance of that certain type of demon. This is more individual rather than all having only the essence of a shapeless 'black mass', orb or other undefined essence in their appearance. Perhaps it is also more unique to them in having a specific appearance. Or again another mockery to God's glory in portraying his creatures in this manner.

I can say that the nature of the animal they choose to represent can be as simple as some cite the reason for Satan's choice of a 'goats head'. The animals own nature as a more "nasty" beast in the animal kingdom. It would seem as these 'negative' entities covet more the negative things in this world. They would certainly favor animals that were leanings to more vile and disgusting habits like pigs, or flies even.

God's Angels

Beyond how the "*Holy Spirit*", in the way that we see it depicted as a '*White Dove*', no doubt a symbol of 'purity'. White, a bird, is a great symbolism for 'spirit' in itself. Doves are also monogamous to one mate for life. Surely these traits reflect in part why a dove is chosen for a representative of the Holy Spirit.

In the same manner the goat is to be for Satan to the opposite.

There are those times when an animal intervenes in saving one's life and then disappears as quickly as it shows to save the person. You could consider a sort of "*prime directive*" to not reveal themselves fully, taking the form of an ordinary canine for example, is quite different than an angelic being making itself known in full form when intervening. So the choice of the animal type is one that will seem less conspicuous to the surroundings. A cow on the city streets that suddenly appears to push you from being hit from oncoming traffic, would clearly be something 'paranormal', especially as it seemed to have disappeared just as mysteriously. A dog can blend in better, so as it can wander in and out of the scene unnoticed, at least this is how we perceive it. As there is at least one encounter in everyone's life where they ask "*Was that divine intervention?*" And we may never know that answer until we pass on from this life.

I also think there is one representing angel for each of the different type of animals on earth. This would be an **animal spirit**, but these are angelic beings of God never having lived on earth as flesh and bone animals. But are representations of these animals themselves.

We still consider that some will go as far as to try to contact their deceased pet, if they believe it's spirit lingers, And by doing so they are snared in that same trap, as others might be trying to come to the aid of children's ghosts, the end result is the same, as you have read, how they chose to show themselves depends on the person(s) they are trying to snare.

THE DEMONIC REALM

THEORY: THE MIRROR WORLD BEYOND

There is evidence that the demonic otherworld is a mirrored one, an opposite in many ways. We see how some demons speak and write 'backwards'. As so when you play the words in 'reverse' or look at their text in the mirror, *(which might resemble a childish penmanship)*, it has a more 'ordinary' sound and look to it.

I knew of one (black witch) who prided himself in nearly being fluent in speaking backwards. As the belief is these demons hear it better spoken in this manner, perhaps to better receive commands, etc. And to perhaps better understand them as they speak.

We know that 'Latin' is often spoken probably as more of a mockery of Jesus, who's primary language was that of ancient Greek/Latin. And to hear it spoken backwards might be done as to 'disrespect'.

This oddity actually first made itself known to many in the 80's when 'backwards *satanic messages*' was all the buzz. And many were boring out the grooves in their records spinning the turntable backwards to hear some supposed 'hidden words'.

The 'speaking backwards' was mentioned as one possibility as to why such a message would become clearer while listening to the LP in reverse. Personally I never heard enough to convince me that such a thing was purposely done by say '*STYX*' on the song '*Snow Blind*' for example. (*I mean, come on! STYX?? We are not talking about Marilyn Mansion here*), however I did find some of the information this fiasco provided to be somewhat interesting in the least. So there is strong evidence, in addition to the theology sense, that the 'demonic realm', simply stated, is a 'backwards' one. As we consider the demon is an 'opposite' by nature. Cold to a warm, darkness to light, a 'positive' to a 'negative', one might even go so far as to say it is possible the reason camcorder batteries,

(Ni-Cads rechargeable), go dead sometimes is a reverse polarity. Say their 'negative' (-) to our side 'positive' (+), simply discharges the battery when they come in proximity with it. Rather than how some say the entity is simply drawing power from it to manifest.

I think that in the case of a demonic 'writing backwards' it is not necessarily done as some display of 'anarchy' or disrespect to God. (*Although much of what they do is*) What it more likely is, is an error in 'perspective judgment' on their part. For example, the demonic of lower ranks are limited by intelligence and wisdom in comparison to a higher order. These same demons are also easier to advert using holy symbols, and things considered 'positive' as they creep closely to dark areas in the night, having repulsion to even brighter incandescent lighting. Not just a natural sunlight. So it may be known these specific types of a lesser demonic have revealed a piece of information about when they interact in our dimension apart from their own.

Imagine how sloppy we might be trying to write backwards on the inside of a window a message that someone could read from the other side. This may very well be how they perceive our world, they are writing forward, yet to use it is appears in 'reverse'.

AS FOR "HUMAN *GHOSTS*"

So we can see the demonic realm is one mirrored, an opposite of our own. Do human ghosts indicate the same? There doesn't seem to be the 'tell tale' signs of this being true as with the 'darker realm'. However, I can recall a case where an apparition appeared with their left hand severed at the wrist, when in life the man was said to be missing a right hand. Is this an example that says what is true for the demonic realm. Although, this case is likely just a fluke, and no real indication of such theory. Consider that food for thought. This dimension that does seem to be more parallel to our own, unlike the world

where demons dwell. So, it is in my opinion that demons are on a different plane than most human spirits that might linger here as 'ghosts', although they at times seem to interact, it is only in certain cases that they co-exist in the same plane.
A demon must 'manifest' to reach this plane of existence, through invitation or by some other means as we discussed. Now this layer between these other worlds is probably much thinner, than the divide that separates this world of ours from the next. And this layer of the 'demonic realm' is indeed a world 'opposite' to our own. While the one where the common ghosts reside is in unison to this world. Even if it does exist as another layer. Conversely, there is also a possibility lost souls (human souls of the damned), may also co-exist in the demonic realm. As the severed arm man did appear to entail a malicious nature, it may have said something of his otherworldly origin. Thus, in saying, perhaps this is an indication this last theory maybe true.

A SIGNATURE COUNT OF "THREE"

In early stages, the demonic may make itself know with a symbol knock, most often in threes. A count of three is indicated, not the number spelled out "T-H-R-E-E", a knock in threes on the door or head board or wall of bed room is a way of saying:

"I am here now, welcome me"
The number three will show up as a sign, this said "mockery of the Trinity", is apparent in these early stages. Some report hearing these 'symbolic' three knocks on their front door, they open the door, and no one is there. The symbolism here is more in the '3' representing 'demonic', the knock a symbolic gesture of:
"I am here, open the door and let me in."
Sometimes these knocks might be on the head board of a bed or on the wall. On the bed, I would say this is more telltale if

the people who sleep in the bed, are going to be the target of 'oppression'. Mainly the one who reports hearing the knock, while the other spouse might be fast asleep.

Another precursor is to hear 'scratching sounds' on the wall. An animal might enter this way if you think about it. Scratching and gnawing through a wall floor or ceiling to gain entrance. We do know that in these stages strange animals could swarm certain areas. Like black rodents or cats. The scratching might entail the sign of a certain type of demon(s) that is often represented by the appearance of one or many of these creatures. There may even result physical marks in these 'scratches' that appear on say the bed baseboards or inside the walls. So here, I understand that perhaps at times this is the 'lower demons' way of 'symbolically' digging into the house through the outside wall or floor, as to show a warning sign of 'intrusion'. As we better recognize it as humans in this world. We can safely say it is 'God's Mortal Law' that likely requires them to 'show signs of their presence' or mark a stage of entry to signify 'infestation', so they can't completely work without detection in some way. These lower demons I refer to, are the 'henchmen' of the 'higher rank' ones who call the shots. Often manifesting themselves as small animals, in dogs, cats, rodents, frogs, and insects, they seem to prefer to manifest themselves as these creatures.

In the morning a home owner may see that there are visible scratches on the walls, and these will often appear to be made with three claws. Just as in more extreme signs where scratches on skin result, following a burning sensation.

THE NUMBER "6" AND "666"

We won't get too much into 'numerology', (*This beyond the biblical sense*), but I wondered who might have encountered the number "666" in a 'haunting' of any type. I find through case histories, personal experiences, study, that it really never indicates this is any special number, say that a demonic spirit likes to display or equate too. Maybe at best some dabbler in the satanic arts, along with the usual Black Metal symbols of inverted pentagrams, goat's heads, swastikas, and so forth. It's part of that 'culture', but really may have little to no meaning to 'Ghost Hunters', 'Ghost busters', 'Exorcists' or "Demonologists". This more so says something of the spiritual/psychological frame of mind of the individual who displays that number on posters, their clothes, bedroom wall, and so forth. It mainly says something about that person as we recognize and relate to that 'triple six number' in its biblical sense of the "Anti-Christ" or the "Number of the Beast".

I wonder about that biblical interpretation, or translation even as this number I feel is not relevant to anything in my line of work, and the number "3" seems to turn up all too often as we know. Or even oddities such as the clock display straight digits (i.e. 4:44, 11:11, etc.) *(Note: Sometimes we do see some numbers that might mean something to us alone, and have no other significance.)*

For example, the trip odometer noting "666", now that number to most of us signifies evil, and because of that biblical interpretation and perhaps we are hinted to notice it on the odometer as a warning (angelic intervention?). But also more like subconsciously we react when seeing this number, because of its noted bad rep, we are more likely to notice that number than say *"867-5309"*. Which is not so universal, especially if you aren't in your 40's.

True, at least until some real anti-Christ does make his/her first public appearance, and maybe that number will make sense as to how it equates to "the number of the beast". But if I were to draft a check list for things to look for that indicates a possible demonic haunt, the number 666 would not be on the list.

The number 6 itself is another matter. We know to keep an eye out for the number six, as it is said to be more of a number of 'Satan' and his minions. But still outside some connections to crime and murder where this number oddly appears often in say the report of a 'body count', details of the crime scene such as 'six stab wounds', and so forth. But as this doesn't apply really to my line of work, I will not go into that theory.

THE SIGNIFICANCE OF 3AM

Always Note the <u>time of night</u> when discerning the 'type' of spirit.

First, I list here a few things to note that relates to 'demonic hour':

- ✓ Sometimes it is 2AM simply because we change our clock due to day light savings time. This is why at times things maybe cited to occur at 2AM when they are reported when it is really the 3 o'clock hour based on the phase of the sun.

- ✓ 3 P.M. is of course when it is said Jesus died and his spirit ascended into heaven until the third day. It is said the Blessed Virgin Mary's assumption into heaven occurred at 3 PM as well. Some say 3 PM is when the veil between this world and heaven is at it thinnest. The same of course can be said in the opposite time of '3AM' and the veil dividing this world and a 'dark realm'.

- ✓ 'Black Masses' (satanic rituals), for example, are notably done at 3AM, not midnight, so these dark rituals are done at this hour providing a gain of strength to evil.

- ✓ 3 A.M. is also a distance enough from sunset-dusk to morning's dawn. Sun light, even in small traces of UV and infrared from the sun can still be seen for well over an hour after sunset. But at 3AM for example, a 'new moon' dark sky can leave a full cover of darkness. Darkness is power to demons and evil spirits. And they prefer darkness as light can be unbearable to them. As we learn somewhat on our own, as children, to turn on a light to get rid of 'monsters'. There is some truth in it. Because with the 'lower demons' especially, as they are easily scared off by such 'positive' things such as light being switched on from darkness. While devils on the other hand appear during daylight hours, turn blessed crucifixes upside down, etc.

Beyond occurrences that are designed to merely to 'disrespect' these things of God, it is also a show of power as a boasting in **"I CAN DO THIS!"** or **"This has no effect on me"**, as to weaken the faith of those oppressed by them. Note that these things always have somewhat of an effect on them; it is more of a matter of how well they can 'suck it up' to display a tolerance to these things. As part of pride, as well as some form of psychological manipulation. The demonic will also like to create more of a ruckus on what are considered 'Christian Holidays' and 'Holy Days', such as 'Good Friday', and 'Easter'. This is just another way for them to show off their power, and here 'disrespect' Christianity, and to 'distract' from the day's meaning.

+ Which brings me to what some say goes beyond a symbolic '3', as stated by others, is indeed a mockery of the 'Holy Trinity'. However, 3 AM still is a preferred time because of the above reasons more so. I always say we should try to '*honor the Holy Trinity*' when we can, since it is so important for them to dishonor God in this way.

+ Essentially, a transition often occurs at these hours of 3-4 pm. In this I am referring to when demons are increasing in numbers, moving from infestation to oppression stages, or onto possession's first stage, etc. So this time set is indeed the most "unholy" time in the day. 3 AM is often a 'mile marker' for these changes as they grow toward a more serious stage of a demonic haunting, say from an 'infestation' to an 'oppression' stage.

In short if you often wake up to see the clock is exactly 3 AM, or clocks may also be found to stop on 'three o'clock', then you might being seeing this as a warning. The number 3 turning up is a demonic symbol, so we take note on a short list when it occurs. As it can often definitely be an indication something is manifesting or already has...

THE 3 AM APOCALYPSE THEORY

I have discussed a rather disturbing notion, a bit of a "doomsday" theory. It is stated that when the sun begins to rise, it breaks them from having more power, diminishes their numbers, portals close and the veil between this world and theirs is no longer as thin.

However if for some reason, the sun was not to rise, the daily event we take for granted as a 'sun-lit morning' will not be there to break the 3AM cycle to close these portals, weakening their numbers and powers. Part of the idea is that as 3 AM comes, a portal begins to open, and just before it opens the 'inter-dimensional doors' all the way, the sun is arriving from the other side of the globe, and sun rise begins to let in some UV light, which we can't see. The portal begins to close. And the demons are forced back in. It sounds like a movie doesn't it? Some apparitions and doomsday prophesies talk about a 'three days of darkness'. If this ever comes to pass we may find out in a hurry that this is true. Let us hope and pray it is not. Again this is just a 'theory'.

MORE SYMPTOMS of the DEMONIC HAUNT

"THE BORROWERS"

You look for your car keys, wallet, things you need to start your day, and they are not where you thought you last left them. You tear the house apart, and become quite stressed out looking for them, then as you sit down to call your job telling them you'll be late, you see there they are, on the end table where you left them. Are you crazy? Didn't you look there already? Now you aren't sure. Under the circumstances you don't have time to sit and think about it, you grab your keys or wallet and you make a mad dash to try to get to work before your boss notices you are late. This account might repeat another time but this instance might have been forgotten in a few days. Passed off as "normal".

When it's an area that is so accessible and open, the search would have turned it up long before. This is more reminiscent of a child's prank. And that can be the type of mentality you feel you are dealing with. But in reality the stress that this incident alone had brought out most certainly fueled any dark spirits that might dwell in the home.
So even when things seem random and chaotic in the way the darks spirits can operate, they are still carrying on a select strategy, a plot toward your undoing. To the contrary, I'll remind you, that it is hard to say 'if' or not it is in fact a trickster spirit, and not just 'carelessness'. Except that this activity will accompany other signs of a 'presence'.

WHEN IT ISN'T 'SUPERNATURAL'

There have been cases where part of the strategy of these spirits was to make the oppressed believe they had more of an effect on things than they did. They would often tell him **"We did that"** or **"It was us"**. So if he lost his 'cell phone' by chance, they would tell him "they took it". Part of the psychological warfare that goes on is to make him believe they are more powerful than they are at the time. I have to remind those I help, that our lives will still have 'hardships' apart from something influenced by a demonic. It is part of living in this world.
Don't look too deep, just *'grin and bear it'*, and try to not give too much credit to them. Follow through with action in *prayers* and so forth as a precaution if you suspect that some things of 'bad luck' might be an effect of a demonic spirit(s). Never hurts saying prayers or stepping up one's spiritual life now does it? Don't wait until you are 100% sure, there is nothing to lose. However, at the same time, you should try hard to refrain from letting it get to you; don't get overboard in blaming things on 'demons' is what I am saying. There is a

fine line of being on watch and aware of things that go *'bump in the night'* versus losing sleep over something that very well could just be a slip of your mind or 'normal' occurrences.

THEIR EFFECTS ON YOUR ABILITY TO 'THINK'

Now I will say this, although your belongings might be misplaced because of your carelessness, we do find your 'thinking' process is affected to such a degree that they can influence where you set things down. Getting your mind 'distracted' as to make it 'drift' to better help us lose those things we try so hard to keep track of. We have to remember even before any stage of manifestation has occurred they are the 'great tempters', and as these stages progress from infestation and onto oppression, the subliminal thought can be very powerful in affecting one's ability to process thought to lead a normal daily routine. They are masters of manipulating thought.

Say the Saint Michael prayer to help limit the effects. Even when making decisions so that your thought process won't be inhibited or influenced into making the less 'bad choices' in life. Choices that are much less obvious to mere mortals as "bad", yet to a demonic who can see a bigger picture, they would take delight in steering you blindly into making choices that largely can affect your life and finances.

DEMONIC EFFECTS ON DREAMS

Darker themes in dreams might be induced or the result of the presence of one or more dark spirits. One night for a case example, I was dreaming the usual dreams; you know the way they can be a bit of obscurity, a sort of gathering at an estate, people I didn't know. I suppose that is irrelevant however. But I wanted to convey the tone of the dream first. Then the over tone and environment of the dream changed, the lights dimmed to darkness, a feel of evil in the air, as a black whirlwind appeared, accompanied by an eerie howl, (odd I have never witnessed this on a personal level previously). I awoke soon after, not to my surprise, there was a presence in my room. The night light's glow in the room was abnormally weak, as though a black veil had encompassed the room. I began to say prayers repeatedly, and over the course of a few minutes the veil seemed to lift slowly, and the light retuned to a normal brightness.

What we can learn from this and other experiences alone is this:

- ✓ The "presence" in your room, might directly affect your dream, it might be your sixth sense or an angelic intervention to make you aware you have an enemy present.

- ✓ The demon is directly attempting to manipulate your dream. More often it is the content, a psychological programming on more minute levels. Not as obvious as my experience.

The timing in awaking for this from a sound sleep was priceless, in order to see what was going on, I otherwise might have slept through as so many have. This is why I might lean more to the idea of a 'divine intervention'. As in I believe that God wanted me to awaken to be aware of what was taking place in my room as I slept. It gave me opportunity to deal with the entity. This is another reason we should pray before bedtime, even if you don't suspect in the least you might have such visitation occurring late night. We always want to take precautions to not allow them access to our bedsides.

I recall another time I awoke and caught a shadowy being streak by and duck on my wife's side of the bed. I wasn't sure if I saw this correctly as half-asleep, when we don't trust our eyes so much. Then as I sat there still, my wife began to twitch like we do when we have nightmares. I quietly started some prayers, and the twitching stopped, and she turned over. The next morning I didn't mention this, I don't tell her what is going on many times as feeding these things with fear is not good. Plus if God wanted her to witness these things she would not be so fast asleep when they went on. She did describe she had some very bad 'nightmares' for some reason that night. This is not typical for her as she stated, and that dream sounded demonic in nature.

SEE ALSO "NIGHT TERRORS" As you read on in the book.

THEIR EFFECTS ON RELATIONSHIPS, MARRIAGE

You might not experience one paranormal occurrence yet in other ways; your family IS greatly affected. Try extra hard to keep the emotions under control, and don't let arguments get heated. Stress between the otherwise loving husband and wife can get intense, because of the way the spirits can manipulate you. Just be ready for this, a family torn apart in such a way is more often the result of their doing, one way or another. Even through stages of temptation, un-manifested levels of inter action.
(*See also section on 'Temptation'*)
As I mention earlier how they might affect our dreams, often the seeds of thought enter our dreams first that might promote 'infidelity' or petty arguments for example by manipulating the dreams of the otherwise loving couple. Be aware of this too in how it can affect the family.

EXPERIENCES ALONE

One way there might be a wedge driven between the spouses, is that one might experience everything, while the other 'nothing'.
In my case, I am glad that my wife is not dragged into 'encounters', it will help keep her life more normal. As my life

never was. With other relationships, they seek validation from their spouse and 'support' and when they don't get it; it can create tension and ill feelings between the two. As I stated, the other spouse may not witness a thing, and they might sleep entirely through even the most horrific events that take place. This is what Ed Warren called a *"Psychic sleep"* it can be the result of an induced sleep to keep the psychological warfare going against 'one person'.

The next morning over coffee and breakfast, there might be made mention of an occurrence, and because the spouse didn't witness it, they don't get as much credibility in it being supernatural. This can occur between parents and children as well. So a form of 'resentment' begins to take hold, when your friends or more importantly your spouse, or other family member(s) do not believe. Hearing:
"It was probably your imagination"
"It was likely a dream" or
"I am sure there is a logical explanation for that",
 This is not really 'supporting', and can be insulting and in the least a sort of a 'patronizing' to the spouse.
Self destructive habits might increase also, further stressing the relationship. All of the matters a family deals with will also directly stress the marriage, and even can give a seed of thought of undue blame on the spouse, further driving a wedge into the family unit.

This is just a warning once again, you may not even realize it 'has' entered your life and 'is' affecting your relationship in ways you don't even know. Look at yourself even. Has your behavior changed? Is 'jealously' coming from nowhere, are you finding yourself 'short tempered' where otherwise you were once a more patient man? Pay attention to these types of changes as you analyze and interview for potential demonic cases. Personality changes are part of a demonic 'infestation', again it is a 'psychological' and a 'spiritual battle' that is

aimed at you and your family's self-destruction. Fight to keep the family together!
(I recommend Bill Bean's book "Dark Force" as he had endured the major effects of demonic oppression on his family.)
An extreme case is a result of murder. Think of Ronald Defeo (Amityville) murdering his parents, brother and sisters as they slept. And with a 'voice' telling him to carry it out. This is classic demonic before the Lutzes have even entered the vacant house , as deeper oppression can drive one to suicide and yes 'murder'. This is to be expected but more so over a period of several months of the spirits attaching themselves to one over a course of a few months, you will not often see a person possessed in a couple of days, then driven to kill at the control of a demon. It is done over a period of time, as many decisions are made to entertain thought, personal choices can lean to a demonic temptation placing one into their control more and more. *(See also my thoughts on "temptation")*

LISTEN TO THE CHILDREN

Since my son could see TV, I avoided exposure of 'scary' programs and movies when he was around, to even the likes of 'Scooby-Doo'. We waited for him to go to bed, he has a 'white noise' sound box, that provides a background noise of waves to help drown out household noises and TV shows as he sleeps.

Protecting him from 'exposure' to such imagery became by chance a bit of an experiment in an old theory I have of 'why children really might be afraid of the dark'. As we know children seem to have a 'natural fear' of darkness, and share a common aversion to darker places such as closets and under the bed. This was my belief as a child as well and countless others.
And as I dove deeper into knowledge of the studies of

Demonology and the paranormal in the 80's, it shed some more light on a notion I already had in theory.

First, many of us already know of, in the least suspect, that children are more 'sensitive', especially at early ages before the 'age of reason' *(6-8 years old)*. Second, to know the nature and habits of demons, one comes to understand these childhood fears have some weight in a paranormal reality. As we understand the very nature of the demonic, we find some truth in how they cling to darkened areas, and advert from light. So when the child turns on the light, the dark shape may retreat into the closet, or under the bed to a safer more darkened portion of the room. It should be noted however, that more often what a child may see is certainly no indication of an actual 'demonic haunting'.

What we have to realize is that demons are around us day and night, waging war in spiritual warfare on a lesser level of temptation through subliminal thought. So we find that there doesn't need to be actual 'manifestations' for the child to see as they are more sensitive, It could simply be what is always lurking behind the scenes, that goes otherwise unnoticed and unseen by us. Such as with our guardian angels that are said to always be there.

I have seen and heard stories from adults who recall seeing in the corner of their eye, a black shape fleeting to the closet upon the click of the light switch. And on more than one occasion where it made them actually jump! Some even hearing a disturbance in the closet at that moment, as if their hasty retreat, in ducking from the light, knocked over some objects. Yes, our kids call in 'dad or mom' when they fear the 'monster' in their closet, then we calmly and rationally try to show the child that the closet is indeed empty and the toy simply rolled off the shelf on its own from sheer gravity. But it is hard for me to tell him it wasn't a 'monster' when I had witnessed something just a moment ago before I heard him calling out. As I have more than once been awoken seeing a fleeting shadow darting from view in front of me, just before he calls out from his room down the hall: "*Daddy!*". I don't try to make him face these fears now; I am more or less letting him trust his own instincts. In this thought I say to other parents. Respect your child's fears if they are afraid of the basement, or his/her closet. Don't push them to face the fear; they are only children after all. The fear will more than likely decrease by default as they get older. But we should listen to what is most often a God given instinct that helps them with say, a temporary gift of true 'discernment'. This is a valued gift in such a world we live in today. To help them as they grow more so to be able to better protect themselves without mom and dad nearby.

When I hear him call I hug my kid, calm him down, say some prayers, and all is well. I more than most, always keep in mind; they may see something we don't. Though I don't give it credit, I don't make him feel foolish either as though I don't believe he saw something. But let us not forget they are only young children. And vivid imagination or not we should try to avoid pushing them into the pool before they are ready to swim…

It is a bit disturbing, as the times I was a child seeking refuge in the small well lit bathroom after fleeting into it's safety. I used to have nightmares about waking up helpless, unable to switch on the light in the darkness, I still find that quite disturbing, afraid to run into something like a person's body that isn't there in the dark.

In the locked bathroom, I would clear the shower curtain. Then I look in the mirror and breathe a deep sigh of relief as I feel safe. I would clean the sink to a shine with a wash rag, and then at some point I would get up enough nerve to go back to my room.

Turing on the lights, and going back to sleep until morning in 'full light'. Good thing when Mom came in as the morning was here, she never complained about the lights being found on all night. Even as I thought it to be only "night terrors" back then, as I was told "just a dream". It was all still truly frightening, and I can remember how that feels even today. To be a kid and feel so alone and helpless at night.

Maybe in part this is what keeps me going today to help a family where their own children can sleep better at night and live a more normal childhood.

See also: "Dealing with Children 'Who See Ghosts' (refer to index)

PRAYER FOR OUR CHILDREN:

We bow humbly before You, heavenly Father, to pray for our children, [names of children], and for our whole family. We bring our children and our family before You in the name of the Lord Jesus Christ.

We thank You, Lord, that You love [names of children] and our entire family, with the love of Calvary. We thank You that You have given [names of children] to us to love and nurture in Christ.

We ask You to forgive us together as parents, and each of us alone in our roles as father and mother, for all our failures to guide our children in the way they ought to go. Help us Lord to be the parents You want us to be; that we may train [names of children] in Your ways, that we may model the Christ-life before them, so that when they grow-up they will love You and live for You.

Accepting our position through You of having "divine power to demolish strongholds" (2 Cor. 10:4) that come into our family, we ask You Father to bring all the work of the Lord Jesus, strengthened by the intercession of the Immaculate Virgin Mary, Mother of God, of Blessed

Michael the Archangel, of the Blessed Apostles Peter and Paul, and all the Saints and Angels of Heaven, and powerful in the holy authority of His name, to focus directly against the powers of darkness that do now or may later bother, influence, and bind [names of children] and our family in any way; and specifically against (name specific areas of troubles or problems).
We pray that You shall bring the victory of our Lord's incarnation, crucifixion, resurrection, ascension, and glorification directly against all of Satan's power brought against us in our family and specifically in the lives of [names of children]. We ask You heavenly Father to bind up all power of darkness set to destroy [names of children], or our family, and we loose [names of children], and this family, from the influence and harassment of Satan and his demons, in the name of the Lord Jesus Christ.

We invite the blessed Holy Spirit to move in the hearts of [names of children] that they may know the truth as they are able at their age. We invite the blessed Holy Spirit to move in our hearts and to convict us of sin, of righteousness, and of our responsibility as parents to raise [names of children] in Your name.

We plead the blood of Christ over [names of children] and this family. We claim for us a life yielded to serve the true and living God in the name of the Lord Jesus Christ. Amen.

DEMONIC ENCOUNTERS - SPIRITUAL ATTACKS

"TEMPTATION" –
The STAGE not often considered HARMFUL

From the time we are first born we are with a Guardian Angel, sadly we also are assigned 'personal demons'. Sometimes more than one, as there is certainly enough demons that exist to give every man woman and child in this world at least five. Part of this is because of the ratio of demonic spirits and their allies outnumber the human in numbers races 5 times over. And that number can change, as for example, some with a calling from God, as with some clergy and those in the ministry will likely have a second Guardian Angel. But, in this they might have more personal demons also.

THEY KNOW YOU SO WELL

You go through your life, and they have been there the whole time, often closely observing to better know your weaknesses. You have been tested throughout your life, to see how you will give into temptation, and this is used against you as you grow into adulthood.

These demons know the sins of your parents, your inherited weaknesses, and are masters of exploiting them. Demons carry a collective intelligence; they have a certain wisdom of the ages.

Temptation is an everyday part of living in the world, and it is more than words whispered in your ear, as often the many thoughts and ideas might have come, that were 'planted' there in our minds on a 'subconscious' level. Basically when the thoughts arrive at your brain at such a precise point, that by the time it reaches our conscious mind we cannot discern if it is our own thought or 'demonic' in nature. So the origin of the seed of thought is hard to discern, except that we should not hinder to any ill thoughts regardless of the sources.

However on the positive side, influence from the other side reaches our mind on the same level as well. That sudden life saving thought that has you 'glance upward' suddenly when you are changing CDs in your automobile. Avoiding what could have been a fatal crash. That is from God. On the flip side, that sudden urge to run a red light, is often from the 'other side'. In cartoons we see a 'Devil' and an 'Angelic' version of 'Fred Flintstone', both trying to convince Fred to go their way.
"Fred, how about you take the money you found and buy that new bowling ball you've had your eye on" The 'red devil Fred' says, while the other side that sports a halo urges him to: *" to give it to the poor".* This is a sort of graphical representation of what in a way goes on. Just not in so visible, small versions of these angelic beings. Obviously, it is all done much more discreetly.
We never really see a time where both sides have equal influence, as by nature we seem to be in more extremes living our lives to empower one side or the other more. Leaning to God more, suppresses the 'darker side', and empowers the 'light side'.
And the reverse is true of course.
We make decisions in our everyday life, and often we are faced with two decisions. Example: Sometimes leaving the house 2 minutes later can help you avoid a traffic fatality. You want those little unseen influences that would delay you in leaving the house. A though like: *"Maybe I should do a shot of mouthwash before we go right quick."*

Temptation accompanies each stage of demonic influence, but rises to a greater level at each stage. <u>Temptation is the key to all demonic activity</u>. It is through one's freewill that demonic activity may center itself around a person. It begins for example with a choice, sometimes appealing to your curiosity.

A late night apparition of a child at your beside for example. You research to find a child may have died in your house. Now you are getting reeled in. The idea of a trapped soul of a child tugs on your 'heart strings' and the demon has gotten to your good side, and is going to exploit it. But it still takes a decision to break Gods 'mortal laws' of not trying to communicate directly to the dead. If you left it alone, it may continue from time to time to show up unannounced, and remain at that stage I refer to a *"roaming stage"*. However the activity will not increase unless you do things that empower it further. You could yet still give it energy by your actions that are unrelated to contact with the spirit. The *'state-of-grace'*, or rather *'state of sin'* of an individual often plays a part as well. As we move more towards a sinful life, we therefore move further away from God's grace, and 'protection'. So the demon will try to get you to self-serve and act on your sins.

So we find with temptation, though it is a common stage of demonic influence, we can better understand that it is indeed the 'key' to all stages of demonic manipulation.

How they do so, through precisely implanting these subliminal thoughts. This can entail powerful images, vivid memories, not just a thought entering your mind as mere words. You basically can't tell your own thought from theirs. Temptation seems to feel like it was your idea. In oppression-possession you might see how advanced these subliminal images can reach as they start to work as though you are dreaming while you are awake. You might seen some horrific and frightening things, or of a perverted nature. Whatever they think might affect you the most, they will seed that imagery into your thoughts.

DEMONS <u>CAN</u> READ YOUR "AURA"

Humans emit a spiritual glow called an aura. However most of us cannot see this. Think of the early depiction of Jesus and his disciples. A spiritual aura so strong it can be seen by many as a brighter "halo" of a sort. The human aura is an encompassing halo that emits from the body. Often more intensely around the head, this is one reason they show Jesus and the saints to have visible halos, since it is said their aura, which also reflects their spiritual state, can be as bright as it can be seen.

The same applies for negative. A grayish almost black aura could be seen around a girl who started practicing the black arts. One attracts people as a positive, the other obviously second example, repels them. *(This also attracts dark spirits)*

There are said to be 7 layers total, each representing, or somewhat metering an aspect of the person they surround. So emotion, anger, lust, envy are all displayed in shades and intensities of colors. Your spiritual state is darker as you turn more away from God and towards sin. **Physical health, mental health,** and so on are indicated in intensity and color. As the more degraded of positive health the darker they might become

Some think "Auras" are merely a 'New age' religion concept, however it is a fact. Now through history apostles and those blessed with a gift such as Padre Pio, can see auras so they can see that person's state of health without them saying it. Also dark auras may be a warning to some to stay clear of that person, which could mean they intend to do harm to you. Fr. Pio could spot fellow clergy from the color of their aura in a crowd of people. Someone who is gifted with this ability to see auras probably.

Several things can tell them to turn up the power of the temptation. The first I will mention is your 'mood' as demons can read your 'auras' and see your mood from anger to lust. Essentially all of the seven deadly sins are in a way 'color coded' in a band of the human aura representing your current state of 'mood'.

There are several bands of the aura, like a rainbow. So in addition to a band for the spiritual state, also the mood of the person.

A persons 'physical health' is revealed as well. Each of these can expand to a more detailed color spectrum. For example, it may indicate your mental health independently of a color, the color indicating overall health.

The same for the spirit, it may be multiple states. Over all, the aura is a meter of your current status of your well being as a whole. But for the demon to have this information and use it against you is a powerful way to manipulate you. And without a need to directly read your mind.

YOU'RE 'ANTI-ANGEL' or "PERSONAL DEMON"

A keen observation of the surroundings can aid the demon in temptation. As I stated, in how at least one demon has been by your side since birth. This is one reason why it is an older Christian tradition, (sadly over looked by other denominations), to baptize a child in their infancy. As it also serves to protect the child better from these evil onlookers. Therefore through early stages of their childhood, they will not have the influence over them as much as they grow and develop into young men and women.

This demon knows you well, and knows well of your parents, relatives, family line going back many generations also. This information is used against you for your entire life. To sum it up, not only do they have a great knowledge, from having lived for over 6000 years, they also know you better than your own parents do.

As I mentioned previously, it is said those taking a 'higher spiritual path', may gain a 'second' Guardian Angel as well as 'additional demons'. The reason is the need of more troops to wage the war from either side. A man of the cloth for example is a trophy to a demon that can bring him down. There is a bit of jealousy also, against one who has given up worldly possessions and a life of sin to serve God. The demon is jealous this person may have a good shot at Heaven, and they may very well take their vacant seat in the hierarchy in Heaven. *(Further reading: The 'Communion of Saints')*. It pains them to know a mere human may indeed occupy a seat they left vacant after they rebelled. So this makes them a special target.

It is said a higher ranking demon, often referred as 'devils' are assigned to priests, monks and nuns to help assure they fall from grace, and quit the priesthood for example. So they never fulfill their 'calling' to serve in the 'Holy Orders'.

So we see that we make decisions that affect our lives. And how mere 'choices' can create a 'haunted environment', or take it to the next level. All the while we are tempted to aid them in the effort as they attempt to gain more power of our lives.

In a final note I want to mention how intricate temptation can become as it will involve more elaborate plans. This will even include your 'friends' and 'family', being used as unwilling 'pawns' as part of a carefully planned sequence of events, to better devise a greater scheme. Demons are 'collaborators', with this collective knowledge, *(though lower ranks are not as powerful)*, or even as intelligent then those in the higher order. They do well with the craft, as they have for the past 6000 years in helping bring the fall of man. Just know as you read this, for every law you break, and bad choice made, every sin committed, was the end result of a carefully executed technique defined as 'Temptation".

CAN THEY READ OUR MINDS?

In short, NO. Not directly.

A little know fact is that demons <u>cannot</u> directly read your thoughts, unless you direct your thoughts to them. Under certain stages of 'oppression', and of course 'possession', the demon has such communed with the individual that they can't tell their own thought from that of the demon. Also possible with such an extreme attachment it is more likely to 'pick up' more of what that person is thinking.

The Exorcist knows that the demon can take a guess at what they are thinking, because they already know all about him, his childhood, and his ancestry. All that knowledge is to be used against him. But it was not extracted from the mind of the Priest here. They may give you the impression they can read your mind because, since they can so precisely place thoughts into your mind that you can't differentiate from your own thoughts. They may influence your thinking and spout off what they have placed in your mind as though they are in fact reading your mind. They also may read body language and human auras as I described previously. But they cannot read your mind directly. *(They can also see the sins on your soul that are 'unconfessed' and 'unrepented' and use this to their advantage.)*

While a person is under possession the inhabiting demon(s) to some extent might be able to read the thoughts of the victim to some level. Still, I will go with the notion that God simply does not allow them to receive our thoughts. This is not so much a physical limitation but a restriction under God's law.

Remember without God's law binding these demons they would all just kill us, strangle us in our sleep etc. So no matter what, God is at work often to keep these evil spirits bound to His 'Mortal Law'. Only people by choice and through their 'freewill' choices will loosen their restrictions.

CAN A DEMON HEAR PRAYERS?

One thought goes to the reason why Catholics for example, do the 'sign of the cross' before and after a 'prayer' is to enclose the prayer in secrecy from our spiritual 'enemy'. It is sort of

spiritually placing a letter into an envelope and sealing it.
To think of it another way, it is an official beginning and a close to prayer, encapsulating it in secrecy between you and Heaven. For us this is a benefit, in a way of speaking of 'spiritual warfare', of encoding transmissions as so the 'enemy' can't understand your message. If nothing else, I don't want them to here a conversation between me and my maker.

DEMONIC ENCOUNTERS: PHYSICAL ATTACKS

SCRATCHES

Often they will appear out of nowhere, you might be even in the shower or lying in bed, bending over in an open area to pick something up. Then you feel a HOT burning sensation or the scratches. More often there will be the appearance of <u>three</u> symmetrical scratches, if not one set. More than one. But again we see the number three show here. There also might be another set that are say two horizontal, but not aligned with the vertical as the 'three'. The presence of the second set isn't exactly known, but there are some indications that it might be a hint of a 'count' as to the number of spirits 'infesting' the home for example.

BITING

Oppression stages might entail bite marks that appear just as mysteriously as the scratches would. More often the size of a child's bite, this might also include a burning sensation as is typical for any 'flesh wound' that might be afflicted. Some report that it felt like a 'bite', while others just a sudden pain, like they were pricked by a nail or 'burned' in that area with a curling iron.

Another element that is common to both of these attacks is the fact that these 'real wounds' heal in an unusually quick timeframe. It is 'supernatural' in itself the way they would "go away" so mysteriously, which can under normal circumstances take a couple of weeks. They might disappear in 2-3 days entirely. In one case they were gone by the afternoon. This is something to note on the check list that says it is a possible 'demonic'.

EYE POKE

In three high profile cases, one of the victims of the demonic infestation experienced an attack that is like being poked in the eye with a pointed object. They say it would then take a few days to recover from this to where they could open it and see clearly with it again. Typically this has occurred with only the 'left eye', again we see how the demonic can favor "left" to "right" in this.

DISEMBODIED PUSH/SHOVE

This is more so a bully move, but on a flight of stairs, or on the roof of your house clearing leafs from the gutters it can be fatal, and sadly, it has been for some.

A shove alone certainly doesn't spell "demonic", as a human spirit could do this, but it would be acting on their command. But we watch for the accompanied situations where it occurred to note if the spirit seems to be trying to cause harm or death in it's actions. And how hard the contact would be. Such actions always point to a `TYPE:EVIL-HUMAN or TYPE: EVIL-INHUMAN`, and should be handled as such.

SPECROPHELIA

This is a sensitive subject for obvious reason, but I need to entail this in this book because such cases are on a rise.

"SPECROPHELIA" is essentially sexual encounter with spirits.

WHAT MIGHT BRING IT ABOUT

The "dream lover" scenarios are a fantasy shared by many women for example, partly fed by those "spicy" Harlequin romance novels they might read, or TV shows and movies they prefer to watch. That entertains the idea of an 'extra marital affair' for an example. When it crosses into a fantasy, the desire for such encounters might be deep seeded and NOT shared with others. However the demonic can read this and try to use this unhealthy desire to create a doorway into their lives. We know how certain forms of 'sinful sexuality' can be a common reason for attracting demonic infestations. But still it comes down to a bit more. The desire has to be more than that. The dream lover might be a way for the demonic to "test the waters" acting in dreams is still a part of you 'accepting' such an encounter, which often could be considered an act of infidelity if in the dream, there is that realization that they are indeed married and still carry on with the scenario. It is a spiritual test you failed, and it might be the beginnings of further stages of a demonic trying to play upon your secret desires.

Beware!

These encounters might be repeated in dreams, not necessarily the same appearance of the "lover" but it more and more opens the mind for such an encounter. Now the manifestation itself will likely find another doorway, but this encounter has already more or less said you are "open to the idea" of a sexy encounter with a stranger.

PROGRESSIVE STAGES OF THE 'SEXUAL ENCOUNTERS'

These things might progress over a period of several nights or even months. As they can vary to the individual themselves, with many variables that will make each case unique. However, the progression can often take the same path of what we considered the more common elements that others had experienced.
It may begin just as a "night terror" that can begin more subtle, of classic *"things that go bump in the night"*. The person might awaken to hear *"footsteps"* in the darkness, approaching the bed, but not see anything yet. The feel of something or someone sitting on the bed might be the next thing experienced. What we are seeing in these stages as they progress is it is moving more and more to you. These things surround you more 'personally', as more of an 'intimate' encounter, as you are in bed being approach by a 'lover'. So with these early 'warning signs', if acted upon with proper prayers for example, can stop it before it goes further. But many times people are intrigued by the encounter, uncertain as to if it was real or not, they often don't even mention them to their spouse, friends or family members until it has progressed much further. Not doing anything is not quite as bad as an 'invitation' of such an encounter, but we have to remember the activity was probably 'already' invited in by another means.

The physical activity moves forward to more intimate contact as some might soon experience the covers being pulled off of them, or begin to feel hands on the feet or lower calf. Or a hand 'rubbing' or 'massaging' your back'*. This is starting the encounter with some light "groping", a sort of trying to get to "first based" (*if you pardon the expression*). Paralysis may start to take hold on further encounters 'if' they have not already. When you are affected physically, it should be considered an "oppression" stage. There has been some accounts where the spirit makes itself known, projecting the appearance of a very 'handsome' and 'charismatic man'. The final choice is made in this scenario, if they welcome the encounter.

If it begins as a 'gentle lover', it will likely turn to an 'abusive' and 'violent' rape at some point. But when we look back, people make decisions in daily life to choose to marry and stay with the wrong people in abusive relationships. And again here they somehow allowed themselves to become a victim.

In interviews with clients of suspected demonic infestations, we are careful to not seem to pry into one's deepest darkest thoughts of such a desire as a dream lover, because it might affect the marriage to have such a thing surface. That is something the demon might want, to break up the marriage and family. So we have to try to discreetly, since we know most of these encounters begin with simple human desires and sin, I make this information known and hope they will be forthcoming, however I note if that is the case, it is something more "*between you and God*", and I ask them to make a contrition to reconcile any sins that might relate.

INCUBUS-SUCCUBUS

Such encounters are a demonic attack, a sex demon, while the act to lure a person into an idea of sexual relations with a 'stranger' might even be aided by 'human spirits', the act is carried out in fact, by a demonic.

Young men might share the same encounters, but for whatever reason I won't detail, it is more common to 'females' than with 'males'. Technically, the 'Succubus' would be the female gendered demon that attacks men. As the Incubus is to a 'woman'.

There are stories of how 'Priests' will have these types enter their dreams to work on them in the same way, to try to weaken them spiritually through sexual desires. This might seem a bit minuscule, but you have to realize how many Priests and Nuns leave the Holy Orders of the church because of such temptations that come from media and more closely in carefully planted dreams. Everyone who receives the sacrament of 'Holy Orders', under the vow of 'abstinence', will have their own personal demon just to try to ensure they fall from grace by that means.

MY PERSONAL ENCOUNTERS

I was a single man for 36 years and because of that I swayed in and out of many relationships, and dated a so many 'women', sometimes looking for 'Mrs. Right'. Other times filling in time on a Saturday night, all the while, down deep inside I still felt 'empty', and unfulfilled. As I have always desired a serious stable and true loving relationship, even as far back as being a teenager, and even when I denied this truth. My mother wondered if I should be a 'Priest ', and although I entertained that idea, in my thinking I always knew that I was to be a husband and father someday as I am now. So eventually, by the time I was twenty years old, I knew that 'Holy Orders' *(The priesthood)* was not my calling.

At some point I realize that my desires and emotions were played upon by these types of spirits. But, remember, because of my upbringing, I was always surrounded with 'holy symbols' where my mother and father offered prayers on my behalf, throughout my life. I sincerely believe that these things might have saved me from things far worse than I am about to entail. (*I have had a Saint Benedict medal since I was in grade school.)* But these things still didn't stop some things from occurring.

Many, many times I was visited by what appeared to be female spirits. Typically in dresses or gowns. They seemed solid when I would awake and see them; I might ask the usual "what are you doing here?" And they would turn and walk through the wall.

Some had posed the idea I might be drawing human spirits that related to my feeling 'empty'. Now I do realize some human spirits might be used as 'pawns' in such a way, but I think the encounters were evil in nature, at least as it would reveal itself overtime.

Back then, there were times when I would wakeup with the feeling that someone was in bed with me. The certain slight movements, the person's breathing moves the bed slightly even. A bit of pressure on my back as though it was an arm or something touching me.

I know what it feels like to not be alone in bed. Especially now that I have been married for eight years, I very well know the way the bed feels when you are not alone. As in this case I speak of, it was very evident that my back seemed to be facing an 'unknown guest'. I should mention that I never was one to get into 'drunken stupors', and invite a woman home with me, then forget what I had done the night before. So these encounters were more of a surprise. Was it an old girlfriend who snuck in? I would eventually 'work up the nerve to turn over and would see 'nothing'. No one, as I was indeed alone with nothing behind me. Not even a pillow.

As I hinted, this type of encounter happened more than once. And sadly I was almost open to the idea of welcoming the advances of an 'unknown stranger' as you can see how I was setting myself up, just as I warn others of now to not do. Now I was never 'sexually assaulted' thank God. But I was 'attacked' by what I can only describe as a 'succubus' in it's appearance.

I woke in the morning, face down in bed. But something was holding me down. A hand was on either side of my face, palms down framing my face into a locked position, face down in the pillow. It's feet on both sides of me as it straddled over my body, I could feel the longer toenails dig into my sides just under my ribs. The feet and the hands held me in position tightly. Although at first I was puzzled and thought *"who might be playing a joke and holding me down?"* And for a moment I was out of body, as a floating disembodied spirit getting a glimpse of my still lying body and what was hunched over me. The body was a pinkish tone, maybe better described as more course, as though scarred all over from burns. A gangly creature with thin, stringy long white hair on its head, and pinkish rough skin all over its body. Disproportionately long legs, with white hair on the heel that was set high above the foot, like a quadruped. I felt a sense of terror, as the tightening of the feet and hand grips holding my face in the pillow was starting to make it hard to breath. So, in my mind, I readied myself to make a quick turn in bed to hurdle the creature off of me to release me. I counted to myself, 1, 2...3 rolling over fast, I fell out of bed. I then opened my eyes, there was 'nothing'. It was 9:30 AM in a place void of anyone except me. Interesting to note, later that morning I had found my 'Saint Benedict medal' had fallen off onto the bathroom floor, at least since the night before. All I can say is a "Succubus" fits my scenario because in part of the lifestyle I was living. And second, it is no coincidence in how the demon took opportunity to attack when I was left more open with my 'extra protection' removed.

Later in life, I haven't seen such an apparition, nor do I expect the creature has not returned either. What I do see is a sort of mockery of my past history of that Rock 'n' Roll lifestyle of *wine, women, and song*. There are times when the demons mock my previous lifestyle behavior by shaping piles of clothes to appear to be a woman in a seductive position. We are not talking an abstract prospective either, but quick detail in proportion and shape highlighting. Whenever I would see this I would stare and look away many times even and it would remain. Amazing how they can carefully and discreetly manipulate your environment, and just as sort of a mockery of you past lifestyles. And to such artistic proportions at that.

Another encounter I can't explain was when I woke lying on

my stomach late one night, to the feeling of a hand rubbing my back lightly. Something as my wife would otherwise do. My hair is longer, lying across the back over my shoulder moving with each stroke. When I lifted up my head to look at my wife, I was surprised to see she was fast asleep and facing the other way. A It was clear that her arms were not near enough to reach across a king size bed, as to be able to touch my back from her side of the bed from that distance.

What was that? Nothing ever came of that. I realize it could have been a deceased relative, paying a friendly visit. However, call me a 'pessimist' in after all I have experienced in life. I don't trust anything as "good" by default, and I take action with extra prayers to be sure such encounters don't evolve into some manifestation on yet another night. Again, *"just to be on the safe side"*

Besides there are enough cases out there that begin with a few nights of ghostly 'back rubs' as mentioned earlier. And that is cause for alarm somewhat. Whereas the clothes piles are another thing, more of a psychological game, typical in spiritual warfare.

'DEMONIC DEATH'

Hitting it right after some key point above. We see how the demonic will try to manipulate our environment, objects, and even 'people' to bring about their strategy.

Our death can be the result of a carefully planned series of events designed to ensure or demise. You're traveling home from work at night, when suddenly a large black animal runs across the road, you steer to miss hitting it, wrecking your car. Dead. Curses can be carried out as a 'death sentence' this way as well.

Many so-called accidents, and even when one seems to have "died in their sleep", can be the result of demonic attack.

You are faced with choices each day. As each choice might tip the scales of fate it always isn't so clear which could save your life, and when danger is abound and you should steer clear of certain choices. But for the most part, we revert again back to free will choices that place us in such a vulnerable state that a demon can affect us to this degree. Regardless if or not it might have come from a curse.

When you are weak spiritually, one way or another they might try to kill you, if you miss one opportunity to serve the task, they will find another. Of course this won't necessarily happen in the same night. But realize how many times we place ourselves in a certain danger driving our car. Or even in taking a shower. Remember, "<u>Demons CAN kill</u>!"

OLD HAG / SLEEP PARALYSIS

The term "HAG RIDDEN", comes from this which is what one refers to another as looking "sleep deprived" would mean that they look like they are exhausted and tired. That was what the victims of this would feel the following day, exhaustion, depending on how long it took place. The HAG, is still called that though many do not see a hag or any entity whatsoever, but when they do it commonly even today fits this description of an "OLD HAG".

This Article is on actual 'paranormal encounters', not debatable cases of what is medical 'SP'.

FOLKLORE AND THE LEGEND OF:

```
"When night falls, the hag is free to
leave her body (or to shed her skin,
depending on who is telling the story) to
wander unseen on land, underground or
through the air. The hag is invisible, but
her presence is warm to the touch, and
feels like raw meat. When a hag chooses
to ride to her victim's house, she will
```

choose a horse and almost never a mule. The hag drives the horse nearly to death, and tangles the poor 'beast's tail into impossible knots. In the morning, the owner finds his horse in a heavy lather, all but crippled from the ghastly ride. What does a hag do when she gets to her victim? She "rides" that person as well! The hag sits on a sleeping person's chest and face, weighing the sleeper down and meaning to choke or smother her victim. The victims struggle, never fully awake, as the hag "swallows" their voices so that not even the screamers themselves can hear their calls for help. The hag's flesh is said to have the bounce of rubber whenever her victim strikes out at her in the dark."

Although this is considered 'folklore', the problem with a 'legend' is that it gets distorted from the truth over time, like with the tale of 'Werewolves' and even 'Vampires'. As it is hard to tell as to where the original root of the lore came from. And how much was mere superstition. This is much as in how 'gossip' can take on some new proportions and details as it is passed on through the 'grapevine'. It takes on a whole new story highly skewed from the original as each person along the way might take opportunity to embellish. So we listen in part to these old myths and legends and see what we can take from them that could be plausible to today's reality.

We find for example that the old 'vampire lore' is more similar to the description of the 'old hag' visitations, than it's own legend of a sort of 'old Witch' on a broom. It was thought to be a spirit once deceased who would feed off one's 'life-force' as they slept. Often the victim would awake in the same way, 'paralyzed', unable to speak, and they find they have a visitor in a 'dark spirit' which comes to their side from the darkness of the room and then sits on the chest of, or hovers over the top of the paralyzed victim. Each morning the person would awake more drained of energy and a depletion of health for no reason known. Typically as it was said, that after the third or fourth attack they were found dead that next morning. These encounters were believed to be (at times) the restless spirit of a recently deceased relative for example. It was thought that driving a wood steak through the heart of the body through the coffin base, and into the earth would keep the restless spirit 'pinned down'. No doubt a solution based on *'superstition'*.

I feel there is some credibility in part in this, that they had seen the deceased to identify them, but it was a classic case of the demonic masquerade, the demon portrayed to be a woman's husband, or lover. Allowing the encounter, she would entail the encounter the next day to friends and family. That she was visited by the 'dearly departed' in the night. The seed of thought speculated from this notion and it grew into the vampire lore. Eventually, it goes without saying, the 'Blood Vampire' lure I think mixed with this specter visitation. Or 'Old Hag' type encounter.

Legends, lore and mere superstitions aside, let us look at some more recent testimony from people who have experienced the OLD HAG visitation. Case examples will help to understand the difference between what is merely a rare medical condition, versus something that is indeed 'paranormal', an early stage of attack.

The simple truth is those who debate it as a medical condition simply don't have enough experience in it to draw such conclusion. Second least we forget the *"science only mindset"* which can be quite a way beyond a 'healthy skepticism', and crosses the line into a 'biased opinion'.

TESTIMONY #1

Recorded cases of vampire attacks in Eastern Europe sometimes feature Old Hag characteristics. For example, a case cited by both Montague Summers and Dr. Franz Hartmann features, as Summers notes, "typical instances of vampirism" and <u>strongly resembles the Old Hag encounter</u>:

A miller had a healthy servant-boy, who soon after entering his service began to fail. He acquired a ravenous appetite, but nevertheless grew daily more feeble and emaciated. Being interrogated, he at last confessed that a thing which he could no see, but which he could plainly feel, came to him every night about twelve o'clock and settled upon his chest, drawing all the life out of him, so that he became paralyzed for the time being, and neither could move nor cry out. Thereupon the miller agreed to share the bed with the boy, and made him promise that he should give a certain sign when the vampire arrived. This was done, and when the signal was made the miller putting out his hands grasped an invisible but very tangible substance that rested upon the boy's chest. He described it as apparently elliptical in shape, and to the touch feeling like gelatin, properties which suggest an ectoplasmic formation. The thing writhed and fiercely struggled to escape, but he gripped it firmly and threw it on the fire. After that the boy recovered, and there was an end of these visits."

MY COMMENTS:
Nothing compares to a 3rd party actually 'witnessing' the attack, of course such accounts of witnesses like the victim's spouse can help validate for the victim that this was 'not' just some hallucination.

TESTIMONY #2

"As I was lying in bed thinking, I became aware of a rustling sound emanating from the turret . I focused on the sound, trying to determine it's origins. A breeze over papers? A mouse? As soon as I dismissed these possibilities the rustling sound stopped and was replaced by the sound of stealthy, shuffling footsteps that were headed in my direction. The sense of a presence was suddenly so strong that it filled the room. I was terrified. The critical detail here is that I clearly remember pulling the blanket over my head (I was lying on my back.) The next thing I knew I was <u>paralyzed</u>—I couldn't move a finger. The footsteps continued their approach and the next thing I knew, a tremendous weight settled on my chest, forcing me into the mattress. I felt that there was a menacing presence, a personality at work that wanted to meddle with me in particular. It was nasty! The intense, dreadful weight continued to press down on me, almost like a large animal settling itself on my body. I thought I would go through the mattress. I knew that I was awake, I was not dreaming, and that something evil was in the room with me. Somehow, my childhood years of Sunday School paid off and I prayed to be released. In that instant, it was over. The following morning, I tried to tell myself that it had been just a dream. To this day, twenty-odd years later, I don't believe I was dreaming.. After that, I slept with the light on and my bedroom door open. Months later, one of my roommates was sick with the flu. Her room was cold so I offered to switch with her until she felt better. That night, she stayed <u>in my room</u> and closed the pocket doors. The rest of us were watching TV. Elsewhere in the apartment. A number of friends were there. Sometime after midnight, we heard the doors of my room screech open on their runners and slam into their recesses in the wall. My roommate came screaming down the hall, saying that something had sat on the bed. She felt the bed sag beneath the weight, though in her case, it wasn't on top of her. She also felt and heard something clawing and scraping at the bedspread. After my roommate's experience, we two scaredy-cats decided to share a room and kept the hall light on. Though nothing like that ever happened again, we did have some exciting times with a Ouija board in that apartment. We left that place at the end of the school year and found another old apartment that proved to be just fine. The students who moved into our former place reportedly had problems there, too. Unfortunately, we never compared stories. I should mention that my fascination with the subject of ghosts led to my getting a Masters degree in Folklore at the University of Pennsylvania. While there I studied with Dr. David Hufford, who wrote The Terror That Comes In The Night. I wrote a thesis entitled "The Old Hag Experience Within A Haunted House

Tradition." I found people who claimed that more than one member of their family experienced variations of the Old Hag within the same house. They only discovered much later that they had shared similar experiences while living there. I also interviewed two people whose Old Hag attacks precipitated out-of-body experiences. IMHO Old Hag attacks occur, or at least are reported more frequently in settings that are considered "haunted." This may be a case of "Which comes first, the chicken or the egg?" Does a house with a reputation of being haunted encourage someone to interpret the experience as supernatural or does the experience itself promote the house to be called haunted? In poring over collections of both contemporary and past ghost folklore from around the world, I noticed that Old Hag attacks accompany other manifestations with startling frequency. I also found that elements of a typical "Old Hag," like the rustling sound, the sound of footsteps or the percipient suffering temporary paralysis, are elements commonly mentioned by people who report seeing an apparition, even in broad daylight. Hufford's book should be read by anyone interested in the Old Hag. Although riveting to read, it is scholarly and gives medical science its due. No conclusions are drawn. If you do read it, however, you may choose never to sleep on your back again."

MY COMMENTS:
We see prayers either are a quick cure for SP, or do as they usually do in warding off real 'night terrors' that attack one in

the night. This also reminds me that those who experienced the 'Old Hag' are the ones best to analyze and research the phenomenon.

Note how multiple people experience the same thing? How far fetched is the notion they shared a mass hallucination. This is telling of a demonic haunting, no question. Not imagination or medical SP which was something that set in 'after' they were already awake and heard and felt something in the room.

TESTIMONY #3

" On the last Thursday in November, Ben looked at the clock by his bedside and saw that it was 11:57. He turned over and went to sleep. About a half hour later Ben awoke. Dazed from sleep, he wasn't sure why he had awakened but he felt there was someone in the room with him. He opened his eyes fully, and at the foot of the bed saw something gray and mist like hovering over him. Whatever it was just a foot from his face. It was slowly moving toward him. Afraid of suffocation, he threw his blankets at it. It disappeared as soon as he began moving. Ben turned on the light but found nothing but his thrown blankets. A half-hour had passed since he had last looked at the clock. Two weeks later, on a Wednesday night, Ben again went to bed about midnight. Approximately a half hour later, he again awoke feeling there was a presence in the room. He looked around in the dim light. By the dresser, directly down from the bed, were two small animate objects. As Ben looked at them, they appeared to be children. They seemed to be aware of him, in that they made eye contact, but made no effort to move from where they were. As Ben watched, they simply faded and were gone. Ben saw nothing for two full months after that. But he did begin to awaken in the morning from time to time, conscious, but entirely unable to move. When he did finally move he would be sluggish for the rest of the day. Ben's roommate, having never seen, nor heard, anything in the house, was a little concerned about his friend. Then on a Monday night, Ben retired close to midnight again. About 45 minutes later, Ben awoke to the feeling of a presence in the room. He opened his eyes, and at the corner of the bed stooped an old man with a wrinkled face and a long beard. The man was entirely white and seemed solid. As Ben rose from the bed, the figure retreated to a far corner and seemed to shrink but remained in the room. Ben threw his pillow at the man. It hit the closet. The door to the room suddenly slammed and the figure was gone. Ben's roommate came in to see what had happened. There didn't seem any way the door could have slammed unless Ben had accidentally and unknowingly hit it with such force it bounced against the closet and then slammed shut. But then, Ben wonders, why wasn't the pillow in front of the door.

MY COMMENTS:
First note how Ben didn't wake to find he was paralyzed, it happened after this figure moved over him. Second I agree with the frustration in letting science and psychology make one feel like it was all a hallucination or simply SP. It goes to show again, that such things are a matter of the spirit, not a matter of science.

This is like many legends and folklore, most people are too afraid to admit there may be truth in this as a paranormal experience with an actual 'evil entity'. It's a fact that most 'regular folks' can't deal with, the idea of ghosts in any form, and simply dismiss it all as superstitious nonsense. This is far too easy to say. If you really listen to the people who tell of these experiences, I mean 'really' listen; you will know that the experiences aren't a simple case of "temp. sleep paralysis". Blinded by science, the 'white coats' often never listen to the truth even when it is right before them. Like with Ebenezer Scrooge claiming his ghostly visitor was due to "an undigested piece of chip beef". Remember the movie "The entity"? Watch it again as this moronic psychiatrist, tries to explain what happens to this woman as a mental problem she is having even after he himself sees this entity, and the attacks happening, ignoring her boyfriend who witnessed all. You will see what kind of approach they have against the supernatural. To get a scientist involved to help with something paranormal, is simply worse than hiring an amateur ghost buster to solve your problem. They are even more so in the dark it seems on the reality of it all because of their bias of 'science only' and atheistic approach to finding answers."

THE DIFFERENCE BETWEEN "SP" AND AN ATTACK:

Medical "Sleep Paralysis", (*cataleptic somnambulism*) I feel is more clearly defined from what is a demonic attack. First realize this is 'always' what the 'Atheist' and 'Demonic/Ghost' skeptics default to, while through others in their personal accounts define it by description throughout history as an 'Old Hag', 'Vampire', 'Succubus', 'Incubus' or another type of 'demonic' visitation. And there we have a 'cause and effect' test accounted for with mere prayers breaking SP, and warding off would-be encounters with this 'evil'. You must consider the source of the explanation as they are in a 'Humanistic'

'Atheistic' theory, from people who believe that everything supernatural in origin is not an intelligent demonic or ghost, but has a 'natural' explanation.

Logically, I thought my first thought if I would wake up paralyzed in bed would be:

```
"OH MY GOD! I AM PARALYZED!"
```

As opposed to something of this detail:

```
"There's something evil in the room,
coming out of the darkness, it's now
sitting on my chest I can't breathe!"
```

See the difference?

Our response to such occurrences in part tell what is going on

A Testimony related to this:

Frank, 40, awoke late one and was unable to move his body. I cite this example, since it can compare with what a person is thinking, feeling, experiencing as they awake paralyzed. This should NOT stray far from any other person's account of waking up feeling actually paralyzed and not 'pinned down'. His first thought was: *"Oh my God, I can't move!"* It wasn't a fear of something beyond being paralyzed, he didn't sense an evil presence, hear disembodied footsteps walking towards his bedside, view an 'old hag' emerging from the darkness, or a similar demonic creature. No descriptions of black shadow mass, a ghost or anything. Such thoughts were the furthest from his mind. As with all humans naturally, the experience had him fearing of things related to being 'paralyzed' and 'immobilized', and nothing more. He was only focused on the helpless feeling of being disabled, especially since this took him by surprise, as he didn't find out until later after a trip to the hospital, that he had a stroke. He thought of how is he going to work? What about the family? Will he be in a wheel chair the rest of his life? *"Will I die next?"* All of this in the first 'five' minutes. Note how the reaction of waking up simply paralyzed is different, from experiencing the 'Old Hag' attack. Tell me where one suddenly gets diverted from the thought of being paralyzed to that of a paranormal encounter considered a physical attack?

LISTEN TO THE WITNESS CLOSELY!

A thing learned here is as an investigator, listen to your witness more closely and you can tell if it was 'medical' or in fact 'paranormal.' The proof is in the pudding' it is beyond normal to fabricate a night terror from the thought of being incapacitated the rest of one's life. Science always goes with 'science', as we know all paranormal can't be explained with mere science, we also must refrain from relying upon it for every case of so-called 'Sleep Paralysis', and maybe accept the fact the one who experienced this phenomenon could have indeed had a true encounter with evil that night, and not simply a case of that more rare 'SP'. The thinking in that person's mind greatly differs from the one who feels there is something paranormal about the whole thing, as opposed to just a 'stroke' or 'medical condition'. Witnesses are offended and rightfully so, in a flat out disbelief from those who investigate their claims who ignore what they are telling them and stick to the "*cataleptic somnambulism*" theory, as though it is always the case.

"I know what I saw and experienced"

They might say in frustration. *(Now grant it we are not going to always tell them what they want to hear)* Bottom line if you had it happen to you, you will know it was unquestionably more than another case of 'SP'. This applies to all paranormal experience, science even goes to say it was our 'imagination', or with multiple witnesses, some said 'mass hallucination'.

Let us all keep in mind that often those who didn't actually experience this phenomenon are the ones telling us it is cataleptic somnambulism. When you have had it happen to you yourself, you know 'Sleep Paralysis' is much harder to believe than a 'paranormal' explanation in something that compares to the stories of the 'Old Hag'. As a child, your parents tell you **"It was only the wind"; and "There are no monsters in your closet"**, this is when we are children. So as adults these people of science <u>patronize us</u> like children. We don't want to do this to clients. Hear them out and carefully weigh the descriptions and accounts from the witnesses always. In truth medical SP is actually much rarer than such similar experiences that are indeed 'demonic' in its nature

Another Notable quote:

"...Now, years later, after learning more about it, [After my own OLD HAG encounter], I was shocked to discover that science says it's a brain disorder. How can that be the case when we both experienced the same thing at the same time? When thousands of people from all over the world have actually seen the old hag, and the descriptions are the same. Call me crazy but I disagree. Unfortunately, I have no way to prove my theories, except that <u>I have experienced it first hand</u>, and it is terrifying."

MY COMMENTS:
I agree with Cindy, a more logical mind would actually go with the OLD HAG not simply being common hallucinations while

having a sleep paralysis. And most have never even heard of it before the experience, and then find many others share the same experience. Again be leery of 'science alone' when it requires physical proof and validation, this is one reason many consider Parapsychology a pseudo-science.

This is from an article on Sleep paralysis:
Surprisingly, though, is the consistency of such reports made by societies and cultures with no previous knowledge of each other or their lore. [Such as the 'OLD HAG'] The main details remain constant. A man or woman is attacked during the night, usually lying on their back, when an evil entity sits upon their body, causes paralysis, and even sometimes chokes or smothers it's victim. Though their motivation may differ, (possession, revenge, or just wanting to upset the living) the attack remains strikingly similar. And these stories are not limited to Western cultures, in fact, quite the contrary. In Thailand people refer to being Phi um (ghost covered) and phi kau (ghost possessed), and these experiences include a feeling of pressure, paralysis, and something black covering the body. In Japan, kanashibara ("to tie with an iron rope") is a common known and accepted experience. In the Far North one speaks of agumangia (Inupik) or ukomiarik (Yupik) in which "a soul" tries to take possession of the paralyzed victim. In Laos, da chor is described as follows: "You want to listen, you can't hear; you want to speak, you are dumb; you want to call out, you cannot; you feel you are dying, dying; you want to

run away. You urine with fear in your sleep.

MY COMMENTS:
This was from an article I felt leaned to saying all 'Old Hag' and 'Night Terrors' were SP related. Then they go onto say the above statement which should help make one rethink this 'SP only' theory, in that many different cultures experience it as more of a paranormal experience or attack.

 Keep in mind most of us never read about this before the first hand encounter. It's not so widely shown in movies that one already makes up an image in their mind then experiences it. The encounter is demonic in nature, that 'suffocation' and 'strangulation' is a common attack in the night by a demonic. And can often result in 'death'. So to see a black shadowy figure do this in the same way, as another witness says the 'lurking black figure hunched over his paralyzed body', then moved swiftly over him like a crushing weight. Others see the 'Old Hag'. These same encounters often begin the same way and end with 'sexual assault' as I describe previously, (Succubus/Incubus). And this is one reason one should <u>say a protection prayer before bed</u>, and to wear the proper protection symbols and medals on oneself as you sleep. My previously described encounter was the only time I was 'physically attacked'; that I can now recall, and later that same morning, I found my Saint Benedict medal had fallen off during the night before I went to bed on the bathroom floor.

<u>TESTIMONY #5</u>

"At approximately two o'clock one morning, I was awakened from a sound sleep. No apparent reason. I had not been dreaming. The bed faced a doorway into the hall, and the door was open. In the doorway I saw a figure dressed in a long robe, possibly with a hood. All I could see, other than

the black outline, was a shining glow where a face would be. I was petrified and found myself unable to move. I seemed to be paralyzed. I kept telling myself I had to be dreaming and, if I could just awaken my husband lying next to me, everything would be all right. All I can say is that there was a feeling of extreme evil that seemed to be coming from the figure. After several attempts to speak my husband's name—my voice seemed to be paralyzed, too—I finally croaked out "John." I managed to say my husband's name a second time, and finally a third time. Each time I said "John" the figure became smaller, and it disappeared completely when my husband woke up. I was shaking from head to toe, my paralysis disappearing with the vision. My teeth were chattering so badly that I was unable to speak coherently for many minutes. My husband is a realist and kept trying to find a logical reason for the apparition—the streetlight, headlights, neighbors' lights—but he never could convince me that what I had seen was a normal phenomenon. I used to get peeved at my son Ed because when I went to his room to awaken him for school or work he was never there. Usually I would find him on the couch in the den. About a year after we moved he told me the reason he would never sleep in his own room: he was terrified in there. He had been awakened on many occasions, usually in the early morning hours, with the feeling that someone was in the room, even though he could see no one. During these times he would be paralyzed, unable to move a finger, for many terrifying minutes. On several occasions he was awakened by being lifted bodily from the bed and dropped. He never saw anything. He just had the feeling of a presence in his room, and the only good night's sleep he ever had was on the couch in the den. After hearing this, I began to quiz my other children to see whether, anything had ever happened to them in this house. My son Mike, before I going into the navy, had had the same bedroom that Ed had his experiences in. He told me that on one occasion he was awakened from a sound sleep early in the morning to see a figure at the end of his bed, just I looking at him. He describes it as an old lady sort of dressed in a 'gown and bathrobe'... "

MY COMMENTS:
A case of a 'black shadowy figure' again, an Old Woman... I have no doubt 'Sleep Paralysis' can happen, but as we began to approach the 21st century I realize they try to explain all 'night terrors' with a bias towards 'science only/humanism' as being purely psychological or medical. (As with SP)It is important that we as an investigative team, weigh all possibilities without such 'bias' and truly listen to the client/witnesses to determine what truly applies to their specific case.

A DEFENSE WHEN YOU 'CAN NOT MOVE OR SPEAK'

People might awaken finding themselves under attack with a form of induced 'paralysis' and are unable to speak. Don't wait! Remember as I spell in this book, **'Demons CAN read your directed thoughts'**, although they can't read your mind in general. Project your thoughts as though you are shouting at whatever is holding you down:

`"In the name of Jesus, begone!"`

Repeat this thought in the same manner.
To extend this further, you might visually picture 'Jesus on the cross'. Quickly these methods have been proven to 'free' the paralysis, then when you can speak say the prayers aloud to rebuke the manifested spirit! We find that when we can't speak these beings can hear thought directed to them, so without words from your mouth you can still affect them with prayers in your own thoughts. True! In addition, a call on Jesus name is a sort of prayer of intercession in itself. So this is considered as well, why mere thoughts, rather than spoken words can have an effect.

MYTHS AND MISCONCEPTIONS: On "DEMONIC SPIRITS"

PHYSICALLY BATTLING DEMONS

I read on an online forum where a Priest answers some Q&A from e-mails he receives. He couldn't help but post an absurd message in one fellow that went on with a delusional idea: `"I am the Demon slayer..."` And believe it or not there are more than one like that, although more likely some naive teen, who is one of those fanatics of the TV's *'Buffy the Vampire Slayer'* series. Or "Supernatural" which is even more confusing as is the movie "Constantine", when in reference to doing true battle with evil. They have a skewed view of the true reality of what in fact humans are battling with *Demons and Devils*, just as they portray *"vampires"* on the 'boob-tube' and 'big screen'.
So, in truth we cannot fight a spiritual battle with our bodies or

with physical means. If we could only master our swordsmanship or 'hand to hand' combat skill and defeat them.

When I was younger I saw so many things to where I got to the point I was annoyed by them. **"Quit bothering me! Let me sleep!"** I flung pillows at whatever it was, and sometimes it would disappear. Others it would pass through them, and they would stay as I stared at it, until it left. At some point, I kept a replica (Unsharpened) Samurai sword by my bed, and I grew so tired of these shadowy visitors, I reverted to rising up from bed and waving the sword through these beings. Foolish I know and I cringe when thinking back after hearing the extremes of how this could have affected me in my physical efforts to defend my space. I could have been killed! The effects of contact can be a sort of 'electric shock', frigid cold, getting shoved back, (*as my friend did for merely being in the path of the fleeing shadow*). As the before mentioned 'paralysis' has effects on your heart that might induce stroke or heart failure, or with the more extreme, as "*spontaneous human combustion*". Which has been chronicled through Catholic Church history as a certain real affect of a demonic encounter.

But somehow God had protected me through these foolish times. Maybe with these reasons it is clearer now. Now as I have a 'visitor' I merely stay put, keep an eye on the being and begin to say prayers to remove it. This is the main reason I have holy water bedside, not just in blessing myself when I rise in the morning and again before bedtime. It is "*In case of emergency...*", and I recommend this for anyone who believes they are 'haunted", as to never assume a 'harmless' spirit is behind the occurrences. Be on the safe side and keep your emergency measures ready in case you are attacked one night.

So the reality is that we should keep our physical distance and not try to make contact with what has manifested, especially an obvious 'demonic entity'. Such arrogance and foolishness will more often not go unpunished, and the 'payback' might be later on not immediately, when you least expect it. Simply having *'no fear'* is <u>NOT</u> protection in itself, it can make one the fool. Just as being fearless cannot help you in a tiger's cage, the nature of the beast is the same, regardless of your attitude about it. Think of it this way, if not for God and his heavenly court of Angels and Saints in Heaven who "intercede" for us to provide real protection and binding of these spirits, demons would indeed kill us where we stand. Our choices to break the 'leash' that holds them back, (*A restraint set there by Gods 'Mortal Law" by default*), by the same means we make a bad choice in taking a swing at a dark shadowy demon, with it comes the backlash.

My great uncle, who was a bitter old soul, an abusive alcoholic, 'mean spirited' as my dad described him, while in the hospital dying he sat up in his hospital bed and started swinging at the air. A concerned son, asked him: **"what are you doing Dad? Lie down please!"** He responded. **"I am fighting off these winged creatures; the little bastards are coming at me, striking at me"**.

He died before long that day. Regardless if you believe the poor old man was simply hallucinating, his defense against demons only resulting in 'swinging' in the air wildly, as I did with my sword. (Side note: The 'Hail Mary' last line **"Pray for us sinners, now and <u>at the hour of my death"</u>.** All I will say for now, is that there is a reason that being stated, as it applies to praying for a 'peaceful' departure in part. The demonic is said to make one last attempt to sway the hearts and minds as we are in passing, again with a last ditch effort. Prayers like this help assure we will not endure such torments for long.

In most cases, with age comes wisdom, and I have learned to not bother to do anything but keep an eye on it, have faith in God's protection, try not to be afraid, don't turn away from it, and pray (in the least) until it leaves. So the bottom line is we should indeed avoid purposely having physical contact with these entities, and leave it as the type of battle it really is. There is also something to 'turning your back on it'. So many times you hear of invisible attacks where investigators turn to leave a room and then they get a scratch on their back for example. Back fighters they may be, although a cowardly act in a human sense they are far from afraid of us and by no means 'cowards'. This is why I don't want to turn my back on them and simply run away. You also don't want to look at the eyes directly. So you have to draw a line between the two.

DEMONS CAN'T KILL YOU

They can kill you in ways you don't realize, your friend who might be "oppressed" might be driving and suddenly an unfamiliar black animal streaks across the road. They steer to avoid collision and crash the car. No one knows what really happened. Apparent accidents of other kinds may also have been at the hand of a demonic. That disembodied hand shoving you when you are walking up a staircase. They can induce heart attacks sometimes by just reaching in and grasping your poor tired heart, or make you experience something to induce stress on your heart. One who dies in their sleep might have been a victim of a nightmarish dream that was too much on a poor old heart. Say your protection prayers before you sleep! I have gone over this extensively throughout this book, so as you read to this point, you are very well aware that they can in fact kill you.

HUMAN SPIRITS CAN'T KILL YOU

Remember that a simple shove on a staircase doesn't have to

be much force to send you off balance and fall down the staircase. You might be tripped in the bathroom, distracted when driving, all of these things can be fatal under the right circumstances, and if the end result was death, most certainly it can be said the action that 'triggered' the events leading to death is the cause. *(Keep in mind 'malicious' human spirits are minions of the devil)*

DEMONS CAN HELP YOU

This statement is only true if it was stated as "demons can appear to help". There will be no "hell boy" hero, or one helping you avoid death without ulterior motives that will result in your undoing. This is in the midst of these liars, who manipulate the truth to better snare us. The view of 'help' must be a misconception and likely not even a direct result of their action. Even a deceased relative, if they are a "condemned soul" they cannot make a move to their own will. For example, in warning you of a most certain danger. Refer to the section "*A Word about Witchcraft*" I mention of how those spirits whom have a clear dark side always want something in return for their supposed "good" they might provide. I also maintain that they might falsify 'protection' by simply calling off their dogs on you for a time being. Again like paying the mafia for protection, when it is really their goons who came to bust up your store, to force you to subscribe to such insurance means.

DEMONS CAN PREDICT THE FUTURE

As I say many times, with the wisdom of the ages, and having known you since birth, and mankind in general since our existence on earth. With this information alone, they can do well to try to predict an outcome to events, and your 'fortune' and 'fate' even.

You must keep in mind that many fortune telling schemes

could simply be a spell being cast on you to make the prediction come true. Another reason to avoid fortune tellers even Tarot readers. As these methods impose the fortune read on you, as to help validate the reader, and therefore send them back for more.

As so with demons, as they have this 'vast knowledge', they can very well take a good guess at predicting the future events based on the information they will have based on circumstances and likely choice, some of which they might affect, or "nudge' to make it occur.

For example, a man, we'll call "Mr. W., might be told he is going to die on the *twenty-seventh of September in the year 2008*, could be accurate to the time and the place even.

What this really entails is:

In knowing Mr. W. travels to work daily, he might cross a certain bridge, they are aware that the bridge is unstable and where the weakest point is. How many more cars can cross over before that will fail, and right near where Mr. W. is passing over that bridge daily. And that the number of cars that will typically pass over that bridge will add up to him being on the bridge when it collapses.

They might even see into his heart and know when the next 'stroke' is to come.
Again, tipping the scales, pushing the fate. To some degree we might see that some variables will be adjusted to see that this prediction is carried out. The man might lose his keys, and delay his crossing the bridge to a more precise dangerous time, as the bridge fails.

As for a weak heart, they can create situations of stress, or even go as far as to reach in to affect his heart rate. How they can affect us in these ways, will depend on how much we more so appease them in our lives. And turn our backs on God.

Limiting God's protection, and therefore empowering their effects on us.

DEMONS CAN REPRODUCE

False. Not technically anyway. While it can be said that a 'Human-demonic hybrid' is the exception, they are not "Demons". Biblically they are called the "Nephilim", they are said to be born of human women, but without an actual soul. The demon which induced the pregnancy will often be the one which resides in this offspring. However, there is more likely to be more than one inhabiting it.

DEMONS ARE SOULS OF THE 'NEPHILIM'

False, this is a myth; there were 'no souls' in the otherwise empty shells of the half human offspring that were a result of that unholy union between demonic beings and human women. The soul was merely that of a fallen angel, it could have been the demon that had intercourse with the human female himself. Or another, likely as I said previously, several will inhabit the same body from birth onward. As there are no new souls that have come from this, as demons cannot themselves reproduce in by 'any' means.

WHAT ARE THE NEPHILIM?

The biblical "Nephilim" were called the 'giants' back in the days of Noah, and if you had seen the movie "*The 300*" this so-called lore is a bit of a factual account, but more so the 'creature' like beings were the result of this 'unholy union' between the fallen angels and human females. All had magical powers and demanded to be treated as "gods". But some can seem just like normal people. There is a certain fear today that the "Nephilim" have begun to return and are already amongst us. And if you are in proximity of one, we don't expect to

"sense" 'evil', or anything usual. This is a greater masquerade and again they can fool all five and sixth senses. You will likely find they are beautiful charismatic people, rather than ugly and repulsive. (Better to blend in) That might serve them better considering the way woman can throw themselves at a good looking guy for a "one night stand".
I myself won't go as far as to say this is actually occurring. But I suppose when it is considered how they came to be it isn't out of the ordinary, as we see "Incubus" accounts plentiful today. It is quite possible that many demonic-human hybrids again walk the earth.

TYPE: GOOD-HUMAN SPIRITS

Spirits we label as **TYPE: HUMAN-GOOD** are not generally associated with what people consider to be a *"problem haunting"*, and I personally generally don't get contacted about that really, beyond simple questions usually more curious in nature, rather than a real concern. The most common things we are contacted of might be a demonic stage of **"Scout And Roam"** as I describe earlier. The main thing I want to tell is don't make mistakes in getting any unhealthy obsessions over these mild hauntings. You might "Open Doors" through your actions, words, or decisions made that will take what seems to be a quieter, simple "haunting" to an "infestation" or worse. Human spirits are often used as "pawns" to get people to cross these lines of God's *'Mortal Law'*, so it can give it an 'invitation' to infest.

We mainly are only concerned with two elements with these types:

- ✓ Correctly identifying it is indeed a 'Good' spirit.

- ✓ Offering prayers, penance, for their benefit, if #1 is correct. (i.e. help them to move on)

The problem is it can't be so methodical even in these two short steps.

NOTE: Rarely, will the drama be played out as factual in where a murder victim's un-rested spirit is trying to reveal it's killer, or an otherwise undisclosed location of a buried body is revealed, and so forth... Don't assume such drama is true, more often it is a snare by a demonic or one of their minions which can be a human spirit as I mentioned earlier.

Generally, the information following is in helping add details of typical fashion as to what a GOOD Spirit often entails in this sort of "haunting".

<u>I recommend</u> that we more spend time on learning the signs and traits in recognizing an **'Evil presence'**, rather than to look for signs of a supposed 'Good'. Mostly because a dark spirit can so well pretend to be an *'angel of light'* or a lost loved one. We have to read between the lines and look for indications it is not what it pretends to be.

In this I am saying we tend to not pay much attention to signs of it being a 'good spirit', if we get even ONE indication that might spell "demonic" or 'evil'. Be leery of making such a judgment, and don't assume it is 'good' as this is in part purely for your own safety, and that of the 'client' you are helping. Because of the extreme difficulty in discerning good from evil, it is best to assume it is EVIL, until we come up clean as to finding no trace and indications of an 'evil presence.'
This is one reason alone why we should avoid communicating with the spirit and begin prayers for intercession to deal with it now rather than later especially. Because 'they' cannot fool God and his Angels and Saints. But they do well to fool most "Psychic-Mediums" and especially those people lost and confused in faith based systems that are misleading on these matters.

A CASE EXAMPLE of A GOOD SPIRIT:

Here is a case example in a story.

The grandmother too be, was excited about the arrival of her first grandchild, she was knitting socks and clothes daily, anxiously awaiting that special day. She was a widow and staying with the daughter for the time being. She was so looking forward to the baby's arrival that's all she talked about. Sadly she passed away in her sleep one night, and before the blessed event with the birth of her first grandchild. About 6 months after the baby was born, the mother had been awakened to the sound of her baby on the monitor 'laughing'. A giggle like she does during the day when getting affection or dad's 'tickling fingers'. Curious, quietly opening the door to the nursery and peeking in to see there was what appeared to be her grandmother, smiling, looking down at the baby. There was interaction, the babies eyes fixed on the face of this apparition. Smiling back, kicking, and laughing. He was wearing one of her outfits she made, and covered in one of her hand made blankets. A tear rolled down her cheek, she said softly "Mom"? And the apparition then turned around and smiled, as she reached down as though to cover him up with the blanket. And then with that, she faded away into the night.

That was the first and last time she saw her grandmother. You could say the *'unfinished business'* was complete. She only wanted to interact once with her grandchild. Somehow by the grace of God she was granted this special privilege.

In this case of the grandmother, she was allowed by God to return in spirit as to get one moment of interaction with her new born grandchild. And we ask why was the deceased grandmother allowed to visit her grand child? As it is clear that God certainly had given her permission to interact with the child and it was indeed meant for the mother to look in and see the two of them interacting. I am sure that the daughter may have had some 'closure' in seeing this in one form or another. I am sure it was disheartening for her to have her grandmother pass away so close to the birth of her first grandchild. This may have validated the afterlife for her daughter, which could have some positive effects on her and her child's spiritually. Seeing the grandmother play with her grandson would be priceless, and one could assume that the grandmother did not pass on as a 'lost soul' by the indications present of her visitation. Let's assume it is an apparition; it passes the check list so it is NOT an inhuman spirit, or evil spirit. Why is the spirit here? First do we all agree that God does in fact control the afterlife? And they are here for a reason. Why are they here?

The 'Unfinished business' explanation which one way or another has it's presence in popular culture nowadays, is partly true. But that business is simply not a goal the person who passes on can simply by choice carry out. It must be allowed by God.

The story of the Girl, who is seen walking on the road in a prom dress, is in purgatory. And least we all forget history where such things prompted prayers for the soul without the apparition itself requesting prayer from beyond the grave.

Don't try to second guess or 'judge' where people go when they die.
What I am doing here is explaining some real reasons a ghost may make itself known.

PURGATORY - "ALL GHOSTS ARE 'NOT' DEMONS"

Shakespeare has pictured a ghost from Purgatory for Hamlet, however he chose rather to throw out suggestions which might satisfy those members of his audience who followed any one of the three schools of thought on the subject. A sort of political correctness, where as he was careful not to alienate or step on the toes of those who believed in the other schools of thought.

"Purgatory is a phase of existence in the after-life that lies between earth and heaven"

This is the best 'short' answer I can give. Purgatory is an important concept to grasp because it can often explain the existence of ghosts manifesting their presence in this world.

HERE I LIST 'SOME TYPES OF 'PURGATORY' GHOSTS.

1. **Attached to People, places or things.** Some might linger because of a certain attachment to otherworldly things, loved ones, or their new home they didn't get a chance to enjoy.

   The understanding here is by God's will, people might be allowed to take time to remove themselves from worldly things and people to better prepare themselves for the next journey.

2. **Unrealized Death.** It does happen where they don't realize they have died for whatever reason, and do not move on until they understand they are now a spirit in passing and no longer flesh and blood. I would have to extend that this alone isn't the reason for them lingering, it is part of a penance somehow and might often accompany

another scenario in this list. This is the typical situation where some dramatize it with a "Go into the light", however we should try to avoid direct interaction as <u>all of these</u> cases here can simply be a demonic masquerading as a human spirit, to snare you.

3. **Doomed to repeat.** A suicide might be seen repeating their act of taking their own life in a scenario some consider to be a "residual haunting". This may also include a murder, or some other act of mortal sin. Some might hold themselves there with their own guilt, or it is more community service in a state of 'Purgatory'. As I state elsewhere in this book, we never see anything unless there is good reason. We should pray for the spirits passing when we see or hear of this. Offer masses to be said, rosaries for the 'poor soul'.

4. **By Special Grace.** A spirit may be allowed to visit a family member one last time, perhaps even on death, or sometime after such as on the anniversary of their death, or to help console a mourning loved one. Since this is a onetime apparition, we don't pay attention to this case, as it doesn't qualify as a "problem haunting" or a "haunting" in general. The act is usually done and over with and they typically never return. I should note this one is common to demons in their masquerade, don't be so willing to think dead relatives visits you more than once!

5. **Warning.** Another very rare case is when an apparition warns of a pending doom, this might apply to case #4 "*by special grace*" however the reason for the appearance is more alarming. The warning could be something to avoid death, injury, or financial decisions. Now I can say if the warning didn't help you in any way to avoid the pending trauma, it was very likely not from a person or angel with God. In every case of a "good" spirit, there was still time to make amends, change plans, make decisions to divert you from the fate.

6. **Messengers.** As opposed to a warning as with the above case, the "message" doesn't warn of impeding danger or future events. Instead the message might be something simple and directed to a loved one saying "*They are OK*", a request to "*pray from them*" or the more dramatic, but extremely rare, revealing a location where their body may lie in an improper burial, such as in a shallow grave in a previously unknown location. The message might also be to locate personal belongings, even 'valuables' such as hidden money, deeds to property. There was an old "Abbot and Costello" movie called "Hold that Ghost" that portrayed Lou Costello as a ghost from the 18th century, who lingered here for 200 years, and tried to reveal a location of a document that cleared his and another person's name of being a "traitor".

7. **To reveal their KILLERS.** Another extremely rare scenario is when the spirit is trying to reveal the killers, as with the movie "Ghost". On a side note. We should note human spirits we considered as "good" will never be the ones to carry out an act of 'revenge' in bringing the demise of their killers. There is strong evidence that such a

revenge might take place, but it would be a **TYPE: EVIL HUMAN** or **INHUMAN** spirit.

8. **General Purgatory Ghost.** As none of the above examples apply, the appearance of the spirit has long been considered by the church as an indication of a need to pray for that soul who lingers in the home or property location. They might be there for a variety of reasons as I detail in part in the section on "Purgatory". And please remember, regardless of the TYPE: 'good' or 'evil' spirit, prayers will only help the situation. To help toward 'deliverance' or helping the spirit to 'pass on' to the next phase, which might be another phase of Purgatory, or onward to Heaven.

The learned Protestant, Dr. Jeremy Taylor, writes:
> "We find by the history of the maccabees, that the Jews did pray and make offerings for the dead which appears by other testimonies, and by their form of prayer, still extant, which they used in the captivity. Now it is very considerable that since Our Blessed Savior did reprove all the evil doctrines of the Scribes and Pharisees, and did argue concerning the dead and the resurrection, yet he spoke no word against this public practice but left it as he found it which he who came to declare to us all the will of His Father, would not have done, if it had not been innocent, pious and full of charity. The practice of it was at first, and was universal; it being plain in Tertultian and St. Cyprian."

WHY WE NEED TO UNDERSTAND

Purgatory is an important concept to grasp because it can often explain the existence of ghost's manifesting their presence in this world. So you need to understand the concept of these other netherworld regions beyond a simple Heaven/Hell. To truly know the origins of many ghosts.

Where does a man go if he dies before he is able to repent his sin(s)?

Do all suicides go to hell? **No.**

A 'Purgatory', to the spirit, is a last hope for the otherwise 'hopeless', a middle road between Heaven and Hell. A place of penance, lessons to learn, or cleansing and preparation before 'meeting your maker', yes there are many levels...

It's the community service sentenced after death, as opposed to life imprisonment (Hell) or getting off without a warning. (Heaven).

Excuse the metaphors, but it is a good way of saying there has to logically be a 'Purgatory'. Not everyone is prepared before death to meet our maker. Say a person dies suddenly in a car crash. No time for absolution or repenting. According to what many Fundamentalist Protestant Christians believe here, that person would therefore go to 'Hell'. However this form of black and white only thinking is far from the truth.

Some might have us believe mass murderer Jeffery Domer, if he converted on his death bed, could go straight to Heaven? And escape a form of restitution for all of the lives he took and the pain he caused? I don't think so. No more than the court system would let him off with only a 'warning'. So beyond the notion of only 'black and whites', there are many shades of gray that Catholics call Purgatory. Just to say there is 'no such place' is the same as saying God is not as fair as man is here on earth in the court system. Does the judge only offer two possible sentences? Death row, or go Scot free? Again there are no such absolutes in life…

…or death. Every person's case is different and will be judged accordingly after death.

It is not ours to judge. Just as some say that 'all suicides go to Hell', but I see this as not 'fair'. Sometimes that person is not in their right mind, and surely God would not hold them to such absolutes? To refuse to believe that there is a chance at Heaven even after death is a thing of hope; I will never be sure why so many are against this two-thousand plus year old belief.

Somehow along the transitions of the new Christian religions, all have forgotten about this place Purgatory. It is an important thing to grasp because it can explain the presence of ghosts many times. It is so much more cozy to think we might all go to Heaven I suppose that a customized 'feel good' version of the Christian faith is going to tell people what they want to hear. Like Billy Graham in a notion all you have to do is "Accept Jesus as your personal savior" and you will go to Heaven. This "Middle" world is to be a place for souls to bear their penance, purifying, cleansing their hearts. A place of 'absolution', of preparation for Heaven for those who are not worthy of Heaven, or deserving of Hell. "Praying for the dead" is mentioned in the oldest existing bible (in Greek) one that existed long before Luther saw it fit to edit the bible to his preferences. Don't try to conceive how long one goes there or who does, etc. -or consider this as a "Catholic" belief as well. Those who refuse to believe this concept of Purgatory simply because "Catholics" believe in it are fooling themselves over a mindless prejudice. No one is asking you to leave your faith, just know <u>what works</u>. Be armed and ready with all you may need.

When I was a teen, I began a short lived study of 'Buddhism', because of an interest in that Chinese 'philosophy' while learning 'Chinese Gung-Fu'. As I also continued to be educated as to the 'origins of ghosts' in unrelated studies, and through personal experiences, I strayed back to my family's religion as "Catholic". Which already had an answer, far back into history with the details of "Purgatory", but not a common thing taught at church as it once was some time ago. Especially in the details of what this 'phase of existence' really entailed.

It was more of the same talk of a sort of 'fire and brimstone', which tells us so little of the true accounts, that I and others might be interested in knowing.

Again, I am not trying to sell, or tell you that you 'must' understand the other realms where the soul can go besides 'Heaven' and 'Hell'.

1) Some departed souls benefit from prayers, and sometimes even appear to relatives or friends to request prayers. Regardless, prayers more often lead to effective "ghost busting" by either helping to release the spirit from this "limbo" state, or by warding them off if it is evil. (You fundamentalists ask yourselves this: **"Now why would a 'demon' ask for prayers?"**

2) The spirits are bound to a routine or state, until a certain time. Often the time never expires during the lifetime of a house owner who frequently sees the apparition. And the generations that follow might report to have seen the same vision over the coming years.

IMPORTANT!
Understanding the real reasons as to 'why' the 'good spirits' would ever make themselves known to the living is crucial in concluding as to their true origins. Therefore you are able to decide how to handle it. A vital tool is a real knowledge of these 'facts'.

'BIBLE ONLY' FUNDAMENTALISM

Fundamentalist will attempt to argue:

"Where do you find Purgatory and praying for the dead in the Bible?"
"Purgatory is a place and state where those go for a time, who die with no un- repented mortal sins on their souls, but

who still have either venial sins, or who still have temporal punishment due either for venial sins or repented mortal sins."
- Rev. Arthur W. Terminiello, 1956.

We can prove the existence of Purgatory from Holy Scripture and from reason.

1. **OLD TESTAMENT** ... in II Maccabees we read:
"And making a gathering, he sent twelve thousand drachms of silver to Jerusalem for sacrifice to be offered for the sins of the dead. ... It is therefore a holy and wholesome thought to pray for the dead that they may be loosed from sin."

Among non-Catholics this book is generally not accepted as the word of God. However, no one denies that it 'is' a reliable book of history. As such, it proves that the Jews believed in the existence of a place in the next world where sins 'could' be forgiven.

We know this cannot be 'Hell' from which there is no escape; nor can it be Heaven, for nothing unclean can enter there. We know also that Christ did not correct this belief as he would have done if it were not true.

2. **NEW TESTAMENT** ...

(a) In the Apocalypse, (XXI, 27), we are told:
"And there shall not enter into it anything defiled. ..."
If there were no Purgatory, this would mean that God would have to send a person who died with only the slightest venial sin on his soul to Hell with all those who have committed horrible crimes.

(b) In St. Matthew's Gospel (V, 26) St. Matthew is here speaking of Hell. But by inference we are told that there 'is' a place we can 'leave' in the next world:

"**Amen, I say to thee, thou wilt not come out from it til thou has paid the last farthing.**"

From this text we conclude that there must be a place of restitution in the afterlife, or a 'third place', where some atonement, can, be made after death. Again, this 'cannot' be Hell as we know it, nor can it be heaven, for nothing unclean can enter Heaven. There must then be a 'third place'. And this place we call "Purgatory."

(c) Again we read in St. Matthew (XII, 32) that the sin against the Holy Ghost cannot be forgiven 'either' in this world 'or' in the world to come. We conclude from this that there 'are' sins which can be forgiven in the next world.

3. **SIMPLE 'REASONING' ALSO PROVES** the existence of Purgatory. Most people are not such great sinners when they die as to deserve Hell; nor are most people prepared to go immediately to Heaven. God's goodness and mercy demands a place of purifying for the slight sins of those who have tried to live according to His law. Again a phase of existence before heaven that is for restitution and is a place of preparation for heaven is not a bad place. It is a second hope.

THE BIBLE IS AN INCOMPLETE BOOK OF CHRISTIAN DOCTRINE

When Nero burned Rome; said 'five-thousand' scrolls of scripture were destroyed by fire. Later, Emperor Constantine, a born again Christian, after declaring Christianity as the "*Official*" religion of Rome, sought the help of higher clergy to compile the first known bible in book form. So when the first book of the bible was assembled, it was incomplete, so those of you who say "that's not in the bible" Read on its history before using that as an argument.

The bible is in fact an incomplete compilation of the scripture, and in being incomplete it should not be used alone to 'reverse engineer' yet another offspring Christian Denomination. Then some 1000 years later along came…

MARTIN LUTHER's REFORMATION

We have to cover Martin Luther since he thought himself righteous in removing seven books from the bible that his own personal beliefs disagreed with, and various texts from the gospels. Martin Luther thought himself to be righteous in taking out *eleven* sections of the bible; including **seven** entire books of the bible that he had also changed the text such as this line in Romans.

First this was translated from the Greek bible from 400 A.D. into English: (*Romans 3:28*)
"for we reconcile that a man is justified by faith independently of the works of the law."

Now Luther's translation, which is changed to help support his view:
"Therefore we conclude that a man is justified by faith alone without the deeds of the law"

Note the words "*Conclude*" And "*Reconcile*" in the first part.
In the second part "*ALONE*" and "*Independently*"

The third part "*without the*" versus "*of the*" a large difference of words.
Almost complete opposites. And definitely changing the meaning of the scripture.

With biased translations, these people interject their own ideas during translation. They read it as they want it to be read.

Sometimes changing a word from "Many" to "One" for example can totally change the meaning of the text and gospel truth. No wonder there is a said twenty-thousand or so errors in the King James Versions.

Another contradiction from a bad translation:

Genesis 23:1 *"God tempted Abraham."*

James 1:13 *"God tempts no one"*.

The word *"tempted"* for some reason, replaced *"tested"*. Although we can be 'tested' through 'temptation', they are not one in the same.

Several others are mentioned here:
http://www.totse.com/en/religion/christianity/contradk.html

It is a huge undertaking in translating the bible, one can grow weary, and they may not do it carefully being anxious to get it done. Some may not be as fluent in their languages but too proud to recognize it? Humans make mistakes, and the fact is if the Holy Ghost truly enlightened these people, even Luther, as they translated the bible, there would be no errors. Some things are considered contradictions when they are merely the old language text misinterpreted. Sometimes you are reading a metaphor, and analogy, not a literal. I believe some become confused over this.

In Jesus Saying 'To turn the other cheek' and '…the body is the temple of the Holy Spirit'. Many think the first means to not defend yourself. This is meant verbal, as we are to defend our well being mentally, physically and spiritually as it is the temple of the Holy Ghost.

BIBLICAL "REVERSE ENGINEERING":

So with an incomplete bible, and with the 'Good Book' with these 'errors', we see every time someone reads the bible, another misinterpretation may occur in addition to being mislead by faulty translations. And again, yet another denomination calling itself 'Christian' evolves.

In Genesis for another example, older bibles have the word "She" in it while all newer bibles have "He". How can you mix up male and female references during translation?
(Genesis 3:15)
So the argument `"That's not in the bible"` doesn't fly with me. Especially when church reformer Martin Luther removed as many as 11 sections, which included the book of *"II Maccabees"* which told of how even before Christ, there was a belief in 'praying for the dead'. So we know that a notion of a 'Purgatory' like existence even predates Christianity itself.

The point here is so many read the bible and interpret something entirely different. I have to say this better supports having a doctrine, and that the bible is a companion to that doctrine. And that bible alone teaching is improper, mainly because it is incomplete, contains many errors. Imagine building a high rise using plans that have these concerns? How stable would it be?

PRAYERS FOR THE DEAD.
Learn from history.

(PRAYERS can be found in back of this book)

MYTH IS OFTEN SEEDED FROM FACT

Many make the mistake in assuming it is of ignorance and mythology, when you'll find that even myth is based often on fact. Overtime it can be distorted just from the grapevine it can deteriorate from person to person. Just like urban legends. It may be better to assume that 'all' myths are indeed based in part on fact and to seek out the origin of truth.

So now that you understand the belief in the other place in the world beyond, you understand a large part of why ghost are here. It will all start to make sense now unlike it never has before. As I said, if you seek to understand why you are haunted by an apparition of a person, you can better deal with it now. I say pray regardless.

UNDERSTAND THESE FACTS AND POINTS:

- ✓ Don't dispel the methodology and faith of other denominations simply because they don't share the beliefs you do. Yes, holy water, and some objects, blessed by certain priests do in fact affect spirits. The Kirlian camera shows that the aura of blessed water is ten times the strength in its 'aura' than it was before the blessing. This is also true of objects and water that are near those who pray. So this can say that the place of worship itself is a holy place and not simply an 'Auditorium' for a gathering. These places traditionally were sought to be a sanctuary against true evil in the past and as also portrayed in many Hollywood movies.

- ✓ Purgatory is a 'phase of after-life existence'. Exactly what it might entail is custom to each individual person. We do know from research ghosts can be temporarily imprisoned there, and also released from there with prayers in which they at times have been known to ask the witness(es) to their visitations to "pray for them" This is a common thought of history, being portrayed as so, in famous stage plays as Hamlet, and A Christmas Carol.

✓ "Ghosts are not always evil", and are not always 'demons'.

CASE EXAMPLE: GHOSTLY APPARITION: PROM TEENAGER.

It is a now common belief that ghosts are sometimes here because of their *'unfinished business*es. You'll soon connect the dots as to why tragic sudden death creates hauntings. Let me throw this case to you, now that you are armed with the belief of 'Purgatory'.

In the story, two teenagers, in a male and female, travel down the dark road just after their *'high school prom'*. They 'fooled around' a bit at a popular but secluded place, while they got drunk on the drinking of 'spiked punch' and bottles of wine. A fatal car crash occurs, and the girl is killed instantly, yet the male driver survived. That was 10 years ago, and locals when driving by the former crash site on occasion report of seeing the girl's apparition walking on the road in her prom dress.
One story had the girl actually get a ride from a local, and she was taken to a house upon her directions. When they arrived the girl was gone from the back seat. Think about this, why would this girl be earth bound repeating her attempts to get home?
To those who don't believe in a phase of existence beyond a 'Heaven' or a 'Hell', where do you suppose this spirit is? Some school of theological understanding dictates that your destination is set and applied within 40 days after your death. So why is she seen here? She died so fast she couldn't repent her sins; her 'Purgatory' could simply be to repeat the last scenario of her life. As I said before, many think the Purgatory is a 'fiery temporary hell'; it is often more of a 'nightmare' for some. The 'purge' of a 'metaphysical fire', is in the least a last

stage to cleanse the soul before entering Heaven. Why is the negative scenario so often 'preached' as though this is what it is like the whole time for everyone in Purgatory? It's perhaps to discourage people from an idea that such a place is a failsafe, therefore it may be viewed as not such a bad place when falling short of Heaven. And to discourage a notion of not trying as hard to follow the commandments and to reach heaven, but allowing yourself to think Purgatory is 'not such a bad place'. And falling short of the goals, in letting one take on a lukewarm lackluster life as a 'Christian' . And to try hard to not even wind up in 'Purgatory' as it isn't a place of 'fun' and happiness' it is indeed 'time served' a place for 'lessons learned', that were not learned in life. A place of penance, that you should focus your life on avoiding.

THE BATTLE BEGINS
SPIRITUAL WARFARE SOLUTIONS

THE SPIRITUAL ARMOR OF GOD:

1) "Loins girded in truth"-
When the truth of God is with us, we do not fall prey to the devil's lies and deceits. We can hold up the truth as a defense, and the truth will win out over the demonic battle we are faced with. Perhaps it is important that it is mentioned as being around the "loins" insofar as we must protect our sexuality since it is one of the important ways in which we are most God-like, through our capacity to participate in the creation of new life.

2) "Righteousness as a breastplate"-
Our Godly, virtuous, holy lives will and can act as a defense against the evil one. In order to participate in the victory won by Christ, we must live as Christ lived, we must live as righteous individuals. It is righteousness that is able to face and overcome evil. The breastplate protects our heart; our hearts must not be infected by sin, but must remain pure through our righteous living.

3) "Feet shod in readiness for the Gospel of peace"-
The Gospel preaches peace, for Christ is named as the "Prince of Peace." We must not resort to physical violence in our battle against evil. We must be ready to live peaceful lives. "Peace" will be able to stand up against violence and overcome, because "peace" does not play according to the rules of "violence." It is only in playing by our Christian rules, not by the enemy's rules, that we'll attain victory over the evil one.

4) "Faith as a shield"-
Faith is able to lead us to salvation. It is able to deflect the lies of the evil one, and thus work to secure our salvation. The one who enters battle without being sufficiently armed with faith will never be able to attain true and lasting victory. Faith gives us the ability to endure the battle of Christian life, move forward, and usurp enemy ground. We must go into battle with faith.

5) "the Helmet of salvation"-
We are able to win the battle against the evil one when we are confident that Christ has paid the price for our sin, thus enabling us to enter into the salvation He offers us. Salvation is for the head- it protects our greatest asset, our head, that member of the body that directs all of our actions. Our lives must be guided by our salvation attained for us in Jesus Christ.

6) "the Sword of the Spirit"-
This is the Word of God. Not only can it refer to the Sacred Scriptures, which we must be familiar with (for, as St. Jerome says, "Ignorance of scripture is ignorance of Christ") but it can also refer to the Divine Word of God, Jesus Christ Himself. We must be knowledgeable about God's revelation in scripture, and about His revelation to us in the person of His Son. This is the only offensive weapon mentioned, the rest are all defensive. We strike with the sword; we wound the evil one through the promises of God as revealed in scripture and in Jesus Christ Himself.

I - PREPARATIONS

To combat evil you yourself have to remove yourself as much as possible from things that are 'negative', in other words:

```
"You can't expect to rebuke one demon
while you yet appease another"
```

BASIC 'SAFE' ADVICE TO "FIELD INVESTIGATORS":

For some of us, it is necessary as a "Field Investigator" to thoroughly investigate claims. For others, "ghost hunting" can be fun, enlightening, a recreational pastime, and even a serious scientific endeavor. I don't recommend it. The fact that you are treading in areas of the unknown is always a concern. To both I say, always be prepared "Just-in-case", as many of the spirits that dwell within these hauntings are not good natured, and can harm you or affect you in a variety of ways.

For 'field Investigators', as this more applies to "ghost hunters", as these are what I call "leisure hunts". Where you are not there to help with a "problem haunting", you are a "Ghost Hunter" more so there for 'recreation' and not a supposed "Ghost Buster" or a "Field Investigator".*(although some of these tips apply there too)*

THE TOP THINGS TO NOTE ARE THE FOLLOWING GOING ON 'ANY' INVESTIGATION:
(These are not in any particular order)

1) Take appropriate measures to **protect yourself**, "Just in case" - as to not bring home attachments (i.e. prayers, wearing holy symbols etc.) Say your 'protection prayer' before entering the premises, and later special prayers to detach any hitch-hikers after the hunt is over. Have someone carry a vile of holy water in case of an emergency, to break off attack that might occur. Be sure each split team has at least one closed vile in their pocket or bag. Wear a "Saint Benedict" medal on a neck chain and concealed under the shirt, as to not 'provoke' intentionally.

2) **Be careful in "assuming"** a type of spirit might reside at any given location. And don't assume a "demon" is merely a "ghost". If establishing communication, and without the before mentioned protection advice followed, then suddenly your life can take a drastic change, as it is affected by the would-be spirit(s).
As I stress throughout this book. Don't be fooled by what they might pretend to be the 'ghost of a little girl', as the evil ones can often pretend to be, to lure you into the drama. Don't "trust" that the spirit is 'harmless'. We all might criticize those who call everything "demonic", but honestly, assuming this might keep one on their toes better than the average person.

3) **RESPECT!** Any outright 'disrespect', in trying to provoke the spirits in order to get "EVP recordings" and other captured

data/evidence. Again as with #2, as we often don't know the nature of the spirits as in, is it good/evil, demonic or not. You might be attacked or affected even much later simply by "disrespecting" in this matter. Show some respect!

4) **Avoid 'Religious Provocation'**. Sporting holy symbols that provoke more than they do protect, is a sort of 'unintentional religious provocation". Which to the demons, is the same as 'picking a fight' with them. Keep all holy symbols tucked away, as with crucifixes and so forth. Even the Saint Benedict medal, you are not there to provoke in any way in ghost hunting. *(Provoking is always a thing considered controversial, even when you MUST attain evidence in a client based situation.)* So keep your blessed rosaries, and relics of saints, out of the pocket and into the glove box of your car when on the hunt. Keep in mind that you are currently doing a "field investigation", and you are not (yet) there to make war and proceed with methods of "deliverance". We also want to avoid saying 'prayers of protection' on-site, as you are there to merely observe, and gather information and it is your responsibility to not do things that might affect the place you are investigating. *(Until you are ready for the battle)* This also includes ANY prayers, or rituals onsite, spoken or performed by ANY faith or belief system.

5) **Don't be so quick to conclude** based on supposed evidence which can be 'misleading'. Be leery of what information would-be spirits might try to convey. Again the "drama" can draw you in 'hook, line and sinker'. Remember "Stir of Echoes?" *(The movie w/ Kevin Bacon),* more often that is 'not' a reality. And they find nothing but an expensive 'financial drain' on tearing up walls and floors to find the supposed spirit's "corpse." Be leery of what you are told by these spirits. Many Hollywood movies can make us believe that these scenarios are more often truer than they are, when they are quite rare. So avoid acting too quick on what could very well be a 'potential wild goose chase', that is in part based on info

received from the 'otherworldly' spirits. And by the same token, what a "Psychic-Medium", might come up with, as many are not gifted with their abilities from 'God'.

6) **Hold on** to stair case rails and potential sections of the building or property where all it takes is a "push' to send you tumbling down a staircase or falling into a hole. Need I say more of this?

7) **Get your sleep**, don't take medicine, drinks, etc. that impair you. This will also open you up to spiritual dangers as well, as merely stumbling around in the darkness. As I mention earlier of the dangers of 'altered states of consciousness', in opening yourself up to spiritual attack. This can include 'step in possessions'.

8) **Go in with FAITH not FEAR**. Obviously, fear might send you running through a dark hall and really hurting yourself. But beyond that, fear also 'feeds' evil. And it might make you more of a target.

9) **If the place starts to "rub you the wrong way"**, don't stay inside the premises, leave even if only for a "breather". For example, some might feel it is 'hard to breath', feel a sense of evil, nausea, or 'feel faint', as the site begins to affect them the wrong way. Get out and away, head to the car, maybe start your 'purging' with prayers and so forth to 'detach' any spirits that 'might be' affecting you. *(Just to be on the safe side.)* Don't try to 'suck it up', tell your team that you need to 'take a break' and get a 'breather'. These things happen often enough don't feel bad, just pay attention your body and mind when you are at these places you might pick up something others don't.

10) Have at least one person **research the location** layout prior. In addition to my recommendation as to try to be aware of the potential 'type' of spirit there, as well as the location's own 'pitfalls'. In larger places, it is important to be aware of

the 'exits', and the layout. It will be easier to get a 'breath of fresh air' as well as to 'vacate' in case of emergencies.

Finally, if you are "hunting" you are not in a "battle phase". You are there more so to observe. Not to feed, poke sticks at, or kick the fence to stir up the spirits that haunt a location. Don't forget that!
The only real 100% safe investigating is to not go investigate at all. Try to consider these more so the 'spiritual aspects' of arming oneself with the knowledge of what dangers might lurk at any given location and what you can do to best protect yourself from them.

DON'T GO IN WITH 'ALL GUNS BLAZING'

Consider this fictitious scenario:

Investigators determine the house has a 'demonic entity'. The owners agree to the offered solution of a 'cleansing', someone walks around the house with holy water (example), saying prayers and so forth. And all is quiet during this process, and then soon it is completed. The home owners thank the team; they pack up and drive home, basking in a glow of accomplishment.
A bit premature however...
So as the evening streams into later hours of the night, it becomes time for 'payback'. The home owners suddenly hear a ruckus downstairs, unlike what they have experienced before. It sounds like a barroom brawl, and it is coming from the family room.
They might call the police and they later find, the room is trashed, furniture overturned, the big screen TV is cracked, stereo receiver is in pieces with the speaker cones punctured. The walls covered with graffiti, as thought scribbled with a red lipstick citing foul language. `"No sign of forced entry, none else has a key..."` The policeman notes, and leaves it as a 'mystery'.

The end result: In all a few thousand dollars in damage and a more distraught family, the retaliation might have also weakened their faith in God.

...And why did this happen?   How were these people helped?

An ineffective 'cleansing' or 'blessing' as well as the other methods of deliverance can often do more harm than good. Especially if it is not done properly, and by the right people. In other words, the 'beehive' was shaken, and not removed, and while the team gloated in a 'job well done', things only got worse upon their withdrawal. What this group did, to a lesser degree, was in effect a 'religious provocation'. A varied by method, sort of ritual some proclaimed "Religious Demonologists" do to purposely force the demon to reveal it's presence, as to better validate a demonic haunting. *(Referred to earlier in the book where I discuss 'Religious provocation')*

In other scenarios, 'payback' can be in the form of a 'physical attack'. The family goes to sleep, and closes their eyes, in a trusting of the 'strangers with meters'. With hope that it may truly be over, and they can live their lives normally. Then around the later hours of night, the attack begins. For one case example, it was 'strangulation' as the woman of the house slept. This is more so done as a 'warning', and show of what you are dealing with, and not a *'demonic death'* to be carried out. But it is indeed a 'punishment' for the failed attempts of a 'cleansing', and we have to realize these things in the least cause the demonic a certain 'metaphysical pain'. If the demon could kill you, it would, it really hasn't gained power from the anger it simply was displaying what it is capable of in the current stage of demonic 'manifestation'. Which at this point would be an 'oppression' stage or later.

Bottom line is to not go in with all guns blazing until you know what you are dealing with. Would you go in with a butterfly net to catch a dragon? Be sure to assess carefully in a possible demonic involvement and at what level it may have already manifested. If it can manifest in a daytime sunlit kitchen and likes to spin wall hung crucifixes upside down. *(As this may be an indication of the work of a higher more powerful demon or "devil").* One solution doesn't fit all demonic cases, so keep the 'blessing' guns holstered, until you learn it is going to help, not make things worse. And doing it yourself is a last resort; remember the guidelines for proper preparation before doing battle. And try to get a true clergyman whenever possible, such as a Roman Catholic Priest. (You'll want to a*void the clergy from the "Old Catholics" denominations here in the U.S. especially.)*

A few note to recap:

- ✓ Try to carefully avoid stirring things up.

- ✓ Do your prayers of protection before entering the premises, and off property.

- ✓ Leave the metaphoric 'guns' in the glove boxes and tool cases. Rather than to flash crucifixes, relics and splashing holy water like some cereal box licensed holy man.

- ✓ You don't want to rattle the cage then leave the poor family to deal with it alone!
  Be prepared to start what you have finished and don't be so arrogant in the thought you can handle it alone without a priest or relevant ordained clergy.

- ✓ Call on your 'prayer groups' to begin prayers for 'deliverance' ASAP, the more people the better.

- ✓ Demonic spirits are not driven away in a timely manner at your convenience. So if you have to be at work the next morning, schedule a set of dates when you can be there for them, say after the initial blessing or 'exorcism/cleansing'.

At least maybe for a couple of days.

✓ Don't forget these aren't the ghosts of mourning Civil War widows; they are malevolent, powerful, dark entities that should not be taken lightly.

Sorry to get preachy here folks, but we can't simply ride off into the sunset, or moonlight, until the job is done. After all, the goal should be as with a 'closer' and not merely some reckless "Ghost Buster" mimicking 'The Atlantic Paranormal Society'.

"PRAYER GROUPS" NEED TO ALSO PRAY FOR THEIR OWN PROTECTION

Simply praying for those afflicted by different levels of demonic infestations can draw a 'pay back' onto you and even your immediate family. You might be visited by a shadowy being, be physically attacked, or more commonly affected with a string of 'financial hardships'. Just be aware, that these things have surfaced from teams that weren't even aware that this scenario 'can be' true. So please note.

Say some of the prayers for yourself as well at least once every three days when offering prayers for these potential demonic cases. Even as if you don't know the haunting is in fact "demonic" don't take any chances! As many of us know, it can be as simple as talking to the client on the phone to draw in a dark spirit that night who is none pleased with your assistance. More often however, and sadly, the "payback" comes in the form of "back luck" and misfortunes. Be aware of this when you are any level of a "Spiritual Warrior" to wear armor and pray for your own protection as well as the others by default. Remember, even as with this lower level role as a 'Prayer Warrior', it still is not to be taken lightly, as you too have an important role in the tasks at hand.

And you too can feel the effects of demonic spirits that are not too happy with your meddling in their affairs in 'spiritual warfare' and you assist in your way.

"FAITH AND GRACE"

Faith is an important part of our lives, but how does it empower us in helping clients in investigations and our own protection against evil entities?

Let me work with some metaphors:
Faith is the control valve, less faith restricts the flow, and more can completely open up the valve. Now as the 'water pressure' is considered as "God's grace", you can have the valve entirely 'open', and yet only get a 'trickle' of water from the source. This is depending on the "state of grace" you are in. This is dependant not on your 'faith' alone, but level of 'spirituality', how devout you are to your God. In this can go as deep as in your words and actions and even your thoughts. You can have all the faith in the world in God, but it will not help you until you live it! So as for some of the 'Christian-Judeo religions', our actions can lower the 'water pressure', as with our 'sins' through certain words and actions, it will certainly weaken the amount of water flow coming through at the source.

Think of how low confidence can restrict your abilities as a person in life, no matter what your education is, or who you are. It is a lack of 'faith' in oneself. Having low self esteem and little confidence in oneself is restricting you from being your 'fullest', just as our weak faith can restrict God's grace.

Now the sad part is, even some Catholic Priests will often go into spiritual warfare while 'weak of faith', therefore 'weak' of God's grace. And therefore are not going to work well as an instrument of God in "Deliverance". A priest, who goes in to bless a house for example, might be suddenly overcome with 'nausea', breaking out in a sweat and then is forced to quickly excuse himself to make an abrupt exit from the premises. Now as we know in 'Demonology', how dangerous it is to merely shake the bee-hive and to leave the swarm of bees for the family to deal with. Yes, in this case, the priest very likely made things worse. Again as I said, once the battle has begun, you can simply make a quick exit and leave the family alone to take retaliation strikes. So today we have to consider that even many priests are not ready to deal with 'demonic haunts', yet they go in with a false notion that as an 'ordained clergy' they are by default immune to the affects of such evil. And a simple blessing can rid the premises of the problem haunts. This is one reason I warn groups of trying to deal with demonic hauntings, if they underestimate the manifested power of the demon(s). Even forty or so years ago, the late Ed Warren would first talk to a priest to see if he was right in his 'faith and grace'.

Lorraine had said that "*a few questions would tell Ed if or not this priest was the 'right one' for helping in this case*". So a few questions, as Ed Warren would ask, could very well reveal the 'man of the cloth', but I wish it was that simple now-a days for the rest of us. It is getting hard to make a choice now however, and at times you find in smaller cities, a shortage of priests has one going between two parishes in two cities or towns that are an hour apart. So if one priest is say 'reluctant' to visit the family, this may be a bigger thorn in the foot of closing the case. Perhaps part of the reason for a rise in laity 'Demonologists', and the need for such a book as this to help educate, as they are far less clergy with the knowledge, understanding of these things I speak of.

And yes, the level of 'faith and grace' does really play a vital part.

So being an ordained priest with the sacrament of "Holy Orders", isn't alone enough to effectively handle the demonic. You have to live your life on a higher path, pray to stay strong in faith and grace. And priests can be dealing with exorcisms for forty years and still will retreat to three days of prayer, and fasting prior to an exorcism. Including rosaries and special masses offered up as to help the victim and to better help him to stand firm in battle. No one is truly safe to where they can simply lay back and do God's work. Much prayer in the least is required before, during, and after closing the case. As clients are often a 'client for life', there is a need to keep in contact with them, for quite some time after the infestation has been cleared, so this is a 'good protocol' for many reasons.

CATHOLICISM FOR DUMMIES

If you surf around the web you find some ignorance that is very offensive about the Catholic/Orthodox faith. This same ignorance separates these two Christian denominations when it comes to methods of "Deliverance/Exorcisms" and the understanding of "Demonology". I see true prejudice, as usual based on "ignorance" of the Catholic faith, and it's history.

CATHOLIC METHODS VERSUS PROTESTANT:
Since this still is a problem in the way some denominations are so "Anti-Catholic" still even today. Let us hope through 'education' this gap in the bridge between Catholic and Orthodox and other Christian denominations can be 'closed'.

The main differences that apply to "Deliverance" are:

1. Intercession of Mary and the Saints. The difference between "Honor and Venerate" (as we do Mary and the Saints, and "Worship and Adore" as we do Jesus.

2. Crucifixes - versus Crosses. Many fundamentalist fear this may be what was referred to as a "graven image", with the figure of Jesus on the cross as it is on a necklace, rosary, on the wall in your home. The demonic will recoil at a site of a crucifix, while with a 'plain' blank cross; it will most often result in no reaction. It varies if it was blessed or often carried on oneself especially when prayers are said. Although one may find confidence and faith in an object of sentiment, the object itself is nothing of power against the demon as the crucifix is. In truth, the image alone of the crucified savior repels demons, even the higher rank demons which may endure the metaphysical pain it causes, still will have a threshold of weakness where they cannot stay exposed full front, in proximity of it for long. Here you must learn from others who have experienced this fact first hand! We cannot turn our backs on two-thousand years of history in 'spiritual warfare'.

3. Holy Water – blessed objects. Universally speaking, praying over objects can energize them with certain 'positive energy' of Jesus/God. A blessing is directing this energy (graces) to that object, place or person. Water is a pure element and in itself already a positive force against evil spirits. Blessed it is charged with even more power. *(See the section where I detail this further)*

4. Baptism - Infant baptism is important enough for it to be a key question when we ask about a child who may be affected by negative spirits. Beyond a mere anointing, christening, or a 'blessing', a Catholic baptism for example has a "minor (simple) exorcism" built in as to break any possible attachments as well as generational curses. Talk about giving a kid a fresh start on life! That is exactly what it does...

5. The Rosary – Hail Mary - I have often said in itself, the rosary is a one prayer fits all. Which means a daily rosary can keep one on the right path in life (if said right) to where our true needs will be met alone. This includes protection from evil spirits. As you will see, the "Hail Mary" is made up of 'quotes' from biblical scripture primarily.

"Hail Mary Full of Grace, the Lord is with thee" - Said by the Angel Gabriel.
"Blessed are though among woman and Blessed is the fruit of Thy Womb Jesus" - As said by Elizabeth when Mary visited her to find she was expecting a baby (John the Baptist).
"Holy Mary Mother of God, Pray for us sinners now and at the hour of our death amen" As I mention this is a part that asks for intercession as when we are most vulnerable at our hour of death. And demons might come calling at a last effort, to try to turn our minds and our hearts away from God.

Some NDE's (near death experiences), have said "Mother Mary had appeared and her bright light ran off these 'ravaging wolves' in demons from the person's bedside.

I can attest from experience alone, that demons do recoil to things that represent our "Blessed Mother". The rosary for example is alone a great tool of "deliverance", the Immaculate Heart of Mary painting can be used for religious provocation in itself. Mary is considered the "New Eve", a biblical prophecy has her bringing defeat to Satan and his minions, just as Satan through a Woman brought the fall of mankind, God will use a Woman to bring the fall of Satan. Mary is also considered the one to take place where Lucifer once sat, as the <u>highest angel in Heaven.</u>

We also read in Genesis:
"<u>She</u> shall Crush your head and you Shall Lie in wait for <u>HER</u> heal".
This is why you see Mary standing on the head of a serpent on some statues. As I mention Crucifixes recoil demons, pictures that are divinely inspired work as the Immaculate Heart image, also are both an object of hatred and fear for the demonic.

Interestingly, this has revealed itself even before the reason was explained.

FORMER CATHOLICS AND CHRISTIANS

I realize that bad experiences from those hard core, 'bible pounding', and 'fire and brimstone' type 'Christian' ministers have been counter productive and drove many people away from the faith. As the Christian faith is poorly represented by many. And instead of the blame merely going only towards these 'negative' preachers, ministers and priests alone. They sadly begin to reject the 'core doctrine' and 'beliefs' entirely, that is Christianity in general. Still, as you might have strayed from the faith, and become an agnostic even.

One cannot argue that at least eight of the Ten Commandments are a great set of universal rules to live by. Lest we forget **`"Love thy Neighbor as thyself"`**. They are guidelines as to how to treat others. What I went on to say was that we should not let a bad experience with hard core types steer us away from the reality of demons. Also do not let your faith detour you away from the truth. These are inhuman, malicious entities, evil by their very nature. No matter if you place a 'fallen angel' original on them or not. It should be understood that their behavior alone suggests that they are fallen angels. And we rely upon this piece of information to better understand how they infest one's lives, from 'temptation' to 'possession'. So as we find that all of the Christian denominations do not agree on demons, and the belief varies enough to say they are missing the whole picture.

As I said, one point here is that the bible is an incomplete book as I mentioned it's history earlier in this book. Most certainly, it would be absurd to believe all of the Christian Theology and teachings are in a bible so short of pages? This is why a bible only teaching can be lacking, even some key elements.

I make this point in saying that some Fundamentalist Christians are judging Catholics/Orthodox, unfairly based on their own derived interpretations of the bible.

History shows in part the validity of the Catholic Church, right at the foot heals of the Protestant uprising in Europe. As with the case of the Exorcism of 'Nicole Aubrey' is a great example of how this new and modified version of Christianity fell short of a successful deliverance. And ultimately it was a Roman Catholic Bishop who in the end successfully freed this woman of the demonic spirits that infested her. My point here is in the Protestant reform a great many things were lost that aid in 'spiritual warfare' and the more extreme in "demonic possession. And this is even evident today. As the 'Roman Ritual' Exorcism performed by a "Catholic Exorcist" (priest) is still considered the 'big guns' when all else fails.

Just try to be 'open minded' and not reject what two-thousand years of Christian history has taught us. Simply because of a prejudice taught by your minister or even your mother about "Catholics" and their faith. And realize if Jesus truly considers the Catholic Church to be the "whore of Babylon" mentioned in the bible for example, He would have forsaken it such as it would be rendered nearly powerless in its effectiveness against these evil spirits. Whereas, again, we know quite the contrary is true, just from case study alone.

7. The sign of the cross - Chronicled by Saint Benedict, the sign of the cross alone has worked to expel demons, and is indeed a holy gesture. Not commonly known is that this is more than merely a show of faith or acknowledgment of the Holy Trinity, when Catholics begin and end prayers with the sign of the cross. It is a way to conceal prayers to where they cannot be heard by 'any' of the unworldly minions of Satan. A sort of 'analogy' is a metaphysical 'scramble' of your prayer message so that only God and Heaven can descramble it and hear it. So in beginning and ending a prayer with this symbolic gesture is also a way to mark the beginning and the ending of the "transmission" so to speak.

8. The "HOLY TRINITY"- confusion again is in the idea that "Trinity" is a reference to a Pagan deity. First "trinity" means "the three". But remember we are referring to the "Holy Trinity", which is the same as saying the "Holy Three". God the Father, God the Son, and God the Holy Spirit, I can say that 'all Christians' can agree exist. The 'Holy Trinity' doctrine simply says these are three entities that are one in the same God. As we humans fail to understand some of the great mysteries of God, this too is scrutinized under a sort of ignorance with a pseudo-logical reasoning which fails atrociously.

"There is but One God, the Father." - **1 Corinthians** **8:6**

So who is Jesus? Why do we worship him as Christians? You can't believe in Jesus as the son of God, and also believe that "God the Father, God the Son, God the Holy Spirit, is merely some Gnostic or pagan belief. The "Three" is the *"Holy Trinity"* Catholics refer to, now if you don't believe in Jesus you are not a Christian. And you might make such an argument perhaps. But this goes to show how the bible can be taken out of context.

I will also mention as demonic entities seek to 'mock' the Trinity, we should take opportunity to take occasion to honor the Holy Trinity in prayers for example, such as the before mentioned sign of the cross. Which has a counter effect on the demonic as a "positive" action, in honoring God in this extra way.

THE "ROMAN RITUAL" VS. 20TH CENTURY DELIVERANCE'

As earlier I mention the exorcism of Nicole Aubrey, which resulted in the first compiled version of the "Roman Ritual", in 1566'. I say 'compiled' - because a majority of it consists of prayers, the use of holy symbols and rituals, that were already in practice, but not necessarily combined 'together' for one session. Words and actions not necessarily designed for 'deliverance' and likely not used together as a 'road tested' formulae for practicing clergy to rid one of evil spirits as it came to be in that 16th century. So, in short, after a successful exorcism by the Bishop of Leon, the Roman Ritual was compiled based on those series of rituals and prayers done to expel the said 26 demons that possessed Nicola Aubrey. So, the Roman Ritual was 'field' improvised to a certain extent, and tested on the fly, using a combination of different prayers, holy symbols and other actions. No doubt divinely inspired by the Holy Spirit, I can say because of it's power even today amongst so many denominations and belief systems that have their own form of "exorcisms". The ritual was originally spoken in Latin, the native language of Jesus from Galilee. Crucifixes, holy water, relics of saints, all these things that affect the demons were used. Providing confession, a mass offered for the victim's deliverance and to give them communion is also a part.

Deliverance with other denominations didn't begin to make a scene again until the 20th century, still using the same means of 'laying on of the hands', praying over the possessed, reading biblical passages from psalms for example. The methods are improvised rather than so organized as the Roman Ritual, and although they can take a longer time before the person is free of the infesting demons, they have been quite effective. Which is why, I say to go to other denominations for help, 'after a clear diagnosis', for these 'deliverance sessions. But be mindful as I before mentioned, some denominations are highly prejudice against Catholics and they view the Catholic faith no much better than 'Satanism', which is absurd. And they will force the possessed to renounce the Holy Trinity, The Blessed Mother, and the "Demon of Catholicism". And this is without even recognizing their own 'demons' that are behind this mindset.

The Bottom line:

Prescreen ANYONE you deal with in this to know they are qualified. This is true for many reasons since we are dealing with people here. Consider how careful you might be before recommending a friend to a trustworthy Auto Mechanic, or a 'good' Physician.

YOUR DELIVERANCE TOOLKIT

Your "ARMOR OF GOD" can also include 'physical objects' as well, in sacramentals, blessed oil, salt, holy water, and other holy symbols.

READ THIS FIRST!
Some are concerned about the use of the Saint Benedict Medal, Miraculous Medal, Relic of Saints and others, and their Catholic/Orthodox origins. As you may know, these 'sacramentals' are common to other Demonologists, Exorcists, Catholic Clergy, etc; as effective in protection against evil spirits and demons. And should be used regardless if you are a practicing Orthodox- Catholic or not. We only pray to Mary and the Saints for 'intercession', as I said only to honor and venerate them, and look to them as 'role models'.
(And not worship and adore as we do Jesus)

We read Paul asking the churches to pray for him in **1 Timothy 2:1-4.** This is 'intercession', as when you ask for others to pray for you. As you might call you mother and family and ask if they will pray that you find a job, or that the operation goes well, or for a healthy baby. In this we ask Mary and the saints in the same manner to "pray for us". In short, you can wear these medals and it is a sort of silent prayer ('intercession'), in asking 'Saint Benedict' for example, to pray to God for your protection.

PRECAUTION: AVOID DEMONIC "RETALIATION"

Weak solutions might invite a sort of 'retaliation <u>often occurring</u> that same night, usually when it can wreak the most havoc at it's hour of power around that 2AM-4AM time period. You never want to go into a gun battle with no armor, armed with a butter knife, as you should NOT do anything less than to go over ALL I prescribe here in this book, and follow the advice given. Don't take any chances!
Sometimes we simply do not know at what level the demons have manifested until they are aggravated by lower level solutions provided by some 'Ghost hunting' team's "Holy man". Also always say protection prayers before coming in contact with people, places or things that are haunted or might be haunted. Then after contact say a breaking curses prayer to separate any attachments that might have resulted. This includes phone conversations, e-mail. Just in helping these affected people you can also be affected. Protect yourself; bind them in Jesus name so that you can do your work to help them without demonic payback.

BLESSING OF OBJECTS

Kirlian Camera research actually shows the effectiveness of a priest's blessing in the form of a more prominent 'aura' that encompasses the object. Also when a group of people said prayers around the object it had similar results. In that it in a way is imbued with the 'positive energy' of God from your prayer, which has energized it. Note that simply being near an object for a length of time temporarily charges it a bit, but not in a way a priest's ' blessing' can do with a special positive power. Now since we are on the subject of 'protection' from evil spirits and demons, it should be noted the priest's blessing is proven most effective in the field. Regardless of what you think of the Catholic church, this notion has been field tested by many non-Catholics. Realize the history with the church in affectively exorcising demons, again, such history should not be ignored simply because of a bias against the Catholic faith.

WHY A PRIEST BLESSING?

The Priesthood is a higher path of a religious life, as they choose a vow of poverty, chastity, charity, absence, for example, as to more follow in the footsteps of Jesus. Living a life of more 'positive' lifestyles. Also as the Catholic/Orthodox church believes that after the priest receives the sacrament of 'Holy Orders' one of the 'gifts' they receive is the power to 'bless' objects. Of course the effectiveness of this 'imbued' or 'positive' energy of God, is directly proportional to the piety of the priest.
Lastly, a priest is ordained, it is believed that they are bestowed with a special grace from God with certain "gifts". One being a certain power to imbue an object with God's 'positive' grace through what we call a 'blessing'.

BEESWAX CANDLES

Available at Catholic supply, bees wax is a 'pure' and more 'natural' wax, again I say how 'purity' is a 'positive' to combat their "negative". Again so many times it comes up; this is a battle of positives versus 'negatives'. Opposites repel. The candles should be blessed. One 'cleansing' method for a room or localized area is in placing a lit candle in the center of a dish of 'holy water', with the candle base submersed, these stay lit a long while so you could leave them lit over night. Some age old stories tell of these being lit during storms and the house being untouched while others were devastated around it. 'Votive lights', lit for the departed is an offering such as a 'novena'. You might want to light one at church (and be sure to donate), while you are handling your own, or another family's haunting case.

BLESSED SALT

Any superstition other faiths may attribute to salt warding off evil, can be said gets its roots from the age old Christian-Judeo faith. However, this is 'not' superstition. Salt blessed by the liturgical prayer of a priest may be used by itself, unmixed, as in exorcisms, and formerly in the exorcism prayer at baptism, or it may be mixed with water to make holy water, as the Ritual prescribes *(reminiscent of Elisha's miracle)*. In whichever form, it is intended to be an instrument of grace to preserve one from the corruption of evil occurring as sin, sickness, demonic influence, or other manifestations.

Greg Myers, a seasoned paranormal investigator, here in my home state of Missouri, had discovered firsthand, the effect sea salt has on evil spirits, even unblessed! As he poured a line in front of himself, when he was confronted by a 'shadowy figure', it effectively backed off. Still it is better to have the salt blessed by a priest to make it more effective.

NOTES:

- Blessed Salt can be used for reasons similar to Holy Water.

- Holy Water is a symbol of our baptism -- a symbol of washing clean.

- Salt is a symbol of purifying, preserving.

- The most common use of laity using blessed salt is probably in doing a lay blessing of one's home.

- The salt can be sprinkled around the parameter of one's property, or in windows ledges and places like that.

- A good practice when traveling is to say a blessing and sprinkle salt or holy water in the hotel/motel rooms. Who knows what has gone on in those rooms?

But this is mainly to note that 'blessed salt', like holy water, can be used to consecrate a place for God such as one's home, property, room, car, etc.

I really don't recommend salt, and need to mention that you try to use it carefully...
Salt is used by some carelessly and messy as 'water', and part of the issue here is salt can cause 'corrosion' and damage some surfaces, especially after prolonged exposure. This is why we would use holy water and even holy oil in some cases, rather than to spread salt.
Salt is also more a preventative, creating threshold barriers for example by running it across a threshold, window sills, gateway entrances to your property. Again it is better to be 'blessed'

THE SAINT BENEDICT MEDAL

Go to www.osb.org, get one for each member of the family involved/living in the haunted location, need to wear it always such as on a chain around the neck, even in the bath/shower *(get the chain blessed too)*. My baby girl has one taped under her crib, hard to put one on her at this age. Get 'four more', that is 'one' for each corner of your property or four corners of your home if in an apartment.

Carry this with you at all times, my son when he was in Kindergarten, had one strung into his shoe laces low below the tongue to keep him from seeing it and getting curious about the 'shiny metal thing'. It provided an extra safe feeling knowing he was protected in yet another way. If not for the medal of Saint Benedict always around my neck since I was a teen, I might have been physically attacked or even killed at the hands of demons and evil spirits. It is hard to say. But based on what I have experienced throughout my life, it is a safe bet to say that is definitely true. And will even prevent demonic possession. This and other protection medals, and 'symbols', that I suggest using for 'protection', and these are consistent with the theological ideals of the field of 'Demonology' through the doctrine of the two-thousand years of church history. You will find that more notable 'Demonologists' and others who do the work we do to some extent in "deliverance', will always carry one of these.

ORIGIN OF THE BENEDICT MEDAL

The origin of the medal likely dates back to the time of St. Benedict himself, of whom we know that, in his frequent battles with "evil spirits", he generally made use of the sign of the cross and wrought many miracles thereby. He also taught his disciples to use the sign of our redemption against the assaults of Satan and in other dangers. *St. Maurus* and *St. Placidus*, his first and most renowned disciples, wrought their numerous miracles through the power of the holy cross and in the name and by the merits of their holy founder. The medal of St. Benedict can be blessed by any priest *(Instr., 26 Sept. 1964; Can. 1168)*. The medal is powerful even without the special Benedictine blessing.

DESCRIPTION OF THE MEDAL

We distinguish two types of the medal of St. Benedict: the ordinary medal, and that of Monte Casino, which is known as the Jubilee [or Centenary] Medal. The latter has been enriched with a great number of indulgences, especially with the famous Toties Quoties plenary indulgence on All Souls' Day. We describe here only the Jubilee Medal.

In the year 1880 the venerable Benedictine Order celebrated the 1400th anniversary of the birth of its glorious founder. The beautiful Jubilee Medal was struck on this occasion, and since that time the Monastery of Monte Casino has the sole privilege of striking this Medal. A so, all Jubilee medals must be procured from the Monastery of Monte Cassino. On one side the medal has a cross, the sign of our redemption, the protecting shield given us by God to ward off the fiery arrows of the evil spirit.

In the angles of the cross are found these four letters: C.S.P.B. They stand for the words: Crux Sancti Patris Benedicti: The Cross of the Holy Father Benedict. On the vertical bar of the cross itself are found the letters: **C.S.S.M.L.**, and on the horizontal bar of the cross: **N.D.S.M.D.**
They signify: **Crux Sacra Sit Mihi Lux,
Non Draco Sit Mihi Dux**
This means: *May the holy cross be my light, let not the dragon be my guide.*

Round the margin of the medal, beginning at the right hand on top, we have the following letters: **V.R.S.N.S.M.V. S.M.Q.L.I.V.B.**, They stand for the verses:
The remaining explanation of the meaning of medal.
**Vade Retro, Satana!
Nunquam Suade Mihi Vana.
Sunt Mala Quae Libas
Ipse Venena Bibas.**

The English words are:
**Begone, Satan!
Suggest not vain things to me.
Evil is the cup thou offerest;
Drink thou thine own poison.**

The reverse of the medal bears the image of St. Benedict holding in his right hand the Cross, in the power of which he wrought so many miracles, and in his left hand bearing the Holy Rule, which leads all its followers by the way of the Cross to Eternal Light.

On a pedestal to the right of St. Benedict is the poisoned cup, shattered when he made the sign of the cross over it. On a pedestal to the left is a raven about to carry away a loaf of poisoned bread that a jealous enemy had sent to St. Benedict. Above the cup and the raven are the Latin words: **Crux S-Patris Benedicti.** *[The initials "C.S.P.B." are found on the other side of the medal in the angles of the Cross -- see above.]*

Round the margin is the inscription:
Eius in obitu nostro praesentia muniamur: "May his presence protect us in the hour of our death."

Below St. Benedict we read:
ex SM Casino MDCCCLXXX (from holy Monte Cassino, 1880).

THE POWER AND EFFECTS OF THE MEDAL

No particular prayers are prescribed, for the very wearing and use of the medal is considered a silent prayer to God to grant us, through the merits of St. Benedict, the favors we request. Although a prayer to Saint Benedict that often comes on the accompanied 'pamphlet' that details a description and history of the medal could be said from time to time, as I would I recommend this:

"O holy Father, St. Benedict, blessed by God both in grace and in name, who, while standing in prayer, with hands raised to heaven, didst most happily yield thy angelic spirit into the hands of thy Creator, and hast promised zealously to defend against all the snares of the enemy in the last struggle of death, those who shall daily remind thee of thy glorious

departure and heavenly joys; protect me, I beseech thee, O glorious Father, this day and every day, by thy holy blessings, that I may never be separated from our dear Lord, from the society of thyself, and of all the blessed. Through the same Christ our Lord. Amen."

The medal of St. Benedict is powerful to ward off all dangers of body and soul coming from the evil spirit. We are exposed to the wicked assaults of the devil day and night. St. Peter says: **"Your adversary the devil, as a roaring lion, goeth about seeking whom he may devour."** *(1 Peter 5)*

In the life of St. Benedict we see how the devil tried to do harm to his soul and body, and also to his spiritual children. Father Paul of Moll, saintly Flemish Benedictine wonder-worker *(1824-1896)* frustrated the evil doings of the spirit of darkness chiefly through the use of the medal of St. Benedict, which has proved a most powerful protection against the snares and delusions of the old enemy. Missionaries in pagan lands use this medal with so great an effect that it has been given the remarkable name:

"The devil-chasing medal." The medal is, therefore, a powerful means:

- ✓ *To destroy all diabolical influences.*
- ✓ *To keep away the evil spells of magicians, of wicked and evil-minded persons.*
- ✓ *To impart protection to persons tempted, deluded or tormented by evil spirits.*
- ✓ *To obtain the conversion of sinners, especially when they are in danger of death.*
- ✓ *To serve as an armor in temptations against holy purity.*
- ✓ *To destroy the effects of poison.*

- ✓ To secure a timely and healthy birth for children.
- ✓ To afford protection against storms and lightning.
- ✓ To serve as an efficacious remedy for bodily afflictions and a means of protection against contagious diseases.

Finally, the Medal has often been used with admirable effect even for animals infected with plague or other maladies, and for fields when invaded by harmful insects.

More info: http://www.osb.org/gen/medal.html

The only time I was physically attacked by an evil entity/demon, was on the night I went to bed without this medal, as it had apparently broken and fallen off of my neck chain onto the floor before I had gone to bed without my knowledge. (*Refer to an earlier topic in this book*)
You can attain these medals here also at:
http://www.penitents.org/giftshopBenMedC.htm
3 medals for donation of 75 cents *(+ 50 cents shipping and handling)* **I recommend that you carry one with you at all times.**

PRAYERS

Don't let anyone tell you that specific prayers are not necessary, when they are vital. Look again at the history of the "*Roman Ritual*", there is a great example of a set of well organized prayers, and included rituals. History can tell alone that some prayers work better than others. Rather than simple, short and generic shouts to "*Begone*". Be specific, as a lawyer. Prayers 'do' need to be more detailed, for example, if you command a spirit to leave 'in the name of Jesus', it might just leave your room only, and then go into the hallway and linger for a time. It has not gone entirely, you are still in it's company if you were to go back to sleep. So as to ensure it leaves your property entirely, you need to add more to your methods. This is from experience and testimony of others as well. Not some theology alone, but fact.

An example of a more thorough prayer is included in the book, as it specifies in part:

"*...to leave me forever, and to be consigned into the everlasting hell, where they will be bound by Saint Michael the archangel, Saint Gabriel, Saint Raphael, our guardian angels, and where they will be crushed under the heel of the Immaculate Virgin Mary.*"

While another states: "*go directly to the foot of the cross of Jesus where he will dispose of you according to his holy will*".

So, again, we want to ensure we don't tell it to leave 'without' a command that tells it to leave completely and to 'stay away' also.

Again words can have a power and binding on earth as in heaven, and at times we must be specific such as in this case. "Leave" doesn't mean it is bound to not return.

Choose words wisely, we look to the forefathers of the church, such as even Saint Benedict himself. These sometimes lesser known saints who have lived and died, passing on their knowledge and wisdom. These who have done battle long before we were born throughout history, they fought the good fight and just as we might do now. The prayers we prescribe are often 'divinely inspired' by God,' tried and true', and 'tested' to be very effective for 'deliverance'. Therefore, it can be said that they have a rich history of usage and success. We don't want to go into a gun battle with a butter knife folks, take all measures in ensuring you are successful the first time.

CRUCIFIXES (NOT PLAIN CROSSES)

There is some confusion in the symbol of a cross, and a crucifix. Two things distinguish the two. One, a crucifix, has the crucified Christ, or the figure of Jesus on it. A 'cross' to a demonic is more so just a fancy letter "T". Second, a cross has been proven to have little to no effect on evil spirits, unless it is blessed by a priest for example, as a crucifix alone, even unblessed may also do little in some cases. *(Recommending a 'wood cross')* You see then turned crucifixes upside down in houses, the fact is the more powerful demons will not be affected by a statuette. But they do get affected at the reminder of Jesus' victory over sin and death. This is how one priest described the affects of a crucifix. Just that again as it might be 'blessed', it will be more powerful as a 'positive' holy symbol of God. I want to remind that some objects get a similar effect from being in proximity of those praying for example. But the effects are not as strong; again it varies to the level of piety, and the long term exposure. *(Read of the 'Kirlian camera experiments' for the 'science' of this)*

A WARNING:
A reminder that when you bring certain holy symbols and such objects on the site of a 'haunting' it may 'provoke' the entities, and is considered a sort of 'declaration of war' to these spirits, like pulling out the guns. You may see an immediate increase in activity after, or it may wait until night to wreak havoc around you.
So one needs to be ready for a 'step up' in activity for an all out spiritual warfare, which is reason to get as much protection as possible, and to recite protection prayers before going to sleep at night.

RELICS

Relics of saints can be another powerful tool of protection as well as provocation. Ed and Lorraine Warren had used a relic of Padre Pio in many cases. I had in my possession a relic of Saint Martin De Pores'. These relics can stir the otherwise quiet demons, which try to hide from being detected as to slow the process of getting help, say through a church sanction. Using it in 'religious provocation'.

For protection, if you could see a metaphysical change in adding it on one person, the aura of the person will become brighter as the relic begins to merge its positive energy with your own. *(Note: This is a graphical representation of what you might see.)*

HOLY WATER

Water dissipates the power of an evil spirit. Unclean spirits hate these pure elements of 'salt and water'. We are the salt of the earth. Remember the flood? Water is God's curse for fallen angels and demons. He used salt water to judge them. Remember the legion in the pigs? He destroyed them sending them into the sea. Water is more of a curse to a devil that is why they seek dry places.
(See Matthew 12: 43-45.)

Contrary to the movie 'The Exorcist', the demonic can tell ordinary tap water from blessed holy water. And this is a 'test' in itself as it was hinted as in the movie. In actual cases of exorcisms, the spirit speaking through the possessed, said the tap water was simply "wet", and holy water as indeed burning like 'fire'. Given both types of water were presented in a vile by the same appearance, the test effectively proved the demon can tell the difference, and helps to validate for an actual exorcism, as well as to validate a significance of water blessed by a Catholic Priest . This in itself should make one think. Even the 'Kirlian Camera' experiments show a 'special property' in an enhanced energy aura surrounding the water, one that does not show on common tap water. Regardless of the science in this, holy water is most effective in protection and expelling demons. And should be carried by all on investigations in a small vile 'just in case' it is needed. And have one bedside as well for easy access in case you are visited at night. You can get holy water from local Orthodox/Catholic churches (for free) from a stainless steel or brass dispenser, usually in the back portion of the church. However, you may want to mention you wish to fill you water vile to one in the church, so as to not look 'suspicious' as one who may steal from the church.

For some this can be another "Taboo", because non Orthodox /Catholics refuse to believe there is something called "Holy water". Please try to get over this prejudice, because you are missing the real truth here which can greatly help in your cause against these evil spirits.

A short story told:
While a man laid in bed asleep, his wife flickered some holy water onto him as he lied under a heavy pile of blankets during one cold winter night. He jumped each time the small droplets hit the bed. She was surprised by the action, and decided to see if regular water from a glass would do the same. She tried with three passed, and with each time dripping even more droplets in a fingered wave of her hand. And he laid motionless. As soon as she resumed with the Holy water, he jumped again as though he was slapped. As the story went, her husband earlier that night came home wild eyed and drunk, he trashed the kitchen in a rage. She had said his face 'looked like a demon'. It scared her and she ran out of the house. The holy water test confirmed her suspicions in her mind that he was in the least with a demon, especially when he was drunk. And he was more 'dark' in his personality and over all behavior.

AURA OF BLESSED WATER: A SCIENTIFIC STUDY
(courtesy of www.kirlian.org)

One of the most fascinating research directions on Earth at present is the study of the aura and 'bio-energetic' structure of water. This research is conducted in Russia by a Professor Korotkov.

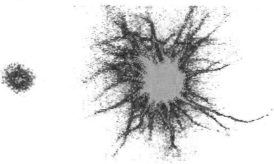

Two Kirlian aura images of seemingly identical drops of water, kindly provided by Prof Korotkov, are shown. The left image depicts aura vibrations around a drop of normal water and the right image shows the aura around a drop charged by the famous Russian healer Allan Chumak. The bio-charged water has more than 30 times stronger aura vibration and significantly altered physical and biological properties.

Contemporary physics cannot explain the above change in water (aura) glow which, technically speaking, is a <u>purely physical process</u> involving an electrical discharge in the ionized air around the drop. The main reason for this is that a great majority of "scientists" on Earth completely ignore our consciousness in their perception of reality. Prof.

K.Korotkov says that the increase in the aura around a drop of water cannot be explained without considering the energy and vibration of our consciousness. Water aura experiments are indisputable evidence ancient tales of "living" or "blessed" water with miraculous properties may have a solid scientific reason in view of the newly discovered secret of water.

So now we see that using the Kirlian Camera we can actually see the difference as though it is indeed somehow 'positively charged' when it is prayed over in other experiments, blessed by a priest. The object or water can't simply be done by a 'healer' unless he is of God. As we know priests are. So that the object or water is charged with the grace of God, and not simple transferred energy from the person's own aura as it maybe in this case.

Or it will not affect the demonic.

So the object needs to be 'charged' with God's grace, it should be noted that the more holy or 'pious' the priest the more power the blessed water or objects. A priest can lose favor with God, and lose his 'gifts', or even go through the whole seminary and not have his heart and mind into it as he did not have a 'true calling'. And at times an ordination can be invalid in God's eyes because of this. History better served Catholic seminaries in filtering out such candidates before 'Holy orders' long before they emerged from the seminary. Sadly now today many are not familiar enough with elements of 'spiritual warfare' to truly help those in peril of a demonic haunting. And thus, one of the main reasons for Fr. Gabriele Amorth to create the "International Association of Exorcists" was to train priests with the age old knowledge of doing battle as an "Exorcist".

THE NAME OF JESUS
Why 'Jesus' name can affect evil spirits

I mention earlier in this book of the connection between *"close encounters of a forth kind" (and later encounter stages)* and how these supposed UFO Alien beings recoil and flee to the utterance of Jesus name. (*As with demonic/evil spirits.*) But I wanted to go into more detail why this would work at all, when it has also worked universally for other people with different faith and belief systems beyond Christian. So here I am going to try to explain this universally, so **all** faith and belief systems might understand this:

Jesus, to a Christian is the '*Son of God*', '*The Redeemer*', '*The Savior*'. His hierarchy is more so where Christians rank him high as the son of God. His word made flesh. But everyone should understand regardless of your faith, is that Jesus was a real person who lived on this earth two-thousand years ago. So as to say this is regardless of your belief as to his 'rank' and 'relation' in the afterlife, he is indeed a REAL spirit, a powerful 'positive' spirit who the negative entities fear and hate. A simple "cause and effect" is at work here we should not ignore. I have been around long enough to find using Jesus name, and not just by Christians, DOES in fact have a reaction on these spirits. Again, this holds truer when you have a stronger faith and grace with God. Which psychologically is a sort of 'positive thinking', and 'confidence'. But, remember 'positive', as the 'law of repulsion' in how everything truly positive will affect these 'negative' evil entities to a degree. So in this we also consider that of 'intercession' in part as to invoke the 'name of Jesus', is essentially asking for a 'positive' spirit to ward off a 'negative' one.

Using the name of Jesus alone is often all people can remember to do in a panic. To where they might forget any and all prayers when in the presence of an evil one. The intense fear that comes with such an encounter may even effect the person where they can't recite their own home address or

phone number even.
But we know simply saying 'Jesus' name alone has released them from paralysis, physical attack, or brought a stop to poltergeist activity in the room for example. This isn't in saying that it will alone always help. It is merely making a good point in stating that people should understand the significance of 'Jesus' as a 'positive spirit', and 'why' it may work for "Non-Christians" as well.

THE MIRACULOUS MEDAL

HISTORY

Zoë Labouré was the daughter of a farmer at Fain-les-Moutiers in France, where she was born in 1806. She was the only one of a large family not to go to school and did not learn to read and write. Her mother died when she was eight, and when her elder sister, Louisa, left home to become a Sister of Charity, the duties of housekeeper and helper to her father fell upon her. When her mother died she chose the Blessed Virgin for her mother, and when she was about 14 or so she heard a call to the religious life. After some opposition from her father, she was allowed to join the Sisters of Charity of St Vincent de Paul at Châtillon-sur-Seine in 1830.

She took the name Catherine, and after her postulance was sent to the order's convent in Rue du Bac in Paris, where she arrived four days before the removal of the relics of St Vincent de Paul from Notre Dame to the Lazarist Church in Rue de Sèvres. On the day of those festivities, a series of visions began which were to make the name of Catherine Labouré famous. On many occasions during mass, Catherine beheld our Lord in front of the Blessed Sacrament and on other occasions she saw symbolic visions of St Vincent above the reliquary containing his incorrupt heart.

The first of the three principal visions took place three months later. On the night of 18 July, when at about 11:30 pm she was woken up suddenly by the appearance of a "shining child", who led her down to the sister's chapel. There Our Lady appeared and talked with her for over two hours, telling her that she would have to undertake a difficult task. On 27 November, the same year, Our Lady appeared to Sister Catherine in the same chapel, in the form of a picture and as it were standing on a globe with shafts of light streaming from Our Lady's hands. Catherine described the event:

"I saw the Blessed Virgin standing on a globe; her face was beautiful beyond words. Rays of dazzling light were streaming from gems on her fingers, down to the globe. And I heard a voice say: 'Behold the symbol of graces which I will shower down on all who ask me for them!' Then, an oval frame surrounded Our Lady on which I read the prayer, in letters of gold: 'O Mary, conceived without sin, pray for us who have recourse to Thee!' The oval frame turned and I could see, on the reverse side, enclosed in a frame of twelve stars, the letter M surmounted by a cross with a bar beneath. Below these symbols were the Hearts of Jesus and Mary, one surrounded by a crown of thorns, the other pierced by a sword. I heard a voice, which said to me: 'Have a medal struck according to this model. Those who wear it, when it is blessed, will receive great graces, especially if they wear it around their necks. There will be graces in abundance for all who wear it with confidence."

Sister Catherine confided in her confessor, Père Aladel, and he, after making very careful investigations, was given permission by the Archbishop of Paris, Monseigneur de Quelen, to have the medal struck. In June, 1832, the first 1,500 were issued. The faith was encountering difficulties in France at this time and it's revival has been attributed to this medal. So many conversions and physical cures were attributed to the medal that the name "Miraculous Medal" was given it by popular acclaim.

The Archbishop of Paris instituted a canonical inquiry into the alleged visions in 1836, before which, however, Sister Catherine could not be induced to appear. Further inquiries took place and eventually the tribunal decided in favor of the authenticity of the visions, taking into consideration the circumstances, the character of the sister concerned, and the prudence and level-headedness of Père Aladel. Until her death on 31 December 1876, Catherine lived unobtrusively among the community at Enghien-Reuilly caring for the sick, the aged and the infirm. Although the other sisters were aware that the one in their midst was the celebrated visionary of the Miraculous Medal, the identity was not made known until Catherine was on her death bed. Her funeral was the occasion of an outburst of popular veneration, and a child of 12, crippled from birth, was instantaneously cured at her grave soon after. Sister Catherine's body had been placed in a triple coffin and buried in a crypt in the chapel at 77, rue de Reuilly where it remained for over 50 years.

Following the announcement of her beatification the coffin was opened and the customary recognition of the relics took place, and it was then discovered that the remains were found to be perfectly intact and incorrupt. The hands and the face were of a pinkish color slightly tinged, but intact. The following day the face had slightly darkened on account of it's first contact with the air. After a cursory examination, the body was borne in solemn procession to the motherhouse. The body was later placed in the motherhouse chapel under the side altar of Our Lady of the Sun, where it still reposes behind a covering of glass, allowing it to be viewed by the many visitors to the chapel.

Saint Catherine was canonized on 27 July 1947 and her feast day is observed on 28 November, the day after the feast of the Miraculous Medal. (It is said that Cardinal Newman began wearing the medal two months before his conversion)

<u>I will note that this is another medal I wear always with the Saint Benedict medal.</u>

More Info:
http://www.amm.org/medal.htm

Go to here to Get a free medal:
http://test.amm.org/submissions/survey/

FRANKINCENSE <u>AND</u> MYRRH (INCENSE)

Blessed by a priest and used instead of 'sage' to cleanse your home/interior. One person I met tried to make a case that adding Myrrh to Frankincense is somehow a lure for evil, rather than a repellant. Not true. This can be lit as incense and used to help clear a home of minor infestations.

WHY NOT SAGE?

Sage might have some effect, but it would only work temporarily, it can be like a smoke bomb clearing a room. Native American's will actually tell you it isn't meant for 'cleansings' and exorcisms as it is being used. It is more of a 'blessing'. Christians need to note this isn't a shared belief and to not MIX faith practices on the same case. Especially as the family for example might be Christian. Part is out of respect for the family's faith. Second is as I cite elsewhere in this book, a 'mix' of belief systems can be a dangerous thing. May people I talk to in this field will also attest this method simply does not work. Not to mention it isn't being done right and without the proper ritual and by a Native American "Holy Man". But, Sage in itself is not a real effective 'positive' as I stress some elements can be. As it fails to have a natural effect against these negative evil entities. Unlike the usage of '*Frankincense and Myrrh*'.

Lastly, when you buy this incense be sure to have it blessed by a priest

PROPERLY DISPOSING OF 'UNHOLY' ITEMS

Many times I hear the question: **"How do I dispose of an Ouija board?"**. Burning it will release the demon(s), likely upon you! Throwing it away will leave the possibility open that someone else might get a hold of it. And let me say that you would be surprised at the garbage that is recovered, might even be by your trash service. Imagine if it made a ruckus like the "Jumangi" Game box did in that movie, as to lure one into uncovering it from burial. If you say, ground into a wood chipper, means pieces can be left behind. Another comes by and gets a splinter in their foot, and brings it home.

I realize it may sound a bit movie'esque but, yes it can be that way! Grant it, it might vary from case to case, and this is under the assumption that the board was used to make demonic contact; the board is not fresh from the box.

As it is disposed of, it is said that you should avoid directly touching the object(s) with your hands, especially objects that might be cursed, and wash your hands with holy water after handling if by mistake. Finally end with a prayer to break attachments and a prayer again of protection as you should also begin this task with.

BURY = SAFEST FOR LAITY

Say an exorcism prayer and sprinkle the items with holy water. Bury it deep, so that no one will find it and the earth will turn it to mulch. Don't bury it where it might be unearthed later, by landscaping, renovations, sewage maintenance. Think this through!

CAST INTO FLOWING WATER

Vatican Exorcist Gabriel Amorth, said he recited the prayers with holy water, burns the items, then empties the ashes into a river of flowing water. But, we have to remember he is an "Exorcist"

II – SPIRITUAL

BUILD YOUR SPIRITUAL ARMOR:

Each member of the household can affect a haunting. Each member needs to review these things that relate to personal issues of spirituality and psychology:

For self help, I ask the client to consider a "spiritual tune-up", and look deep and think of all and anything they may have done in the past that is not pleasing to God. Make a good contrition with God, anything that might not be pleasing to God, ask for his forgiveness. If you are Catholic go to "Confession" and be sure to attend 'Mass' every Sunday with 'Communion'.
Some are so hard hit with problem hauntings they resolve to attend mass every morning. This is great! God helps those better who help themselves. In your case you likely don't need to go every day. (Assuming) But some are better off if they do. It builds spiritual tolerance and graces, faith, etc. as it can after all, only do well. Such prayers should be done in private on your knees as a sign of reverence, and humility. And this is a great way to 'rekindle' your relationship with God.

PRAYER: The "ACT OF CONTRITION"

```
Oh my God I am heartily sorry for having
offended thee, and I detest all of my
sins, because of the possible loss of
heaven and thy just punishments. But most
of all I have offended thee my God, whom
```

are all good and deserving of all my love.
I firmly resolve, with the help of thy
grace. To confess my sins, to do penance,
and to amend my life amen.

III – UNIVERSAL

What I mean by "UNIVERSAL" – Is in explaining to be more commonly understood, generalizing on some aspects of 'deliverance' not specific to any faith.

I found that I am not going to convert all people to *'Catholic'* or even *'Christian'* belief systems. Sometimes we can't "*lead a horse to the water*", and will settle early on for pointing them in the right direction. After all, it's a start! The extreme can fail atrociously, while one metaphorically tries dragging them to the water hole, it will most often make them 'run away' to another *water hole* perhaps. So the approach is lightened on the first meeting (depending on the person and their faith/belief system). So in saying, that sometimes simply easing in the 'faith' part, where it isn't so 'hard hit'- is a vital and necessary early step. So, as often in this way I place the 'seed of thought' in their mind, not so much like the typical "evangelical", who so often will rub people the wrong way with that "In your face" ministering.

I can try to make even those considered as 'Pagans' understand a portion of the significance of 'Jesus', in that a few stepping stones closer might even play a significant part in later life. Especially when they see that often merely just uttering Jesus name can have an effect on these "dark spirits" they might be experiencing, while nothing else seems to affect them in the same manner.
They may ask "Why" later, and then I try to explain in a more easily understood way, as I can't assume everyone was brought

up or even familiar with a *"Christian-Judeo"* belief systems.

- ✓

  Another point of 'universal' is in that idea I have been conveying in that 'Negative' versus 'Positive' way of thinking. That in itself can be more universally understood. So as I might first advise on a 'universal' level I also tell them the simple truth in how **"Without a more 'faith based approach', this advice alone is limited in its effectiveness"**.

  Some examples are:

- ✓ Light versus dark, how letting in more sunlight and leaving lights on have an effect.

- ✓ Pure elements are 'positive' salt, water, olive oil, even before getting 'blessed' in their natural essence, they are more pure, as these spirits avert from these things to a certain extent "as-is" by default.

All of these things can weaken the infestation and are understood universally, as there is so much of a belief system attached to it.

I explain also how "purity' is a 'positive', in that all of these things I mention are to bring in 'positive' (God) things to counter the 'negative' (evil). I mention that more severe haunts will not be as easy to weaken or 'cleansed entirely'. I might tell them straight out how they will have to take a 'higher spiritual path' to God if they really want this gone. By saying that they know what I mean, and the choice become theirs to make, as I said : *"you can lead a horse to water...."*

In other words, we can help people understand why some things work without "getting preachy", and <u>not</u> at the expense of the truth' as some may do.

SO IN SHORT BY 'UNIVERSAL' I AM PARTLY REFERRING TO:

1. to help them better understand why some things work, from a more common perspective.

2. Have them make changes to their lifestyles, home and personal, that may have an effect. These things that are not specific to any faith, <u>rather than to not try to help them at all.</u>

When people come to me of other faiths (*Including self-described agnostics, atheist*), I realize that a "universal approach" can only help so much. But it has made progress, and some walk away with an understanding that 'Jesus' is real, based merely on the "cause and effect" in results.
And that is a 'good start' for someone who was an "Atheist" for example. As I don't want to run people away as I have heard so many times, stories of people going to get help and hearing: **"have you been saved"**?

There is no printed template for handling all people, each have different levels of faith, egos, personalities, we have to be empathetic and try to get a feel for who they are, to better succeed in helping them. So part of 'deliverance' is through effective 'ministering', and it should vary from person to person in how we approach and represent the 'Christian' or 'Catholic' faith.
If you have ever talked a suicide from jumping off a rooftop, and here we are dealing with the human mind as

well, and often the direct approach will be counterproductive. This I find as a parent as well.

IV. PSYCHOLOGICAL.

A profile of the 'psychological state' as well as the overall 'mental health' of each person who might live in, or frequently occupy the property, can often play an important part. This can be a matter of the overall 'tone' of the household, as in if it is a 'positive' or 'negative' environment. Is the mood a happy one? Or more somber?

Let me break down some elements to consider below:

1) **STRESS**

　　Even as you might have to change jobs, if it will hurt 'money matters' around the house, it might make things worse. Reducing stress will be more than learning to change your overall attitude, it is a matter of better managing your life, and handling the very things that help to build stress in your life better: To further detail.

　　a. Money matters - Money is the root of many of a 'divorce'. It is how we react to 'stress' due to a tight budget. The demonic plays into this, they might have manifested so that your household can endure somethings that would otherwise be considered to be *"bad luck"*. A slew of expensive car repairs for example, the car is vital to your daily life, like an appliance, so it needs immediate attention. And it can't wait like saving for Christmas presents.

    *b. **Job related** -* During oppression you might lose your job, it could be that you have changed because of severe 'oppression'; you might be showing up for work late, become careless. Just as the demonic might influence decisions, they can help you to forget important things that can result in you losing your job. At home, simply forgetting to pay a bill is not severing the income flow, so this is more critical.

    *c. **Marital problems**-* Divorce and Separations– consider your marriage to have a heavy strain on you, and also the way they feed on these things supernatural. And a haunting can have a likewise affect on your marriage. My advice. Don't split up and let it win! You are not truly a 'survivor' of the haunting unless your family stays intact when it is all over with.

2) **How they may work to 'increase stress' and 'negative emotions'**

    *a. **Your property**-*Intermittent Car problems can cost a fortune to track down when it might be a diabolical problem. More common for cars I have found is brake lines, hoses, compromising the integrity of these systems. People can go for years being forced to bankruptcy, not realizing a certain evil is manipulating your life to bring you to financial ruin.
    Some cases leave more obvious signs of 'supernatural' destruction, where they have the car damaged as though some jaded hoodlum had ransacked it. Tires slashed, windows broken, the rage taken out on your car. Authorities can be baffled that the car remained locked in the garage, and you might even

suspect a member of your own family, which will bring about more tension. *(Part of the plan often)* As it may be extremely rare, it is still just another example what we can be dealing with in having demonic forces directly affect our finances. As you read next in how our thought process can be affected, where you forget to pay important bills, bringing further unnecessary financial burdens upon yourself. Car accidents are often the result of bad judgment, pray before taking your car out. A totaled car and a huge hospital bill is the quickest way to financial ruin.

b. ***Tipping the decision scales***-When faced with a choice that could tilt either way, you will be more nudged to make the bad choice by decision. During oppression and later stages the demonic subliminal voice is much stronger, as temptations can be also much harder to endure. The same reason that 'suicides' are pushed over the top into following up with that final moment of *"going through with it"*. In a smaller way they might affect our day-to-day decisions. And certainly they know the outcome of many choices you make in life and would indeed try to sway you to the wrong decision. *(one of the 'pitfalls' of "free-will" is being faced with the consequences of your actions)* Before making decisions, it is best to pray, maybe even wait a few days, and then 'sleep on it'. While praying the whole time, as it will weaken the 'influence' that may be there, to enable Heaven's voice to be stronger in helping you to make the right choices. *(A 'daily rosary' is highly recommended)* We have to understand that even if our personality doesn't seem to have been affected, that your day-to-day thought process as it can relate to even the mundane tasks, might be more prone to suddenly falter.

    c. A **Death in the family** or of a friend. This might hold two things. One, emotions might be played upon by a demonic, sometimes even preying on this hard time to try to get you to drink to get your mind off of it, or even suicide. When an opportunity arrives, the demonic might try to take full advantage of your state. Like the way a shark smells blood. This death might bring the spirit to you as well, sadly, some souls who pass on to become condemned souls, might be forced to bring torment and temptation to those they cared about in life. On the other hand, *they might make themselves known if they are in need of prayers (see the 'poor souls')*

3) SLEEP, REST AND NIGHTLY PRACTICES

Avoid that habit of not sleeping nights and sleeping during the day when at all possible. Being terrorized nightly by unseen spirits might force such a habit I realize, but we have to consider also that there are psychological effects of not getting the exposure to sunlight and more exposure to the night. This is actually part of their strategy; to have you awake during these night hours you can be better manipulated and affected. Especially during their hours between 2-4AM.

A NIGHTLY CHECKLIST:

- ✓ Say the proper prayers to protect you while you are in your sleep.

- ✓ Wear Saint Benedict medals, and other forms of protection. Better to protect you physically.

- ✓ I can attest they will stay back 3-6 feet when I have it on.

- ✓ Have a vile of holy water ready near your bedside in case you need it. One that you can open a spout and 'sprinkle the water' from.

- ✓ Pray for 'faith' and not 'fear' so that you can feel safer closing your eyes at night.

- ✓ Sleep with the lights on. Light electric bills really don't add up to much, you can change to more efficient bulbs. And even lower wattages such as with a 40w or a 25w.

- ✓ If they are 'audible', play 'positive' music, or TV. Some say that running "White Noise" can help, try it, in some cases 'voices' come through. Some health food stores carry these, and your local Toys are us, Walmart, and Kmart as well.

- ✓ As you close your eyes, picture yourself kneeling at the foot of the cross with Jesus on it, then imagine further a 'white light' comes from him and surrounds you.

- ✓ Don't eat before bed, especially sugar snacks you don't want the mind to be a bit restless and you are trying to peacefully sleep. We also don't want a *'piece of undigested beef'* to lend a hand to your nightly experiences.

4) GET HELP FOR CLINICAL DEPRESSION, ANXIETY.

Better to try to deal with it without 'medication' if at all possible. Perhaps looking for the 'source'. Remember also often depression and other ailments are caused by demonic oppression, as the spirit and the mind are one, and one indeed directly affects the 'other'. You will find spiritual solutions actually will help your moods, as well as some psychological ailments. Also again I need to note if you see a medical professional, keep your paranormal experiences 'apart' from your counseling sessions. 'Unless' you have one who understands 'spiritual warfare'. Check with the swords of Saint Michael .org and we can try to find you such individuals that qualify in this in your area.

5) BUILD YOUR FAITH, AND NOT YOUR FEAR.

Fear is indeed the opposite of faith, so don't feed it! Faith can move indeed mountains, but it isn't so easy to have much in faith while in these times of crisis. Part of the 'three days' of prayer, fasting, special masses and penance a Priest will do before an exorcism is to keep his psychological state 'sharp', his 'faith' strong. He will need it, when the exorcism begins it can be very draining. Demons attack the mind with string temptations like you have never seen to try to bring you down. It is indeed a 'spiritual battle' and again, as the mind and the spirit are connected, each affects the other.

6) RESOLVE CONFLICTS WITH OTHERS

Don't let deep seeded resentment, anger, unsettled arguments dwell in the pit of your stomach. Deal with them in a peaceful manner and prayer for that. This might also mean settling old differences by being the first one to offer an 'apology'. We need to forgive in our hearts, and not hold these grudges and ill feelings against others inside. Remember 'to forgive'; doesn't mean you have to 'be friends' again, or even 'like' the person.

7) **DON'T WORRY BE HAPPY**.

Keep your positive thinking going! The glass is half full not half empty, look to the bright side of things. This in itself is a self help that might be part of removing negatives from your environment. Such as with Darker music. I found Talk radio left me more of a pessimist, more cynical. This isn't good. I stopped listening. Your friends and family can scope as to how positive you are, listen to them. Help each other to stay 'upbeat', and pray for this too!

8) **RESOLVE CONFLICT WITHIN YOURSELF**

Yes, "confessional is good for the soul" and the mind, deep seeded 'guilt' and your self image can play a part as well. Remember, no matter what you have done God will forgive you and he loves you regardless.

V. ENVIRONMENT.

Analyze the overall environment and tone of the overall surrounding atmosphere.

Evaluate it with the points I mention here:

a) **Horror movies** might be fun, but they invoke that level of fear and emotion of insecurity you don't want to feed **them** with.

b) **Avoid darker music, rap, death metal, etc.** By the same token playing 'Hymns' might actually stir things up, get an assessment of your situation from a qualified demonologist before taking certain actions which might unintentionally "provoke" the spirits into a sometimes violent retaliation. Playing 'Gospel music' is to be a 'preventative' at some point, as a thing to do 'after' the spirits have been removed, and also as so to prevent them from coming back.

c) Try to find ways to let in **more sunlight**, get lighter weight and brighter curtains. Clean windows, open up the drapes and let the sun shine in. Sun provides more than 'vitamin C', as it is in a way 'God's light' in how it affects all living things.

d) **Get outdoors more.** And away from the house, where it has more of a foothold in that environment, best to get away more.

e) **Cleanliness** is next to Godliness – Cleaning your house is good work, for the mind and the spirit and can be a good work out for tired bones. But we also find that cleaning up actually affects activity, it might drop off drastically, if not only for a few days. They love a mess, like pigs in slop, again consider clean, a "positive", a mess "negative" as they prefer negative, it should only make sense.

f) **Lay off the ghost hunting**, at least for a while. As soon as such things can rub you the wrong way, it is time to back away from them. Ghost hunting for the 'adventurous', might be fun, but if you suspect your haunting is a result from such activities, it is time for that to end. Consider it like an allergic reaction, and it is time to remove it from your diet. Or more metaphorically speaking, where after you break your leg 'skiing', you will need some 'recoup time' in the least, as your bones mend to where your leg is 'fully healed' and reconditioned.

g) **BLACK is not in.** Avoid black. Darker curtains and so forth even, replace with brighter colors. This also has a psychological effect as well on a person over time. I am not saying to not wear some cool basic black when you are out of the house from time to time. Just to avoid it around the house. I have seen demons slither their way to hide in hung black shirts, and black dresses draped over a chair back, they definitely like black as they cling to its 'darkness' partly to conceal themselves perhaps. On the other hand, it appeals to them I think, as well as the fact they harbor more power in 'darkness' than in 'light' as you read in this book.

h) **Books in print** – use your sense. Books on black magic, pornography and so forth should be removed. Yes, even the "Illustrated 'Karma Sutra' book you might have to spice up your marriage. Regardless of the manner of which you use certain books, the content is the issue.

VI. BREAKING CURSES

You might find objects or symbols under you bed, behind pictures, in your pillow case, under your mattress, inside your car. Expecting the objects to be where you spend more of your time is the idea.

The objects can be things such as a small piece of parchment, wrapped in a ribbon. Or hair tied in such a ribbon you might find attached to the back of your family portrait on the wall. Symbols might be drawn or even etched into your floor under the bed, pentagrams and certain voodoo symbols. These 'objects' must be removed and disposed of in the same manner I say an Ouija board should. Exception, these should be often 'burned' as I describe, and better if by a priest.

Do breaking curses prayers, and on anything unusual you might have found in your home that further validates someone has placed a curse on you. I will add additional prayers to my website over time:

http://www.catholicdemonologist.com/breakingcurses.htm

Curses aren't just bestowed upon one from some 'old Witch', as simply visiting near an 'unholy gravesite' or even being in proximity of someone evil can also incur one. This can be enough to get a demonic 'attachment' as curses are essentially a 'demonic attachment'. So these prayers can break that spirit's ties with you, or prevent it as it may have tried to attach itself to you. So as a curse can be from a person, place, or thing and not just one placing a 'curse' or 'spell' upon a person.

PRAYERS:
Breaking Household Curses and Spells
I **recommend** that anyone should say these prayers first, just in case it's something you believe to be demonic infestation or and influence of, is related to a possible 'unknown curse.' *(Note: Read more about "curses" in an earlier section of this book)*

PRAYER ONE:
In the name of the Lord Jesus Christ, strengthened by the intercession of the Blessed Virgin Mary, Mother of God, of Blessed Michael the Archangel, of the Blessed Apostles Peter and Paul, and all the Saints, and powerful in the holy authority of His Precious and Wondrous

Name, We ask, O Lord God, that you break and dissolve any and all curses, hexes, spells, seals, satanic vows and pacts, spiritual bondings and soul ties with satanic forces, evil wishes, evil desires, hereditary seals, snares, traps, lies, obstacles, deceptions, diversions, spiritual influences, and every dysfunction and disease from any source whatsoever, that have been placed upon our family and household; [and particularly upon [person's name] , whom we love very much.]

Father in Heaven, please rebuke these evil spirits and their effects and cast them away from this family [and particularly upon [person's name]] so that we may continue to do Your Will and fulfill the mission you have for them to Your Greater Glory.

Thank you, Father, for hearing our prayer. We praise Your Holy Name and worship You and Love You. Thank You for the wisdom and light of Your Holy Spirit. Thank You for enabling us through Your Holy Spirit to be aggressive against the works of the enemy. Thank You for Your Hope, that takes away discouragement; thank You for ongoing victory. "...in all these things we are more than conquerors through Him who loved us" (Romans 837).

Father, We now place our enemies into your hands. Look with mercy upon them, and do not hold their sins against them. Anyone who has cursed our ` family and household, we now bless. Anyone who has hurt us, we now forgive. For those who have persecuted us, we now pray

Our Father...
Hail Mary...
Glory Be...

O My Sweet Jesus, forgive us our sins and save us from the fires of Hell. Lead all souls to Heaven, and help especially those who are most in need of Thy Mercy.
Holy Michael the Archangel, defend us in battle. Be our protection against the wickedness and snares of the devil. May God rebuke him, we humbly pray; and do thou, O prince of the heavenly hosts, by the power of God, thrust into hell Satan and all the other evil spirits who prowl through the world seeking the ruin of souls.
Amen.

PRAYER TWO:
Heavenly Father, I love You, I praise You, and I worship You. I thank You for sending your Son Jesus Who won victory over sin and death for my salvation. I thank You for sending Your Holy Spirit Who empowers me, guides me, and leads me into fullness of life. I thank You for Mary, my Heavenly Mother, who intercedes with the holy angels and saints for me.
Lord Jesus Christ, I place myself at the foot of Your cross and ask You to cover me with Your Precious Blood which pours forth from Your Most Sacred Heart and Your Most Holy Wounds, Cleanse me, my Jesus, in the

living water that flows from Your Heart. I ask You to surround me, Lord Jesus, with Your Holy Light.

Heavenly Father, let the healing waters of my baptism now flow back through the maternal and paternal generations to purify my family line of Satan and sin. I come before You, Father, and ask forgiveness for myself, my relatives, and my ancestors, for any calling upon powers that set themselves up in opposition to you or that does not offer true honor to Jesus Christ. In Jesus' Holy Name, I now reclaim any territory that was handed over to Satan and place it under the Lordship of Jesus Christ.

By the power of Your Holy Spirit, reveal to me, Father, any people I need to forgive and any areas of unconfessed sin. Reveal aspects of my life that are not pleasing You, Father, ways that have given or could give Satan a foothold in my life. Father I give to You any unforgiveness; I give to You my sins; and, I give to You all ways that Satan has a hold of my life. Thank You, Father for these revelations, thank You, for Your forgiveness and Your love.

Lord Jesus, in Your Holy Name, I bind all evil spirits of the air, water, ground, underground, and netherworld. I further bind, in Jesus' Name, any and all emissaries of the satanic headquarters and claim the Precious Blood of Jesus on the air, atmosphere, water, ground and their fruits around us, the underground and the netherworld below.

Heavenly Father, allow Your Son Jesus to

come now with the Holy Spirit, the Blessed Virgin Mary, the holy angels and the saints to protect me from all harm and to keep all evil spirits from taking revenge on me in any way.

(Repeat the following sentence three times; once in honor of the Father, once in honor of the Son, and once in honor of the Holy Spirit.)
In the Holy Name of Jesus, I seal myself, my family, my relatives, this room, our home, our out buildings and the valued contents within, our property, all places in which we live, dwell, work, and travel upon. Our Automobiles, our appliances, furniture, *(place, home, church, car, plane, etc.)*, our financial matters and all sources of supply in the Precious Blood of Jesus Christ.

(To break and dissolve all satanic seals, repeat the following paragraph three times in honor of the Holy Trinity because satanic seals are placed three times to blaspheme the Holy Trinity.)
In the Holy Name of Jesus, I break and dissolve any and all curses, hexes, spells, snares, traps, lies, obstacles, deceptions, diversions, spiritual influences, evil wishes, evil desires, hereditary seals, known and unknown, and every dysfunction and disease from any source including my mistakes and sins. In Jesus' Name, I break and dissolve any and all links and effects of links with: astrologers; bohmos; channelers; charters; clairvoyants; crystal healers; crystals; fortune tellers; mediums; the New Age

Movements; occult seers; palm, tea leaf, or tarot card readers; psychics; santeros; satanic cults; spirit guides; witches; witchdoctors; and Voodoo. In Jesus' Name, I dissolve all effects of participation in séances and divination, Ouija boards, horoscopes, occult games of all sorts, and any form of worship that does not offer true honor to Jesus Christ.

Lord Jesus fill me with charity, compassion, faith, gentleness, hope, humility, joy, kindness, light, love, mercy, modesty, patience, peace, purity, security, serenity, tranquility, trust, truth, understanding, and wisdom. Help me to walk in Your Light and Truth, illuminated by the Holy Spirit so that together We may praise, honor, and glorify our Father in time and in eternity. For You, Lord Jesus, are, ".the way, the truth, and the life" (John 14:6 NAB), and You " have come that we might have life and have it more abundantly" (John 10:10 JB) "God indeed is my savior; I am confident and unafraid. MY strength and courage is the Lord, and he has been my savior" (Isaiah 12:2 JB). Amen. Alleluia. Amen.

VII - THE "DELIVERANCE"

NOTE: PRAYERS FOR **TYPE:** *GOOD-HUMAN SPIRIT HAUNTINGS can be found on page 284*
Pray AFTER getting your metals of protection I mention above.
More prayers will be added later please refer to:
http://www.catholicdemonologist.com/DELIVERANCE.htm

PRAYERS FOR DELIVERANCE FROM EVIL:

PRAYER AGAINST EVERY EVIL

Spirit of our God, Father, Son , and Holy Spirit, Most Holy Trinity, Immaculate Virgin Mary, angels, archangels, and saints of Heaven, descend upon me. Please purify me, Lord, mold me, fill me with Yourself, use me. Banish all the forces of evil from me, destroy them, vanquish them, so that I can be healthy and do good deeds. Banish from me all spells, witchcraft, black magic, malefice, ties, maledictions, and the evil eye; diabolic infestations, oppressions, possessions; all that is evil and sinful, jealousy, perfidy, envy; physical, psychological, moral, spiritual, diabolical ailments. Burn all these evils in hell, that they may never again touch me or any other creature in the entire world. *I humbly ask for the aid of God and his Angels and Saints in heaven, to command and bid all the powers who molest me -- by the power of God all powerful, in the name of Jesus

Christ our Savior, through the intercession of the Immaculate Virgin Mary -- to leave me forever, and to be consigned into the everlasting hell, where they will be bound by Saint Michael the archangel, Saint Gabriel, Saint Raphael, our guardian angels, and where they will be crushed under the heel of the Immaculate Virgin Mary.

(*modified for a 'non-clergy' to recite)

PRAYER FOR DELIVERANCE

My Lord, You are all powerful, You are God, You are Father. We beg You through the intercession and help of the archangels Michael, Raphael, and Gabriel, for the deliverance of our brothers and sisters who are enslaved by the evil one. All saints of heaven, come to our aid. From anxiety, sadness, and obsessions, We beg You: Free us, O Lord. From hatred, fornication, envy, We beg You: Free us, O Lord. From thoughts of jealousy, rage, and death. We beg You: Free us, O Lord. From every thought of suicide and abortion. We beg You: Free us, O Lord. From every form of sinful sexuality. We beg You: Free us, O Lord. From every division in our family, and every harmful friendship. We beg You: Free us, O Lord. From every sort of spell, malefice, witchcraft, and every form of the occult. We beg You: Free us, O Lord. Lord, You Who said, "I leave you peace, my peace I give you," grant that, through the intercession of the Virgin Mary, we may be liberated from every evil spell and enjoy

Your peace always. In the Name of Christ, our Lord. Amen."

SAINT MICHAEL PRAYER

Holy Michael the Archangel, defend us in battle. Be our protection against the wickedness and snares of the devil. May God rebuke him, we humbly pray; and do thou, O prince of the heavenly hosts, by the power of God, thrust into hell Satan and all the other evil spirits who prowl through the world seeking the ruin of souls. Amen.

NOTES ON FURTHER TAKING ACTION

Remember no 'sage smudging' as so many do, that is a pagan ritual. If you must, use incense or like methods that are 'Catholic.'
Again use Frankincense and Myrrh instead, and be sure it is 'blessed' for best results, you can use it all over the house. *(And it doesn't stink like sage either.)*

Get a vile of Holy water, keep it bedside, to cleanse the house carry your lit Frankincense and Myrrh incense into each room and say:
"In the name of Jesus Christ, and by his precious blood, I command all evil and unclean spirits to leave this place, go back to where you came from and never return!" (Always say three times.)

End with a Saint Michael prayer in each room. Open closet doors, cabinets, open a window in each room. Go into the attic and the crawl spaces also. *(NOTE if you don't OWN the house these are not as effective, the owner of the house has a bit more authority in this case*)

'Begin' and 'end' with the deliverance prayers on my site, start in the room that is most active, end in the room where you spend most of the time. Get a priest to 'bless' each room in the house next. Better to time it so the priest is there later that same day. Don't wait until darkness to do these prayers.
After all is done, a rosary would be best, thanking for deliverance'.

MORE ON "CATHOLIC EXORCISMS"

First, it is important to remember to not refer to yourself as a "Demonologist" to the Catholic Church, use the word "Deliverance Minister" or "Spiritual warfare Counselor". Second, for the same reason don't identify your "*Ghost Hunting*" or "*Paranormal research group*" with your introduction.

Keep yourself and your affiliation of such groups behind the scenes. Simply introduce yourself in such a manner as this: **"My Name is Kenneth Deel, and I am a Spiritual Warfare Counselor"** And maybe make mention of your '*Christian Denomination*' if it comes up.

Third, never ask for an "Exorcism" outright, that is for the church to decide. Simply contact and ask for 'assistance', and let them suggest having a local priest 'check it out'. We use the word 'deliverance' when talking to the church, the theology actually is a house cannot be "possessed" therefore it is not an "exorcism" that would be done.

One of the reasons for this 'self-help book' is that Roman Catholic Exorcisms are more difficult and often as lengthy of a red-tape process as say to 'annulment of a marriage'. In other words it can take up to 12 months, even a couple of years as I mentioned in the beginning of this book. How does a family in peril have this time? This is why sometimes the evidence can be so crucial, as you would prefer to provide something to prove to the church how grave the situation has become to help try to expedite the process. Through some validation through hard evidence and 3rd part witnesses they deem trustworthy and credible.

Keep log files of occurrences; and get witness testimony as when a friend spends the night and something significant to proving the haunting occurs. Remember, the more witnesses the better. You can be assured if one person is experiencing it; a psychological/medical screening would be recommended. From my experience I agree with that. Sad it can be more money and time wasted, when they need help now. But while this is underway, you can organize your prayer teams and have them follow this guidebook for example, to outline steps in a sort of 'self deliverance'.

We hope that in the process we don't really have to go so far as requiring a version of the Catholic Roman Ritual to be performed to end the demonic 'infestation'. But in keeping that option open by collecting the proper information during the time as you try to solve it outside of the help of 'church authorities', would be a recommended action.

Don't forget, the process regardless requires self-help:
"GOD HELPS THOSE WHO HELP THEMSELVES."

BEGINNING THE 'RED TAPE'

If you honestly take all steps in this book and it doesn't have an effect, I will be suspicious as anyone should. Beyond that, you would contact a priest first, perhaps after your own investigative results are in and there is enough testimony from witness(es). I say this because this priest will be 'your representative' or 'intermediary' to the local archdiocese bishop, who is the one to authorize an "exorcism" or "deliverance".

As the home owner afflicted with the 'haunting', typically your parish priest would be the first thought, they would tell you to go to him by default. Or a local priest. And if you stray from your town to another to get one who is really going to consider your problem and really try to help, this can be a problem, and it may be referred back to a more local priest. *(However testimony of the 'other' priest will not be ignored)* Yes, sadly, it is hard to find a priest who can truly deal with these things. In some cases I have met liberals who simply say:
```
"The devil doesn't work that way now a days"
```
Others might be 'too old' and frail, and near retirement. And they seem truly frightened at the idea of merely checking the place out when they hear what might be going on there. They may have never experienced such a thing their entire life as a priest. Regardless of experience, if they lack a certain 'faith' or 'belief', it would be better they don't enter your home anyways. That will not be good for anyone in the long run.

So the first priest will take his findings to the bishop, who will review it and may ask you questions next, and will likely send out a church sanctioned 'field investigator' for a better assessment. This is quite common, but it can also vary as to the bishop or as to whom the priest was who initially reported. It is not a procedure at this point preset.

As I had mentioned, we don't expect the process to move along much in a timely manner. But in smaller rural areas, perhaps you will hear a quicker reply. But understand in the last ten years so many of these come in now, they further scrutinize all and the real cases of demonic infestations get put in the same stack as ones involving someone's overactive imagination.

If you can't find help through a local priest you'll want to try to go directly to the bishop. The bishop might try to send you back to your parish priest again… But in the second time, you may get them to at least show up at your house. At times I have found that the priest might have a certain 'attitude' as though he doesn't want to be 'bothered', or as though this is all "ridiculous".

You might pick up on this, but you can make mention of this to the bishop if you think the priest was less than helpful, and ask for another priest to look into your issue. Even if it takes a few phone calls and e-mails in all, and a 'field investigator' or 'paranormal investigator', or other third party REP cannot often do this on behalf of the family. This is just a note for those others out there trying to get help from the church. They will ask you to ask the family to make the initial contact. And it is part of the protocol.

Remember we can only do so much leg work in this case before they will ask to speak and meet with the family. Expect this more so if they don't personally know the people who are helping you and they are not Christian clergy.

Just remember to patiently work with them, and you might get things moving. But I have to say, likely your case can't wait, and a solution such as ones in this book might already be having an effect. What I am saying here, is only approach the church with the most severe cases, and cases of "possession". Not to mention these will be easier to validate with investigations.

VIII – POST PREVENTION

Taking measures to ensure they don't come back, do the protection prayers daily.

I update this online prayer list from time to time if you want to keep an eye on this URL:

http://www.catholicdemonologist.com/protection.htm

Do the "**Hedge prayer of protection**" to seal your household. You can lay **blessed 'sea salt'** across windows and doorways, establishing some boundaries, as I said they oddly seem to enter the home in more 'traditional ways', rather than simply being able to 'slide in through a solid wall' from the outside. Say the ***Saint Michael prayer*** printed in this book, and do the deliverance prayers daily. That is every morning and night for some time after the 'successful deliverance'. You may reduce this to being nightly after say three months have passed.

The "3 KINGS" BLESSING

`http://www.boundless.org/2005/articles/a0001191.cfm`

This blessing of the home and inscription of the initials of the three Magi: *Caspar, Melchior and Balthazar*, above each door can be performed either by a priest or the *father of the family*. The feast of manifestation, or Epiphany, is traditionally celebrated the 12th day after Christmas, January 6th. In the dioceses of the United States this feast has been moved to the Sunday between January 2 and January 8.

The custom in Germany is that of the children's festival between January 1-6 (Three Kings Day). After a service at the churches the children go from house to house to gather offerings for poor children in poor countries. They are dressed as the three kings and carry sticks with stars on the top. At the homes they sing songs and recite messages of Christmas. At each house they paint the letters "20+C+M+B+08" which are for the Latin *Christus Mansionem Benedicat* (Christ bless this house).

PRAYERS AND METHODS

The owner of the house, should be the leader, if not a 'priest'.

On entering the home:

<u>Leader (priest , if present, or father of the family)</u> : Peace be to this house.

<u>All:</u> And to all who dwell herein.
<u>All:</u> From the east came the Magi to Bethlehem to adore the Lord; and opening their treasures they offered precious gifts: gold for the great King, incense for the true God, and myrrh in symbol of His burial.
<u>All Pray:</u> The Magnificat. *During the Magnificat, the room is sprinkled with holy water and incensed. After this is completed,*
<u>All:</u> From the east came the Magi to Bethlehem to adore the Lord; and opening their treasures they offered precious gifts: gold for the great King, incense for the true God, and myrrh in symbol of His burial.
<u>Leader:</u> Our Father. . . And lead us not into temptation
<u>All:</u> But deliver us from evil.
<u>Leader:</u> All they from Saba shall come
<u>All:</u> Bringing gold and frankincense.
<u>Leader:</u> O Lord, hear my prayer.
<u>All:</u> And let my cry come to You.
<u>Leader:</u> Let us pray. O God, who by the guidance of a star didst on this day manifest Thine only-begotten Son to the Gentiles, mercifully grant that we who

know Thee by faith may also attain the vision of Thy glorious majesty. Through Christ our Lord.
All: Amen.
Leader: Be enlightened, be enlightened, O Jerusalem, for thy light is come, and the glory of the Lord is risen upon thee—Jesus Christ born of the Virgin Mary.
All: And the Gentiles shall walk in thy light and kings in the splendor of thy rising, and the glory of the Lord has risen upon thee.
Leader: Let us pray. Bless, O Lord God almighty, this home, that in it there may be health, purity, the strength of victory, humility, goodness and mercy, the fulfillment of Thy law, the thanksgiving to God the Father and to the Son and to the Holy Spirit. And may this blessing remain upon this home and upon all who dwell herein.
Through Christ our Lord.
All: Amen.

After the prayers of the blessing are recited, each room of the home is sprinkled with Epiphany water and incensed. The initials of the Magi are inscribed upon the doors with the blessed chalk. *(The initials, C, M, B, can also be interpreted as the Latin phrase "Christus mansionem benedicat" which means "Christ bless this house".)*
Example: 20 + C + M + B + 08

THE BOUNDARIES OF YOUR PROPERTY OR HOME

The Home owner cannot take the place of a priest exactly, but we are often the ones who cleanse our own homes out of a necessity to do it immediately now, rather than later.

However, rather than these prayers we would do the others I recommend and at times simply recite a basic command again with:

"In the name of Jesus and by his precious blood, I command all evil and unclean spirits to leave this place and our property and never return" <u>saying it three times, sprinkling holy water, each time it is said.</u>

THE 'FOUR CORNERS' BLESSING

(ask the priest, to do this blessing rather than the blessing he might bring)

A St. Benedict medal is buried on each of the four corners of the property, (optionally adding 4 more at halfway between each corner). So this will involve at least eight medals if the property is expansive. At each burial point for the medal, bless the property with the sign of the cross and then bury the medal an inch or two in the ground sufficient that it will remain there undisturbed. Then the owners of the home should recite at each burial point:

"O God, omnipotent and never-ending, who in every place subject to Thee, pervades all and works all Thy Will, comply with our entreaty that Thou be the protector of this dwelling, and that here no antagonism of evil have power to resist Thee, but that, by the co-operation and virtue of the Holy Spirit, with the intercessions of St. Benedict, Thy service may come first of all, and holy freedom remain inviolate.

Through Jesus Christ Our Lord..."

Recite the prayer one time in the center of the property:

"Glorious Saint Benedict, sublime model of virtue, pure vessel of God's grace! Behold me humbly kneeling at your feet. I implore you in your loving kindness to pray for me before the throne of God. To you I have recourse in the dangers that daily surround me. Shield me against my selfishness and my indifference to God and to my neighbor. Inspire me to imitate you in all things. May your blessing be with me always, so that I may see and serve Christ in others and work for His kingdom.

Graciously obtain for me from God those favors and graces which I need so much in the trials, miseries and afflictions of life. Your heart was always full of love, compassion and mercy toward those who were afflicted or troubled in any way. You never dismissed without consolation and assistance anyone who had recourse to you. I therefore invoke your powerful intercession, confident in the hope that you will hear my prayers and obtain for me the special grace and favor I earnestly implore to help deliver us from all evil manifestations and cast them away in Jesus name. Help me, great Saint Benedict, to live and die as a faithful child of God, to run in the sweetness of His loving will, and to attain the eternal happiness of heaven. Amen."

In a sealed container, you can bury with the medal with a small bag of blessed salt, and a blessed crucifix. I used baby food jars with the lid sealed, when we moved into our home seven years ago.

"HEDGE PRAYER OF PROTECTION"

THE PRAYER (FOR HOUSEHOLD/FAMILY)

Trusting in the promise that whatever we ask the Father in Jesus' name He will do, I(we) now approach You Father with confidence in our Lord's words and in Your infinite power and love for me(us) and for our household and family, and with the intercession of the Blessed Virgin Mary, Mother of God, the Blessed Apostles Peter and Paul, Blessed Archangel Michael, my(our) guardian angel(s) and the guardian angels of our household and family, with all the saints and angels of heaven, and Holy in the power of His blessed Name, I(we) ask you Father to protect our household, our property, and the members of our household, and keep us from the harassment and affects of the devil and his minions.
Father I(we) ask in desire to serve You and adore You and to live our lives for You that You build a hedge of protection around our household and our property, like that which surrounded Job, and to help us to keep that hedge repaired and the gate locked so that the devil and his minions have no access or means to breach the hedge except by your expressed will.
Father, I(we) am(are) powerless against

the spiritual forces of evil and recognize my(our) utter dependence on You and Your power. Look with mercy upon me(us) and upon our household and family. Do not look upon our sins, O Lord; rather, look at the sufferings of your Beloved Son and see the Victim who's bitter passion and death has reconciled us to You. By the victory of the cross, protect us from all evil and rebuke any evil spirits who wish to attack, influence, or breach Your hedge of protection in any way. Send them back to Hell and fortify Your hedge for our protection by the blood of Your Son, Jesus. Send your Holy Angels to watch over us and protect us.

Father, all of these things I(we) ask in the most holy name of Jesus Christ, Your Son. Thank you, Father, for hearing my(our) prayer. I(we) love You, I(we) worship You, I(we) thank You and I(we) trust in You. Amen.

PRAYER: SAINT MICHAEL PRAYER

History:
It is said that one day having celebrated the Holy Sacrifice, the aged Pontiff Leo XIII was in conference with the Cardinals. Suddenly he sank to the floor in a deep swoon. Physicians who hastened to his side feared that he had already expired, for they could find no trace of his pulse. However, after a short interval the Holy Father rallied, and opening his eyes exclaimed with great emotion: "Oh what a horrible picture I was permitted to see!" He had been shown in spirit the tremendous activities of the evil spirits and their ravings against the Church. But in the midst of this vision of horror he had also beheld consoling

visions of the glorious Archangel Michael, who had appeared and cast Satan and his legions back into the abyss of hell. Soon afterward he composed the well-known prayer.
Always say at least daily the Saint Michael prayer *(go back a few pages for the prayer)*

GUARDIAN ANGEL PRAYER

Angel of God, my guardian dear, to whom God's love commits me here; ever this day (night) be at my side to enlight and guard, to rule and guide. My Angel of God, by God's will and grace, please watch over my dreams and myself as I sleep. Amen.
Said nightly, before bed.

A WORD ABOUT "MIXED FAITH SOLUTIONS"

You should never confuse the practices of "Santeria" (voodoo) with true Catholic practices. *(They have mixed VooDoo with things Catholic)*. Bottom line, it is best to never mix the faith with pagan rituals and methods or more trouble might come from it.

This is a somewhat generic, but alone an effective solution list, in it being more severe. This is partly done out of respect for the client as well. I realize that when people are so troubled by activity, they will try ANYTHING. This might be when a Baptist tries Catholic solutions. However, don't stray outside their belief systems with any *"Non-Christian-Judeo"* solutions. At best we can point them to the proper clergy according to their faith, and only as they request it. We should always note how much we can help is very limited to their faith. However, it is never a waste of time to try to help, rather than to do nothing.

HOW LONG WILL A DELIVERANCE/EXORCISM LAST?

Part of the problem is people often don't follow the advice well, and may leave many things out. They stop saying the prayers and resume in old 'bad habits' and so forth that can lure in or 'empower' these spirits, as soon as activity seems to cease. In other words they begin to back off on the prevention measures as prescribed and soon they begin again to feel the effects.

Remember they can LAY low a while to make you think 'success', when it is only a way of 'playing dead'. Beware! And <u>keep the battle going</u> even when you think you won! And do so for some time after the battle seems over for a few months.

The lasting success also depends on the people themselves, as we can have a great many variables in the question of *"why the house was haunted"* to begin with. Note that 'three days' is <u>not</u> a definite indication it was indeed 'successful', and having a 'Psychic-medium' tell you **"this house is clear"** isn't a verification the spirits won't be back that same night. These spirits need to removed and bound so they don't return. The true test is going past the first night, especially past 'three AM' , the second is after the first three days. At three weeks I would better say it was successful. Now that might seem to be a bit long of a wait, but by then if it starts to come back it is often because of the people themselves. Perhaps even over a longer period they have come to regain a foothold in the house. Did the team miss a haunted object? Something over looked? This is why it is important to be through the first time. So you don't have to go back because something was missed. This is easy to do, with so many ways our culture has mixed things of the occult into toys, books, movies etc. Hard to say where it might play a part as we over looked a few things tucked away in the closet. But don't get carried away on this as some fundamentalist might do who might make you burn your rock music. Stick to the things I say are significantly affecting your lives 'negatively' and notability should be removed from your house.

SIDE NOTE: Now as some are in a hurry to haul off some of your valued antiques as 'haunted' you can always relocate them to a storage facility until this is verified.
Be leery of people or groups that urge you to part with items they might personally collect for their own usage. What was once for education in the Warren's museums, I see others try to mimic this for the wrong reasons as to glorify themselves, to promote and 'showcase' these like prizes or trophies. Be more concerned at anyone who might charge to 'bury items on sacred ground' for example. This is not a person doing God's work.

We have to realize there are also many reasons why it may come back. I will go over a few more common reasons shortly. The most common might be a decline in the spiritual solutions. When the prayers start to slip, the firewall comes down and they might start up again. The second is free will choices that reunite it back in again.

WHY DO THEY RETURN SOME MONTHS AFTER A CLEANSING?

The way a haunting can affect some severely and not seemingly affect others who follow in the least, at all, is not a mystery in itself, as there are many reasons for this to be true. As for exactly the reason it can be a combination of many, some of which I will try to outline below:

- ✓ The Demon(s) may lay low for a few days so that those who did the /deliverance/exorcism' won't bring in the bigger guns and therefore effectively rebuke them from the house.

- ✓ 'Lying low' can alone be a good strategy in many ways as they may choose to work behind the scenes from then on, without making themselves known. People may see 'behavior changes', old habits become addictions. Depression may reach clinical and even suicidal over time. The point is the decrease in activity may not mean they are gone; you have to read deeper than physical manifestation to see if they are still, in fact there.

- ✓ The 'cleansing/deliverance/exorcism' worked, however the home owners continue to fuel demonic activity through their own lifestyles and habits. *(i.e. free-will choices)* Yes, the client may make changes in their lives, but if you have a roach problem, you certainly would get out of the habit of leaving fallen food crumbs on the floor now wouldn't you? Hence those 'positive' changes must be made. Also consider that if one does 'occult practices' that may have been either the where the 'invitation' occurred for the infesting spirits, or it may have simply fueled it to increase a 'current infestation'. These 'practices' might still be going on for their own selfish reasons even soon after the deliverance. As they may have ignored the sound advice to 'stay away' this is to say that such practices were forthcoming in the investigation phases.

- ✓ The effectiveness of the 'deliverance', as it may have 'scared them off' but it didn't 'rebuke' them. Some find a variety of ways can run them off for a short time, but they might come back soon after. And with a vengeance, *(see 'payback')* be ready with prevention measures to ensure they can't come back!

- ✓ The client is not forthcoming in the initial interviews as I briefly touch on in point number '3'. That is answering in truth or to the best of their knowledge on all of your questions, this can be a problem as to the success of the 'deliverance'.

  If they leave something out, certainly this could be a reason overlooked for a demonic presence to resurface again shortly after the first attempts have been made. With a practice of 'black magic', as I mention elsewhere in this book, a 'red eyed' shadow demon is a strong indication of a past or present occult practice, even if in contradiction to what the client says. And if it RETURNS, most certainly far too often we find that someone is 'dabbling' in it again, especially if a curse is not suspected. We usually do not disclose this info to the client, because we find that the client may decide to lie about 'not' seeing a red eyed shadow. As to lead us to believe they are not dabbling in such practices. We have to carefully consider questions to not be loaded with an obvious answer. Do this with 'any' questions you ask when possible during the client interviews.

- ✓ A curse returns. A curse can be broken and the person can place one again on the client and the family. This should be considered, and is one reason why in the questionnaire, the client should really think if they have any true enemies. If this is suspected as true, you can make prayers to break curses (as the ones in this book) a daily or weekly part of the prescribed prayers. Just to be sure a curse isn't 'ongoing' from some individual. After all we can never tell who might be doing this evil remotely.

- ✓ A cleansing and then a blessing should be repeated every so often. And the head of the household needs to carry on a daily ritual of prayers or more to keep it beaten down. This is necessary often as spraying insecticide as a precautionary measure, rather than to await the return of the roaches first.

Remember: No one said roaches are easy to deal with and neither are spirits!

THE LORD HELPS THOSE WHO HELP THEMSELVES

In closing I want to mention this, when I talk to people and find the activity has not diminished much, I might boldly state that they are not following through with the advice I gave. In this I am quite certain this is the case, and as it might rub them the wrong way, these things can be plain and simply in not following through with tried and true sound advice given. Ironically, they at times admit to this notion by saying **"How did you know"**
I would answer with something like:

"Because your case isn't so unique, as 100's have been through your type of haunting, and by now, if something isn't working, it mostly is do with the people involved not taking appropriate action such as I advised, or they continue to do things they were advised to stop doing"

True in what the late Ed Warren used to say in how you **"can lead a horse to water, but you can't make him drink"**. So true, as often we lead them to water and they stand there and don't take hardly a 'sip'. I have to resubmit instructions of prayers and other guidelines to break the foothold the spirits might have in their lives. And they will take 'small doses', and when they see little results, they back away totally as though nothing is working.

Imagine if you took only one pill a day as opposed to 4 as the doctor prescribed for your heart? Would you be on the phone the next day telling the doctor of your 'heart palpitations' acting like the meds he prescribed are not working? Absurd to say, but a close analogy is said in that. It saddens me how people will succumb to a lackluster version of true battle plan, and then complain it isn't working.

Let us hope and pray whoever may read this book will not take this side note lightly.

****

Lastly, I wanted to make mention, that I make myself available to ANYONE who feels a need to ask for help, or in asking honest questions on the before mentioned topics. This includes question about the Catholic faith. Although I come from a more 'traditional' view, I will try to answer to a post VATICAN II reply. ;) So feel free to contact me: At
Help@catholicdemonologist.com
Or through help@SwordsofsaintMichael.org

DEMONOLOGY TODAY RADIO SHOW

I have an (Internet) Broadcast stream for a radio show called "Demonology Today", which features myself and co-host Deborah Johnson *(Haunting survivor of the well known case "The Devil in Connecticut")*
Visit http://www.catholicdemonologist.com/radio for more information.

You can order the CD with MP3 Audio files of the show with at least 20 episodes for $5.00 plus $1.00 shipping (Lower U.S. States) $2.00 Canada.

QUESTIONS OR COMMENTS ABOUT THE BOOK

As I have stated previously, I am retired from this work fully now, and devoted my time to my loving family. I recommend signing up at the http://www.SwordsOfSaintMichael.ning.com community and asking any questions you may have about content in the book. I will detail the "Swords of Saint Michael" a bit more shortly.

God bless you and your family, and may God give you the blessings and the courage to face "The enemies" that afflict many.

Sincerely,
Kenneth Deel - SOSM
(Retired) Catholic Demonologist/Spiritual Warfare Counselor

APPENDICES:

I - Supplemental

A) Dealing with Children "Who See Ghosts" *(draft v.08)*

In this book each of these points have already been mentioned, but parts are scattered. You can read further on each of these points in the book in various sections where I will go into more detail on them. Such as on "Baptism".

With all the bad info from TV shows and movies I felt an extra need to bring all of the help information into one "supplemental' book section. So the entire book doesn't have to be combed over to begin help on our most precious assets. Our children.

Please don't take your child's experiences at night lightly. TV shows and movies are making people think these are somehow special gifts, when it is more of a "curse", and should be treated as such.

1. Baptism.

    Are they baptized? As I mentioned, baptism is more than a mere "christening" or an "anointing" of a child, it is indeed a 'blessing' and also a "simple" and lesser level "exorcism" to help break

2. generational curses and possible attachments. If this is not done, the child can be affected by these 'negative' spirits. (***See related section for more info***) Children after the age of reason can so choose to renew their baptism vows, or become

"confirmed" if they are to be Catholic. There is nothing wrong with giving a child a positive blessing in such a way, contrary to later choices they might make in life towards another "Belief system" perhaps. I am unsure why people choose to hold off on this when it can affect their child's life to not have these possible "attachments" removed.

2. **They should be taught to 'ignore'.**

It is true that "recognition" can play a part, as they should not acknowledge the presence of any would-be "spirits". We can be aware of their presence, but again we don't want to make eye contact, they should at most just begin to take a defensive action while sitting still and keeping in mind they are there. I would tell my child to *"come and get me"*, rather than to face it alone. They should not invite or be friendly but to tell them to leave when necessary.

3. **Tell them they are not welcome here!**

As a parent you need to make it clear that any and all spirits are not allowed in your house, and they are to stay away from your child. Make such a declaration, when you do, you take steps in deliverance as outlined in the later pages of this book. Remember if they are seeing spirits, you have beings "Uninvited" in your home that are scaring your child. Tell them to leave and never return!

4. **They should be taught to NOT BE AFRAID.**

   Build on their faith and not their fear. We must avoid exposing children to **R Rated** movies, and horror flicks for example. When they begin to realize their guardian angels, and other good spirits are in God's army for intercession, it will be like having an "invisible" body guard. Prayers and talks with them will help to build faith over fear. Always let him/her know they can come to Mommy or Daddy or a resident family member if needed. Again always leave yourselves "accessible" at night.

5. **Get them protection.**

   A Saint Benedict medal on a metal chain around the neck, with a Miraculous medal is recommended. Teach them to bless themselves with holy water daily. Blessed rosaries, crucifixes, positive symbols are always good also. Just that if there is a haunting more apparent than what the child sees, there may be a danger of "Provocation" of the spirits, which might draw retaliation. These two medals I mentioned, should be worn tucked under the clothes. They are designed to protect and will not provoke if 'tucked' away.

6. **Catholics: The sacraments.**

   If they are in the age of reason, time to get them to first communion, and confession, (the sacrament of reconciliation), confession, and "confirmation" if they are over the age of twelve.

7. **Holy water bed side.**

   In case of emergency… This and other measures are to remove the unwanted 'strangers' as we would a pest with a can of insecticide or intruders with mace. The type of bottle with the spout that can be closed off. Go to a Catholic church and the stainless steel vat in the back is where the holy water is. You might have to teach them how to use this also, empowering him/her this way to a certain extent is going to also relieve fear. We never want to assume they can get Dad or Mom if a spirit gets *"Too scary"*

8. **Teach them prayers.**

   Teach them the easy prayer first ***"Leave this place, In the name of Jesus and by his precious blood (sprinkle holy water near where the offending spirit is appearing), leave this place, and go back to where you came from and never return."*** Angel of God prayer, Saint Michael prayer, Hail Mary. We teach kids about ***"Taking candy and car rides from strangers"*,** dealing with dark spirits for some will be part of daily concern. Sometimes the spirits might not make it easy for them to leave. Don't assume they always can run to you at will.

9. **Don't assume it is a "Gift", more often this is a "curse".**

   Do look to the positive, try to solve this problem, don't consider it a gift. Your child is most likely

NOT an oracle assigned by God to help spirits in passing. Regardless of your more 'positive' view or mere ignorance, it doesn't change that there is a grave danger a foot. Remember how I stress "better safe than sorry"? It applies here. We want to weed out any possibility of a negative spirit's influence and affect first by following all suggestions. Keep in mind the way Reverend Mother handled the case with Lorraine Warren as a child at that Catholic school.

10. The child should NOT be taught or practicing "magic" or occult practices.

Some are far too impatient to impose their faith onto their children. My son attends church with me every Sunday and I don't force him to participate. He doesn't understand allot of it. And I don't expect him to. Even as he kneels when the blessed sacrament is open, during the communion rite. Not a "PC" thing here they are too young to deal with fickle spirits. Be sure a baby sitter, or a family member isn't getting them involved with occult practices at an early age.

11. Listen to your child.

...And without giving too much recognition to what they are seeing is real. Trust me it is better they don't think you believe in it entirely. We are trying to teach them how to not be afraid while advising them in how to deal with this. Ask your child questions without raising fear, so you can better judge if it is imagination or real concern.

12. Don't buy into the masquerade.

Dead relatives revisiting more than once, the ghost of children all can be part of a demonic ploy. Don't buy into it. And neither should your child! They must avoid contact with these spirits, God will not have children do tasks that adults should do. There is no business for a "good' spirit to bother a child. I always suspect it is evil regardless of the description. There is nothing to lose by assuming it as such.

13. Pray for them nightly.

I never need to tell a parent to pray for their child, but we have to do more than usual if they are affected by supernatural circumstances. Say the "prayer for our children" (In this book), the Saint Michael prayer. And the other prayers to "break curses" and deliverance.

14. "Cleanse" their room daily if you feel the need.

15. Consider changing their room.

Switch rooms with them, the experiences might actually be favoring one room in the house. If this can't be done consider rearranging the furniture. This has proven to slow down or stop activity for at least a couple of days. It is also good for the psychology to give the scary room a less notable similarity to relate the bad dreams and encounters with.

16. Keep the room very clean.

It is true, that activity and appearances have increased in many cases in a 'mess' versus a more clean room. Seriously!

17. Prep the room for them

Remove dark black clothes, or hangings draped over chairs, etc. Close closet doors, drawers and cabinets, and lock them. Close window shades, etc. Check their bed and in the closet, this is to indirectly show them nothing is in there. And while you are at it, you can sprinkle some holy water even in those places.

18. Provide Night lights.

Fifteen watt night lights aren't bad. I might even go with a small lamp with a 40 watt bulb. So long as it doesn't interfere. Don't make them sleep in the dark! Your electric bill won't notice a difference.

19. Don't let them play video games…

…or talk on the phone so close to bed. There is something to that "electro-magnetic chaos" the guy in the natural food store might have mentioned to you the last time you picked up some vitamins. It might be a matter of stimulating the brain, as being near EMFs might cause. So help the child stay away from too much of these exposures, especially after supper time and closer to bed. Some "adrenalin" might also play a part in these interactive games and can stir up the brain and body. Not something you want to do before bedtime.

20. No snacks!

Sugar snacks, especially just before bed time should be avoided to keep the mind from being more fed to enhance experiences at night *(i.e. "Scrooge- Marley's" supposed "undigested beef")*

21. Are they Active enough during the day? Getting enough sleep at night?

Consider how active they might be, and are they 'sleepy' before bed? If you can help them to be asleep the entire night soundly it would be better. Especially as the other points here are covered. Prescribed medicine might be in order to help them sleep so long as they are wearing protection and other means. Do that as many other things are being done to ensure there safety. And I would consider moving them to your room to sleep if things are so bad that medication is being considered.

22. Turn on the TV

Let them fall asleep watching it. I can say

sometimes this works as it did for me, while with others, they suspected it caused an 'increase' in apparitions. Without going into details as to why, sometimes we try these things. In this try one way or another.

23. Get them a "White noise" sound box.

You can get them in stores in the baby supplies sections. This has also helped to prevent the "voices" from being heard. Again sometimes one key thing to do is to not give attention and if something works to "drown them out" that is good.

24. In CONCLUSION.

Some of these tips assume it is the right thing to teach the child to defend itself against these unwanted visitors. Now that isn't always the right thing to do. Especially as the child is much younger. Use your common sense as a parent, and pray about it. If you feel it is better to protect the child, then proceed…

B) PRAYERS FOR TYPE: GOOD-HUMAN SPIRIT HAUNTINGS:

Prayers for the departed, that might linger as a "Haunting" can be helped without trying to initiate "communication", through prayers of "intercession". These can be said, 'remotely' for others who might have a "Good" spirit haunting their home or property, or, 'on the site'.

Insert the appropriate details within the braces "[ ]" for each prayer. Remember this is for a **TYPE: HUMAN-GOOD**, this is not a "rebuke" or "deliverance", but prayers to help with the passing and transition of the spirits who might linger, onto heaven. Keep in mind only God knows how long a spirit may be destined to "linger", however these prayers often will remove their presence, (haunting), from the premises, even if they are not yet free entirely to transcend into heaven.

Eternal Father,
I offer Thee the Most Precious Blood of Thy Divine Son, Jesus, in union with the masses said throughout the world today, for all the Holy Souls in Purgatory,
for sinners everywhere,
for sinners in the Universal Church, those in my own home and within my family.

Amen.

(Prayer: St. Gertrude)

Follow with:

My Jesus, by the sorrows You suffered in Your agony in the Garden, in Your scourging and crowning with thorns, in Your journey to Calvary, in Your crucifixion and death, have mercy on the souls in purgatory, and especially on those that are most forsaken; deliver them from the torments they endure; call them and admit them to Your most sweet embrace in paradise, where You live with the Father and the Holy Spirit, one God, for ever and ever.   Amen

Then say for seven days, one for each day:

SUNDAY
O Lord God omnipotent, I beseech You by the Precious Blood, which Your divine Son Jesus shed in the Garden, deliver the souls in purgatory that might linger [state the location of the premises and who you suspect the spirits names might be here], and especially that one which is the most forsaken of all, and bring it into Your glory, where it may praise and bless You for ever.   Amen.

Say here: one "Our Father" and one "Hail Mary"

Eternal rest grant unto them, O Lord; and let perpetual light shine upon them. May they rest in peace. Amen.

Merciful Father, hear our prayers and console us. As we renew our faith in Your Son, whom You raised from the dead, strengthen our hope that all our departed brothers and sisters will share in His resurrection, who lives and reigns with You and the Holy Spirit, one God, for ever and ever. Amen.

MONDAY
O Lord God omnipotent, I beseech You by the Precious Blood, which Your divine Son Jesus shed in His cruel scourging, deliver the souls in purgatory that might linger [state the location of the premises, and the names of the souls, if known, that may apply], and among them all, especially that soul which is nearest to it's entrance into Your glory, that it may soon begin to praise You and bless You for ever. Amen.

Say here: one "Our Father" and one "Hail Mary"

Eternal rest grant unto them, O Lord; and let perpetual light shine upon them. May they rest in peace. Amen. Merciful Father, hear our prayers and console us. As we renew our faith in Your Son, whom You raised from the dead, strengthen our hope that all our departed brothers and sisters will share in His resurrection, who lives and reigns with You and the Holy Spirit, one God, for ever and ever. Amen.

TUESDAY

O Lord God omnipotent, I beseech You by the Precious Blood of Your divine Son Jesus that was shed in His bitter crowning with thorns, deliver the souls in purgatory, and among them all, particularly that soul that might linger [state the location of the premises, and the names of the souls, if known, that may apply], which is in the greatest need of our prayers, in order that it may not long be delayed in praising You in Your glory and blessing You for ever.   Amen.

Say here: one "Our Father" and one "Hail Mary"

Eternal rest grant unto them, O Lord; and let perpetual light shine upon them. May they rest in peace.   Amen.

Merciful Father, hear our prayers and console us. As we renew our faith in Your Son, whom You raised from the dead, strengthen our hope that all our departed brothers and sisters will share in His resurrection, who lives and reigns with You and the Holy Spirit, one God, for ever and ever. Amen.

WEDNESDAY

O Lord God omnipotent, I beseech You by the Precious Blood of Your divine Son Jesus that was shed in the streets of Jerusalem while He carried on His sacred shoulders the heavy burden of the Cross, deliver the souls in purgatory that might linger [state the location of the premises, and the names of the souls, if known, that may apply], and especially that one which is richest in merits in Your sight, so that, having soon attained the high place in glory to which it is destined, it may praise You triumphantly and bless You for ever. Amen
Eternal rest grant unto them, O Lord; and let perpetual light shine upon them. May they rest in peace. Amen.

Merciful Father, hear our prayers and console us. As we renew our faith in Your Son, whom You raised from the dead, strengthen our hope that all our departed brothers and sisters will share in His resurrection, who lives and reigns with You and the Holy Spirit, one God, for ever and ever. Amen.

THURSDAY

O Lord God omnipotent, I beseech You by the Precious Body and Blood of Your divine Son Jesus, which He Himself on the night before His Passion gave as meat and drink to His beloved Apostles and bequeathed to His Holy Church to be the perpetual Sacrifice and life-giving nourishment of His faithful people, deliver the souls in purgatory that might linger [state the location of the premises, and the names of the souls, if known, that may apply], but most of all, that soul which was most devoted to this Mystery of infinite love, in order that it may praise You therefore, together with Your divine Son and the Holy Spirit in Your glory for ever. Amen.

Say here: one Our Father and one Hail Mary

Eternal rest grant unto them, O Lord; and let perpetual light shine upon them. May they rest in peace. Amen.

Merciful Father, hear our prayers and console us. As we renew our faith in Your Son, whom You raised from the dead, strengthen our hope that all our departed brothers and sisters will share in His resurrection, who lives and reigns with You and the Holy Spirit, one God, for ever and ever. Amen.

FRIDAY
O Lord God omnipotent,
I beseech You by the Precious Blood which Jesus Your divine Son did shed this day upon the tree of the Cross, especially from His sacred Hands and Feet, deliver the souls in purgatory,

that might linger [state the location of the premises, and the names of the souls, if known, that may apply], and particularly that soul for whom I am most bound to pray, in order that I may not be the cause which hinders You from admitting it quickly to the possession of Your glory where it may praise You and bless You for evermore. Amen

Say here: one "Our Father" and one "Hail Mary"

Eternal rest grant unto them, O Lord; and let perpetual light shine upon them. May they rest in peace. Amen.

Merciful Father, hear our prayers and console us. As we renew our faith in Your Son, whom You raised from the dead, strengthen our hope that all our departed brothers and sisters will share in His resurrection, who lives and reigns with You and the Holy Spirit, one God, for ever and ever. Amen.

SATURDAY
O Lord God omnipotent, I beseech You by the Precious Blood which gushed forth from the sacred Side of Your divine Son Jesus in the presence and to the great sorrow of His most holy Mother, deliver the souls in purgatory that might linger [state the location of the

premises, and the names of the souls, if known, that may apply], and among them all especially that soul which has been most devout to this noble Lady, that it may come quickly into Your glory, there to praise You in her, and her in You through all the ages.
Amen.

Say here: one "Our Father" and one "Hail Mary"

Eternal rest grant unto them, O Lord; and let perpetual light shine upon them. May they rest in peace. Amen.

Merciful Father, hear our prayers and console us. As we renew our faith in Your Son, whom You raised from the dead, strengthen our hope that all our departed brothers and sisters will share in His resurrection, who lives and reigns with You and the Holy Spirit, one God, for ever and ever.
Amen.

II - FIELD INVESTIGATIONS

B) Demonic Haunt Questionnaire *(draft v.06) © 2006 Kenneth Deel*
Something incomplete, but as you will see this is a sort of check list to help reveal "demonic' or 'evil' spirits are present in a supposed "Haunting" case.

Who

The Household members:

Relevant Family information

Relation	Denomination	Baptized?

    a. Are all of the Christians in the household baptized? (y/n)
    b. Have you recently acquired any used items that might be considered 'occult' in nature? (y/n)___ If 'Yes' what item(s)?_____
    c. Does anyone in the household own, use or practice what is considered by many as the 'Occult'. (Examples: Tarot, Crystal balls, etc.)

Object	Own?	Use?	Bought new	Details

(Second hand objects can have spirit 'attachments)

When

    a. When did you first notice activity? (Date and time, relevant event)___
    b. Does the activity occur more so at night? (y/n)___
    c. Does it occur day and or night? (y/n)___
    d. If you note a pattern as to day, or time the occurrences happen ? (y/n)___
    e. If so, please note here:_____
___

    f. Does the hour of 3AM have occurrences? If so describe:_____
_____
_____

    g. Do you have a log of the activity, and can we review it?(y/n)___

HOW: The five senses

Sight:

Black shapes

[ ] Black figures, like robed, hooded. – First noted appearance Date: __ / __ / __
[ ] Shadow being with RED EYES – First noted appearance Date: __ / __ / __
[ ] Full black silhouettes, head to toe appear human, sometimes the outline of a
hat on the head.
[ ] Small black, shapes looking like cats, or strange unidentified smaller mammals.
[ ] Do you see these black shapes at the corner of your eye?

GHOST AND APPARITIONS

    a. Have you seen what appears to be a Ghost of young child? (y/n)___
       (Age guess=____)
    b. Do any of the apparitions seem to be void of eyes?
       (A black recess, where the eyes should be) (y/n)___
    c. Can you see <u>legs</u> down to the <u>feet</u> on the ghost? (y/n)___
    d. Are the feet touching the ground? (y/n)___
    e. Do family pets react? Or seem to be in a deep sleep where they don't at all wake up during an occurrence?
    f. Untimely death of pets, especially birds, rodents, smaller pets

Other Manifestations
- Have you seen smaller strange black or brown animals (in your home) that disappear when you go to look where they went? (y/n)___

Physical Activity
[ ] Have you experienced an object being moved that weigh more than 5 lbs.?
[ ] Levitating objects
[ ] Occurrences that clearly defy the laws of physics as we know it.
    (i.e. Glassware crashing loudly onto the floor, but not broken. A cup falls off table but does not spill its contents)

If yes, describe,
_____

[ ] Awaken to a feeling of the Bed Vibrating, clearly supernatural.

[ ] Have you witnessed Objects move in plain sight? (Direct view)
[ ] …witnessed by more than one member of the household?
[ ] …witnessed by family and friends that live elsewhere.
[ ] Door bell rings with no one possibly there
[ ] Knock on the door

Touch:
[ ] Experience frigid cold spots
[ ] Hair pulled
[ ] Pushed, shoved, slapped, etc.
[ ] experience any 'Hot spots'? (You felt an abnormal localized higher temp)
[ ] Paralysis – Body is unable to move.
   If "Yes", please detail_____

[ ] Restrained (i.e. arm grabbed by unseen hands preventing you from moving it)

Sound:

[ ] Door bell rings with no one possibly there.
[ ] Knocks on the door, no visitor(s).
[ ] Whispers
[ ] Sounds of object breaking when nothing is found broken. (glass, pottery)
[ ] Your name whispered, or softly said in your ear (sometime said 'backwards')
[ ] Knockings [ ] in counts of three?
[ ] Scratching coming from inside wall, appears to move.
[ ] Footsteps
[ ] Moaning
[ ] Animal: Pig squeal or "snort"
[ ] Dog growls

Smells:
Do you experience the repugnant odors and smells? (y/n)__:
If yes check all that apply:
[ ] Sulfur smells
[ ] Urine
[ ] Fecal Matter
[ ] Burning flesh
[ ] Rotting meat
[ ] Spoiled milk
[ ] A smell of "Death"
[ ] The smells seem to move around the house? (*rather than to stay in one location for long*)

Other Senses:
[ ] Do you feel you are being watched?
[ ] Have you ever awoke at night and felt a 'presence'?
[ ] Have you experienced a sudden sense of 'Doom' or 'Dread'?
[ ] Are you beginning to have notable vivid nightmares since the suspected haunting began?
    If "Yes", please explain: _____
_____

[ ] Do you consider yourself a "sensitive"? (*i.e. Clairvoyant, etc.*)

What is the general 'feeling' when you encounter one of the 'spirits':
(Check all that apply)
[ ] Calm and peaceful
[ ] Puzzled
[ ] A bit concerned.
[ ] Confusion
[ ] Sadness, sorrow
[ ] Fear of Death, or well being
[ ] Of an evil presence…
[ ] Very Irritated at being bothered again by another encounter

C) CLIENT INVESTIGATIVE QUESTIONAIRE
(Reformat draft v1.1)
Compiled and edited by Kenneth Deel/ Gregory Myers of Paranormal Task Force © 2008 all rights reserved
www.paranormaltaskforce.com

Case #:

Date:
   Client Name:
   Address:
City, State & Zip:
Contact Phone Numbers:
   Email:

Please answer all questions, write in 'DNA' on ones that do not apply to you.
Try to answer in detail the best you can and please carefully read and answer each question.

PART I – PEOPLE & PROPERTY - FACTS & INFORMATION

1. Please list the names and ages of all those living/working in the situation where the disturbances have taken place.
2. Please list the relationships of all those in the household/business to one another.
3. Are there any pets? (If so, list types.)
4. What are the occupations of those in the location who are or have been working?
5. Please give educational background of all those in the location.
6. What hobbies do those in the location have?

7. What faith/spiritualism do those at the location believe in? Practice? (list for everyone)
8. What faith/spiritualism beliefs have they had in the past if different than current beliefs? (list for everyone)
9. If there were past different beliefs, then why were such beliefs changed? (list for everyone)
10. Who at this location has been baptized? What denomination? (list for everyone)
11. How long have you lived/worked at this location?
12. Are you renting or buying the property?
13. Do you know what year the building(s) involved were built?
14. Are you aware of any significant history such as past deaths, murders, suicides, etc. on this property? If so, please list to the best of your knowledge.
15. Please list any current or past renovations, remodeling, construction, development, etc. that has occurred on this property? When they occurred? Describe please.
16. Have any strange artifacts, inscriptions, symbols, etc. been found on this property? Please describe.
17. Have any items been added or removed at this location such as antiques, etc. near the time that activity was first noticed? If so list.

PART II – PARANORMAL OCCURANCES

History

1. Were any disturbances noted at previous locations? If so, list them and approximated years.

2. When did the disturbances begin in your current residence/business?
3. What sorts of things went on at the beginning?
4. What did you think of them?
5. When was the most recent incident? Describe Please
6. Do the events occur more in one spot (or in more than one place) than in others (certain rooms or parts of the room)? Where are these places?
7. Do the disturbances follow you or others to other locations?
8. Has anyone from outside the residence/business experienced these occurrences? Please list who. What did they experience, as far as you know?
9. Have you ever talked to past occupants or owners of this property about unusual happenings? If yes please describe in detail.
10. Have you ever talked to neighbors about the unusual occurrences or have they told you of such on their property? Please explain.
11. Please describe the disturbances/experiences in terms of what you actually observed. Also, have others describe their observations.
12. Who first noticed them? When were they first noticed? Under what circumstances?
13. Have you contacted any "experts"? (such as, obviously, a parapsychologist, or psychologist, police, priest , rabbi, psychic, etc.) If so, what did they say or recommend?

Frequency

1. Would you say the occurrences are frequent? Are they occurring with any apparent regularity? How often do they occur?

2. Do these occurrences happen at a specific time of the day, day of the week or month, season of the year, etc.?
3. Can you associate these occurrences with the anniversary of someone's death or another tragedy?
4. Have the disturbances been increasing or decreasing in frequency and severity since they first began?

Movement and Manipulation of Objects

1. In terms of movement of objects, describe the movements and what was unusual about them. Did objects seemingly take flight or visibly move by themselves? Were there unusual flight patterns (in other words, did they move like someone had pushed or thrown them, or did they make unusual curves in the air or on a surface, such as making right-angle turns)?
2. Has any one person appeared to be very close to the starting points of moving objects?
3. Could someone have been near enough to an object to move, push, or throw it, either purposely or by accident?
4. Did objects hit their final resting point with unusual force?
5. Did they make unusually loud noises when they struck something?
6. Were breakable objects seen to move and strike something without breaking?
7. Were heavier objects seen to move or rearrange themselves (such as furniture being piled up, especially in such a way that one person could not have done it)? Describe, please. Were these objects seen in motion, or were they simply

discovered in rearranged fashion after they had been moved?
8. Has anyone seen an object start its motion? In other words, have there been any witnesses to an object disturbance beginning with the point just before it took flight or began to move?
9. What were the objects affected? Any particular kind of object affected more than others? Any particular single objects affected more than others? If yes to either one, are there any relationships between the object(s) and any of the people in the household/office?
10. Have you noticed any metal objects particularly affected? Bent silverware, for example? If yes, are you certain no one could have had access to the pieces and bent them normally? Any chance that the pieces of metal/ silverware could have already been bent through normal use (and that you simply never noticed the bends)?
11. Have objects disappeared and been found in another location?

Electronics & Appliances

1. Have there been any unusual electrically related effects? Have appliances, TVs, stereos, lights, or computers been affected? If so, to what extent and how frequently? When any particular person(s) were around?
2. Have unusual interferences been observed while on the telephone? Does the phone ring and when answered there sometimes are just static or other unusual noises with no one on the other end?

Audible Sounds & Voices

1. Have there been any occurrences of unusual noises? Have these sounds been found to have a cause connected with them, or have they occurred with no seeming cause? Describe the sounds and why you think them unusual.
2. Have any of the sounds been connected in any way with the movement/disturbance of physical objects?
3. Have voices been heard, either with or without the appearance of an apparitional form? Were attempts made to see if the voices had a (living or mechanical) source? Are words identifiable? Male or Female?

Visual Sightings & Ghost/Apparitions

1. If nothing was seen, yet you (and others) are sure there is something there (a presence or "entity" or "force"), what makes you so sure?
2. Have there been instances where one or more person saw an apparition (ghost)? If yes, please describe what was seen.
3. Have the images encountered been associated with particular people or events? Have they been associated with particular people who are witnesses to the events or whom you know (example, maybe the ghost is that of your Uncle Harry from Cincinnati)? Were these images connected with the past (the past of the people present or of the house) or with the present (could the images represent living persons or current/future events)?
4. In the case of images seen, did everyone who saw something see the exact same thing, or were there the kinds of differences one would

expect if the apparition had been a living person, there in the flesh? (In other words, if one person stood in front of where the apparition appeared, and another behind it, did the people see the figure from the proper perspective [front and back] or not?)
5. Describe the behavior of the apparition(s). Does the apparition repeat the same activity every time it appears? Or does it seem as if it is aware of your presence as well?
6. Is there attempted communication on the part of the apparition? Have you or anyone else who has experienced the apparition tried to communicate with it? Any results (like communications back, reactions on the part of the apparition, changes in behavior of the phenomena, etc.)?
7. Would you say the apparition seems to be one that is conscious or aware of it's surroundings, that it is an intelligent "entity"?
8. If not, would you say that the experience may represent a past event repeating itself like a video "instant-replay"?

Odors

Have unusual smells been noticed? What was unusual about them? Have they appeared at only certain times or only in certain areas? Have they been localized, yet mobile (confined to a specific area in the air, yet that area has been observed to move about)? Were attempts made to find a natural source of the smell?

Environment

   1. Has the temperature of the location been affected unusually? Have normal causes been looked at as being behind such effects?
   2. Are heaviness feelings or a change in barometric pressure noticed?
   3. Have you or anyone else gotten unusual feelings in a particular place or at particular times (example, do you sense a "presence" or get "cold chills" under certain conditions/in certain locations)?

Analysis

1. Who has been around in each instance of a visual apparition? Of voices? Of unusual smells?
2. Were there any unusual feelings or emotions associated with the disturbances/experiences?
3. Have you connected the disturbances with any particular people witnessing or living/working in the location? With any particular visitors?
4. Are there particular activities going on when the incidents occur (such as eating, watching TV, arguments, etc.)? Explain.
5. Is anyone's behavior affected during the occurrences? Animal's behavior affected? If so, explain.
6. Are certain people seemingly more affected than others? Who? What reactions do the people in the situation have when confronted by one of the disturbances?
7. Do all witnesses to the events have to be around for anything to happen? If not, give examples of such incidents where not everyone was around, and who was there.
8. Have any disturbances been noted to have occurred when no one was around (i.e., has anyone noted the aftereffects of a disturbance that may have occurred with no witnesses, perhaps by objects having been moved)?

9. Have there been times when apparitions/ghosts, smells, voices, footsteps, or odd noises have been experienced by only some of the people (or just one person) and not by others at the same time? Please describe these instances.
10. How about the noises or the smells (if present)? Could they be connected with persons not present (living or dead)? Or can they be connected with the house or building (past or present)?
11. Did the witnesses who had the experience of seeing or hearing a ghost know about that person (whom the ghost represents) before the experience?
12. When the others who have witnessed the events had their first experiences, were they aware of previous encounters or observations or experiences by those who first noticed them? What did they know about them, if anything?
13. How did you feel just before the experience(s) (physically, mentally, and emotionally)? Any common factors between each of the experiences?
14. How did you feel while the experience was actually happening?
15. How did you feel/react after the experience(s) was completed?
16. Did you discuss the experiences with anyone (witness or not) just after it happened? Describe the discussions.
17. Have you looked for ordinary, normal explanations? What makes you sure the events are paranormal?
18. Does anyone involved have a theory as to what may be going on?
19. Is there any reason to think that someone in the home/office might fake the events?

PART III – Humanistic Interactions

1. Do you see the events as representing any emotions or tensions that you or others may have at the moment?
2. Have there been any changes in the daily routine/ lives of the people involved (such as new job, new school, divorce, marriage, death of relative or friend, etc.)? If so, what are they? When did they happen in relation to the disturbances?
3. Do you see the way the disturbances/experiences are happening as being symbolic of anyone's emotional state or thought processes?
4. Are the events perhaps symbolic of any problems that may be going on between people in the affected group (here, not just direct witnesses, but all those with relationship to the people having the experiences)?
5. If you were to pretend this were all happening in a dream, what would you make of it (the "dream," that is)?
6. Are there any visible problems between the people having the experiences and anyone else?
7. Is anyone particularly tense or frustrated or under some stress? What do you think this may be related to (job, friendships, housework, sexual relationships, school, lack of leisure time, etc.)?
8. Have you or anyone else in the home/business experienced sleeping difficulties and/or unusual dreams/nightmares? (If so, please explain.)
9. What would you say your overall health (both physical and mental) was before the experiences began?
10. What would you say your overall health (both physical and mental) has been since the disturbances started?
11. Are you taking any medication or non-prescription drugs? What are they?
12. Are you drinking alcohol, drinks with caffeine, or taking in a lot of sugar, or smoking tobacco? Which one(s), and how much?

13. Have you ever had a 'bad trip' on taking a hallucinogenic drug like LSD? IF so describe the experience.
14. Was there any change in your diet or use of the above substances before the initial experiences?
15. Has there been any change in your diet or use of the above substances since the disturbances began?
16. Are you or any of the others currently under the care of a doctor or psychological counselor/therapist?
17. Do you practice: yoga, meditation, self-hypnosis, biofeedback, relaxation exercises, or physical exercises?
18. Do you believe in Ghosts?
19. Do you believe in Demons?

PART IV – PARANORMAL & OTHER INTEREST

1. Have you or any of the others involved had any psychic experiences in the past?
2. Have you (or anyone else who witnessed the events) been interested in psychic phenomena for a while? Has your family discussed psychic phenomena in the past? If so, in what context?
3. If so, what did/do they have to say?
4. What kinds of books or articles have you read about psychic phenomena or the occult/supernatural/unsolved mysteries?
5. Have you seen films like Ghostbusters, Poltergeist, The Entity, The Amityville Horror, Dreamscape, Resurrection, The Exorcist, The Fury, Carrie, etc.? Which ones? (Name ones that more so may compare to your experiences)
6. What did you think of them (in terms of how they portrayed psychic experiences/disturbances)?
7. How about others involved? Reading? Films? TV shows?
8. What are your feelings/beliefs regarding psychic phenomena or the spiritual world? Religious background (both family and your present religious status)?

9. Have you ever taken any courses on parapsychology, the occult, or any self-development or psychic-development courses? The others?
10. Have you or any of the others ever been to see a psychic?
11. Have you or anyone else within the home/business used any device such as an Ouija Board, Scrying Mirror, Tarot Cards or other such devices on the premises or elsewhere? (If so, please list each and when & where last used.)
12. Have any séances or rituals been performed in the home/business or on the associated property that you are aware of? (If so, please explain.)

PART V – GOALS & ASSISTANCE

1. What would you like done to help you?
2. What is the best time of the day to contact you? How?
3. Would you allow me and perhaps some colleagues to do a serious investigation of the occurrences in your home/office if we feel it would be needed to better assess your situation?
4. Would you be willing to see a counselor, therapist, faith/spiritual practitioner or doctor if that is the most positive way to help deal with the experiences?
5. Would you be willing to follow advice from a priest or spiritual/faith practitioner that is different than your faith/spiritual practices and belief system?

D) ABOUT THE "SWORDS OF SAINT MICHAEL"

What are the goals of the Swords Of Saint Michael?

I created the Swords Of Saint Michael (SoS) organization and community, with the goals of building a network of qualified members and Affiliates in Deliverance, ministers, Exorcist, Demonologist, Christian Clergy. Along with Medical and mental health professionals, all into one network to act as a referral service.
Also Education is key, as there are few resources out there that can arm one with the knowledge needed to truly do the work in "Spiritual warfare" and "Deliverance".

Why the name? Swords of Saint Michael?

To be more universal across more Christian denominations, not just Catholic/Orthodox Saint Michael is a recognized icon across all of Christianity, where Saint Benedict for example is more exclusive to the Early Christian/Catholic. The idea is to bridge to gap and to not start with a name of a person not recognized so much by other denominations. Saint Michael the Arch Angel Warrior well represents what we stand for.

This org is NOT to be confused with another org on the web headed by one who calls himself "Brother", yet is not even recognized as a Catholic Monk by the church in any way. That org is tarnished as it's creator also did a year in jail for possession of Child porn. In there again be careful were you go for help and study...

Why the Social Community/Forum?

To socialize to learn, it will also act as a level of recruitment, some might demonstrate the "right stuff", a sincere desire to do this work for the "right" reasons, and convey a knowledge and understanding of these topics that will qualify them possibly as an "affiliate" or even working later as on an Administration level within the Org itself.

What makes this social community different?
The site will have it's affiliate members, in Exorcist, Demonologists, some "Top names" and those with a vast knowledge and understanding of Ghost and demonic haunting, exorcisms, and other related paranormal phenomenon. The rules state that ONLY posts that don't contradict Christian teachings are allowed. This helps to filter out the confusing mix we find in so many other places when someone may just want to hear from Catholics or other Christian Denominations about these topics. Some feel it is a safe place where you can share your Christian views and learn from others without getting 'attacked' or criticized by others who don't believe as you do.

Where can I sign up for the Social Community?
http://www.SwordsofSaintmichael.org Click on the "Forums" tab. or directly at **http://SwordsOfSaintMichael.ning.com** Please read the site rules before posting.

ADDITIONAL CREDITS and BOOK ACKNOWLEDGMENTS:

A Special thanks to **Lorraine Warren and Debra (Glatzel) Johnson,** for their work, shared experiences, and friendship. And another special thanks to Dawn Marie Ceja for proof reading this book.

Recommended reading:

The Demonologist – By Gerald Brittle
- **Paperback:** 238 pages
- **Publisher:** iUniverse (September 13, 2002)
- **Language:** English
- **ISBN-10:** 0595246184 / **ISBN-13:** 978-0595246182

If you haven't read this, get it. When writing this "Handbook", I actually was considering the material in this book, so as to be a "companion book".

****

"The Devil in Connecticut" – By Gerald Brittle
- **Paperback**
- **Publisher:** Bantam Books (Mm) (November 1983)
- **Language:** English
- **ISBN-10:** 0553237144 / **ISBN-13:** 978-0553237146

A great case study of Possession and a Demonic oppression.
Not to be confused with the "Haunting in Connecticut" movie.

****

An Exorcist Tells his story - Fr. Gabriel Amorth

- **Paperback:** 205 pages
- **Publisher:** Ignatius Press (March 1999)
- **Language:** English
- **ISBN-10:** 0898707102 / **ISBN-13:** 978-0898707106

I consider this book and the follow-up volume, the "Demonic possession handbook"
****

An Exorcist: More Stories - Fr. Gabriel Amorth

- **Paperback:** 203 pages
- **Publisher:** Ignatius Press (February 2002)
- **Language:** English
- **ISBN-10:** 0898709172 / **ISBN-13:** 978-0898709179

A second "Demonic Possession handbook"
****

"I never believed in ghost until... 100 Real-life encounters"
-by The Editors of USA TODAY Weekend edition.
Paperback: 240 pages
Publisher: McGraw-Hill; 1 edition (September 1, 1992)
Language: English
ISBN-10: 0809238403
ISBN-13: 978-0809238408

A Great case study!
****

"ESP, HAUNTINGS and POLTERGEISTS a

Parapsychologists handbook"
-By Lloyd Auerbach
Publisher: Not Avail (October 1986)
Language: English
SBN-10: 0446340138
ISBN-13: 978-0446340137

Lloyd is the quintessential "Parapsychologist" out there. For a "Science only" aspect, you might dive into some of his books.

****

The Haunted: One Family's Nightmare

– Robert Curran

- **Hardcover:** 260 pages
- **Publisher:** St Martins Pr; 1st edition (March 1988)
- **Language:** English
- **ISBN-10:** 0312014406 / **ISBN-13:** 978-0312014407

A Good "case study" of a Demonic infestation another true story

****

"The Catholic Demonologist Handbook"
[Underground Edition] v1.0h
© Copyright 2008-2010 Kenneth Deel, All rights reserved.

Made in the USA
San Bernardino, CA
02 September 2014